ISLAMIC SURVEYS 7

AN INTELLECTUAL HISTORY OF ISLAM IN INDIA

Aziz Ahmad

EDINBURGH
at the University Press

EDINBURGH UNIVERSITY PRESS
22 George Square, Edinburgh
North America
Aldine Publishing Company
529 South Wabash Avenue, Chicago
Australia and New Zealand
Hodder & Stoughton Limited
Africa, Oxford University Press
India, P. C. Manaktala & Sons
Far East, M. Graham Brash & Son
85224 057 0
Library of Congress
Catalog Card Number 69-16010
Printed in Great Britain by
T. & A. Constable Ltd, Edinburgh

FOREWORD

IN 1939 the prospect of a war which would involve many Asian nations made men in positions of responsibility in Britain suddenly aware of the meagre number of our experts in Asian languages and cultures. The Scarbrough Commission was set up, and its report led to a great expansion of Oriental and African studies in Britain after the war. Thirty years later it is clear to an ever-widening circle of readers that they need more than a superficial knowledge of non-European cultures. The appearance of many independent African states with a Muslim majority or a Muslim head of state and the growing political importance of Pakistan and India have shown the desirability of a fuller understanding and appreciation of the Islamic world in all its aspects. Since past history counts for much among Muslims, a journalistic familiarity with present conditions is not enough; there must also be some awareness of how the past has moulded the present.

This series of 'Islamic Surveys' is designed to give the educated reader something more than can be found in the usual popular books. Each work undertakes to survey a special part of the field, and to show the present stage of scholarship here. Where there is a clear picture this will be given; but where there are gaps, obscurities and differences of opinion, these will also be indicated. Bibliographies will afford guidance to those who want to pursue their studies further.

The present volume is intended to help to counteract the relative neglect until recently of the achievements of Islam in the Indo-Pakistan subcontinent. South Asia is not a mere frontier of Islam, but an integral part of the Islamic world, making a distinctive contribution to the life of the whole. For many centuries it has been interacting with Hinduism by way of both attraction and repulsion, but it has not severed its links with the heartlands of Islam. More recently Indian Islam preceded the heartlands in receiving and responding to the European impact. With the creation of Pakistan in 1947 it moved into a significant new phase. The following chapters, leaving aside political history, outline the principal religious and cultural features of Islamic life in the subcontinent through eight centuries.

The transliteration of Arabic words is essentially that of the second edition of *The Encyclopaedia of Islam* (London, 1960, continuing) with three modifications. Two of these are normal with most British Arabists, namely, *q* for *ḳ*, and *j* for *dj*. The third is something of a novelty. It is the replacement of the ligature used to show when two consonants are to be sounded together by an apostrophe to show when they are to be sounded separately. This means that *dh*, *gh*, *kh*, *sh*, *th* (and in non-Arabic words *ch* and *zh*) are to be sounded together; where there is an apostrophe, as in *ad'ham*, they are to be sounded separately. The apostrophe in this usage represents no sound, but, since it only occurs between two consonants (of which the second is *h*), it cannot be confused with the apostrophe representing the glottal stop (*hamza*), which never occurs between two consonants.

In the case of Indian names, where a man has written a book in English (or has been written about), the aim has been to keep the form of the name used on the title-page. Where names occur in different forms, that closest to the system of transliteration has usually been adopted. Names from languages other than Arabic have been assimilated to the Arabic system. Common geographical names have been given their usual form. This is a complex matter, and it is hoped the inevitable inconsistencies will not cause undue pain to any purist.

W. Montgomery Watt
GENERAL EDITOR

THE CONTENTS

LIST OF ILLUSTRATIONS

ACKNOWLEDGEMENTS

MY thanks are due to Professor William Montgomery Watt and the Edinburgh University Press for editorial assistance in the preparation of the typescript.

I am grateful to the American Council of Learned Societies for a research and travel grant which enabled me to collect material for this book in the libraries of the United Kingdom.

A sub-chapter of this book is based on material previously published in the form of an article in the *Zeitschrift der Deutschen morgenländischen Gesellschaft*. I am obliged to its editor for agreeing to its use in this work.

Aziz Ahmad

THE publishers are grateful to the following individuals and institutions for permission to reproduce illustrations: Victoria and Albert Museum, London, plates 1 and 6; Vikin Kumar Jain, Delhi, plate 2; Pakistan High Commission, London, plates 3 and 13; Roger Viollet, Paris, plates 4 and 11; Rolof Beny, Rome, plate 5; Metropolitan Museum of Art, New York, plates 7, 9 and 14; Mr Elwell Sutton, Edinburgh, plates 8 and 12; and the Museum of Fine Arts, Boston, plate 10.

ONE

SUNNĪ ORTHODOXY

1. Ḥanafism

The vast majority of the Muslims of the Indo-Pakistan sub-continent are Sunnīs of the Ḥanafite school or rite.

The first Muslim conquerors of north-west India were Ghaznavids, who were Sunnīs of the Shāfiʿī school. But under the sultan Masʿūd (1030–40) the Ḥanafī school had already begun to supplant the Shāfiʿī in Ghazna. Under his patronage Abū-Muḥammad Naṣāḥī wrote a book supporting the Ḥanafī school of jurisprudence.[1] But Shāfiʿism remained strong under the Ghūrids, and the fact that Nūr Turk the Ismāʿīlī agitator attacked both Ḥanafī and Shāfiʿī doctrines during the reign of the Sulṭāna Raḍiyya (1236–40) shows that the religious and political élite of the realm under the Slave Sultans of Delhi (1206–90) adhered to the culture of the two schools, though no doubt by that time Ḥanafism was definitely in the ascendancy.[2] Under the early Tughluqs, Ḥanafī *fiqh* (jurisprudence) had precedence even over rulings based on the *ḥadīth* (Traditions of the Prophet), according to the evidence of the eminent mystic Niẓām-ad-dīn Awliyā.[3] Ghiyāth-ad-dīn Tughluq's code of administration based on a Qur'ānic foundation and the custom of the earlier Delhi Sultans was undoubtedly strongly Ḥanafite in complexion.[4] His son, and successor, Muḥammad ibn-Tughluq is credited with a thorough knowledge of the Ḥanafite juristic manual, *Hidāya*, by Burhān-ad-dīn al-Marghīniānī, and the law in his government was entirely based on Ḥanafī jurisprudence.[5] His chief *qāḍī*, Kamāl-ad-dīn Ḥānsawī, was a staunch Ḥanafite.[6]

Two great classics of Ḥanafite jurisprudence were compiled during the reign of Fīrūz Tughluq (1351–88): *Fiqh-ī Fīrūz-shāhī*, a manual for the administration of the state, which was ruled as a theocracy; and *Fatāwī Tātārkhāniyya*, a voluminous collection of juristic rulings, structurally modelled on the *Hidāya* and compiled in 1375 by ʿĀlim b. ʿAlāʾ under the patronage of a nobleman, Tātār Khān.

As the Delhi sultanate disintegrated, successor states rose all over the subcontinent, and most of them followed the Ḥanafī law in administration. A comprehensive work of jurisprudence, *Fatāwī Ibrāhīmshāhī*, was compiled under the patronage of Sulṭān Ibrāhīm Sharqī (1402–36) at Jawnpur.[7] As the Delhi Sultanate re-emerged into some prominence in the fifteenth century, Bahlūl Lōdī (1451–89) made a special study of Ḥanafī jurisprudence, on which he could model the legal and administrative policy of his state.[8]

The Mughals were Ḥanafī, Sunnī Turks from Central Asia. Under them Ḥanafism remained, and continued to grow, as the legal rite of Muslim India. Neither the eclecticism of Akbar (1556–1605) nor his heresy seems to have interfered with the continuance of Ḥanafī conformity, which was reinforced by the scholarship of ʿAbd-al-Ḥaqq Muḥaddith Dihlawī, who stressed the precedence of religious law over the mystic path, despite the fact that he had been initiated into three Ṣūfī orders.[9]

The State was run as a theocracy, for a second time, by the Mughal emperor Awrangzīb (1658–1707). During his reign and under his auspices was compiled the third great collection, made in India, of juristic rulings, *Fatāwī-ʿĀlamgīrī*, known outside India as *Fatāwī Hindiyya* and edited by Niẓām-ad-dīn Burhānpūrī and twenty-four other ulema. It follows the classical pattern of the collections of juristic rulings. The line dividing laws relevant to religious ritual and the ordering of social and individual life is blurred. Whereas sections dealing with the ritual are classical in pattern, a more practical orientation is given to the sections dealing with the criminal and civil law of the state, though the edicts prescribed in all legal cases are purely traditional. The work is authoritatively documented and based on the classical collections of Ḥanafī jurisprudence. In the mass of juristic detail the state is conceived as Islamic, and there are prescriptions regulating the treatment of non-Muslims of three categories: hostile, rebellious and protected.[10]

Ḥanafism remained the legal rite of the vast majority of the Muslim élite and the masses during the decadence of the Mughal empire and the rise of British power in the eighteenth and nineteenth century. Challenges to it were peripheral, doctrinaire and without any mass appeal. One such challenge was that of the fundamentalism, in respect of Traditions, of the Ahl-i Ḥadīth,[11] and this was countered by the ulema of the theological school of Deoband, especially its founder, Muḥammad Qāsim Nānotawī.

The historian Shiblī had so personal an intellectual attachment to Abū-Ḥanīfa, the founder of the Ḥanafite school, that he chose to call himself, Nuʿmānī, after him, though the place Shiblī gave him among the pioneers of Muslim scholasticism (*kalām*) is debatable. Ḥanafism hardly needed any rehabilitation in modern times, but a few works championing its cause were written in the later nineteenth and early twentieth century by scholars like Aḥmad ʿAlī Batālawī,[12] Ẓahīr Aḥsan Nīmawī and Asad-Allāh Tilharī, whose work supports the position of juristic *taqlīd* (conformity to precedents) which was under attack in the late nineteenth century by fundamentalists like Ahl-i Ḥadīth.[13]

2. Theological Studies in Medieval India

In theological studies the contribution of India,[14] compared with that of other countries of Dār al-Islām, was meagre and of regional rather than universal importance. In India, Ṣūfis rather than the ulema were the religious inspiration of the Muslim intelligentsia and the masses.

Theological studies began in Arab Sind with the arrival of Abū-Ḥafṣ al-Asadī of Basra (d. 780), one of the earliest authorities on the *ḥadīth*.[15] The first scholar of Sind who distinguished himself in the study of the *ḥadīth* was Abū-Maʿshar Sindī.

In Ghaznavid Lahore the study of Qur'ānic exegesis and *ḥadīth* was introduced by Shaykh Ismāʿīl Bukhārī (d. 1058).[16] A number of theologians had migrated to Delhi to escape the Mongol onslaught during the thirteenth century. Among the theologians during Balban's reign were Burhān-ad-dīn Balkhī and Sharaf-ad-dīn Lālwājī – whom he held in great esteem – even though sometimes, for reasons of state, he disregarded their advice.[17] Conformity to the externalities of religious prescriptions was enforced by ʿAlā'-ad-dīn Khaljī (1296–1316), who put down such vices as alcoholism, gambling, prostitution and homosexuality, and appointed as his public censor Ḍiyā'-ad-dīn Sannāmī, who had a certain anti-Ṣūfī bias. Being illiterate himself, 'Alā'-ad-dīn was no patron of theologians, and an Egyptian Traditionist who had come to Delhi returned to his country because of the lack of patronage. The curriculum of schools during the Khaljī period included the theological sciences, such as Qur'ānic exegesis, *ḥadīth* and Ḥanafī jurisprudence, as well as Arabic linguistics, literature, logic and scholasticism. Literature, which was popular among the Muslim élite, consisted mainly of Ṣūfī classics. Among the theological classics Ghazālī's works held an undisputed position, and guaranteed the channelling of mystic trends into Ash'arite Islam.[18]

It may be surmised that the Tughluq revolution (1320) conserved this pattern of religious life, which had been jeopardized by the apostasy and usurpation of Khusraw Khān. But it underwent a curious mutation under Muḥammad ibn-Tughluq, who himself passed through various religio-intellectual phases.[19] Orthodoxy was enforced by the arrival of 'Abd-al-'Azīz Ardabīlī, who was a disciple of Ibn-Taymiyya; and other traditions of religious disputation, including the rationalistic and the scholastic, were introduced by 'Ilm-ad-dīn, who had returned after a long sojourn in the Hijaz, Egypt and Syria. To these may be added the multiple influx of Muslim religious ideas and nuances of belief brought by foreigners from all over the Islamic world during Muḥammad ibn-Tughluq's reign.

Orthodox as well as scholastic theological trends were reinforced in India in the reign of Sikandar Lōdī (1489–1517), whose court welcomed divines from other parts of Dār al-Islām. Chief among them were Rafī'-ad-dīn Salāmī, a disciple of Dawānī, who introduced the critical study of *ḥadīth* in the schools, and paved the way for 'Abd-al-Ḥaqq Dihlawī, and the rationalist, 'Abd-Allāh Tulanbī, whose lectures Sikandar Lōdī sometimes attended.[20]

In the Deccan and the Gujarat, theological studies had close contact with the Yemen and the Hijaz. Zayn-ad-dīn Abū-Yaḥyā (d. 1521) founded a school and a hospice at Ponānī in the Deccan, which attracted scholars from as far as the East Indies, and his works were well known in Egypt (where they were published in the nineteenth century). One of these, *Hidāyat al-azkiyya*, received commentaries both in the Hijaz and in Java. His grandson, Zayn-ad-dīn ibn-ʿAbd-al-ʿAzīz al-Maʿbarī, won renown as the author of *Tuḥfat al-mujāhidīn*, a historical account of the struggle against the Portuguese from 1498 to 1581, dedicated to ʿAlī ʿĀdil Shāh I (1558–80) and describing in its earlier chapters the history of the advent of Islam in Malabar. His commentary on Shāfiʿite law gained recognition in Egypt and the East Indies.[21] The rulers of the Deccan invited Arab scholars from the Hijaz and the Yemen, one of the most distinguished being the Meccan Ibn-Maʿṣūm (d. 1705).

On the theological plane Gujarat remained close and sensitive to the scholarly trends in the Hijaz, especially through scholars like ʿAbd-al-Wahhāb Muttaqī, who travelled to and fro; and it also produced scholars of exegesis and *ḥadīth* like Shaykh ʿAlī Mahāʾimī. An Arab family – that of al-ʿAydrūs – which had settled at Ahmadabad remained in constant touch with Arabic scholars and invited some of them to Gujarat.[22]

This was the state of theological and related scholarship before the advent of the Mughals. But on the whole its foundations were weak. Unlike the great Ṣūfīs, the ulema were an integral part of the court of the sultan and his nobles, and, instead of exercising a moral influence on the state, were largely its tools. On the theological plane all that they could accomplish was piecemeal reiteration of imitative theology (*taqlīd*). They concentrated entirely on externals, and even in Muslim jurisprudence they were unable to break any fresh ground.

Theological schools were in a sense vocational. They were attached to mosques or hospices or run by state or private charity. These schools kept the state supplied with *qāḍīs* and *muftīs*, judges and jurists, who were described in official terminology as *dastār-bandān* (turban-wearers).

The professionalization of the theologian sapped to some extent the strength of exoteric Islam in the fifteenth and sixteenth centuries, and this explains to some extent the rise of a number of heresies then. But that period merely marks the culmination of a process of failure, which was already felt by Balban towards the close of the thirteenth century, and by Amīr Khusraw at the beginning of the fourteenth.[23] As early as 1257 the ulema, who conspired with Mongol protégés,[24] showed that as a class they were capable of betraying Muslim political power in India instead of safeguarding it. This unreliability of the ulema explains Balban's decision to regard himself as head of state and the fountainhead of its legal authority. It also explains 'Alā'-ad-dīn Khaljī's curtailment of the jurisdiction of the ulema to purely judicial or theological matters, and Muḥammad ibn-Tughluq's treatment of them on the same footing as other citizens of the state, without any special privileges.[25]

After the decentralization of the Chishtī Ṣūfīs, forced by Muḥammad ibn-Tughluq, the two succeeding centuries experienced a spiritual vacuum, in so far as Islam in India was concerned. On the one hand, the spiritual energy of the Chishtī and the Suhrawardī orders had declined, and the Qādirī and the Naqshbandī orders, which were to give to Muslim India a fresh spiritual momentum in the seventeenth century, had not effectively arrived on the scene; on the other hand, the ulema of India had sunk to the most contemptible depths of hypocrisy, simony, greed and degeneration. The spiritual vacuum of sixteenth-century Indian Islam gave rise to a heretical neurosis – the view that Islam after its first thousand years of existence needed a rejuvenation and a rejuvenator, a Mahdī or a quasi-prophet, to enliven it again, possibly in a modified form. This spiritual malaise was partly a reaction to the popular Bhaktī movement in contemporary Hinduism; it has also been suggested that it may have been influenced by some features of Hinduism.[26] The powerful ulema of the time, Shaykh Gadā'ī, Makhdūm-al-Mūlk and Shaykh 'Abd-an-Nabī, challenged these Messianic trends not by disputation or dialectics or strength of spiritual character, but by polemic and persecution, and in this case these eventually failed. The responsibility for this sorry state of affairs has been squarely placed on the shoulders of the wicked divines (*'ulamā-i sū*) by Muslims of divergent views and beliefs such as the historian Badā'ūnī, the mystic Shaykh Aḥmad Sirhindī and Akbar himself.[27]

The migration of the more sincere ulema to the Hijaz coincided with the period of Akbar's heresy but was not necessarily a direct reaction to it. Deeper reasons must have operated to cause this migration; perhaps the spiritual necessity of close contact with Islam's cognizable centre, and a desire to escape from the threatening chaos of spiritual bankruptcy in Muslim India. Travelling to the Hijaz had been made easier by Portuguese navigation. Eminent among the immigrant Indian ulema in the Hijaz was Sayyid ʿAlī Muttaqī, whose chief field of study, like that of his great Meccan contemporary Ibn-Ḥajar, was *ḥadīth*. His disciple, ʿAbd-al-Wahhāb Muttaqī, who also lived in Mecca, was the preceptor of the great Indian divine of Akbar's age, ʿAbd-al-Ḥaqq Dihlawī.[28] Among other Indian scholars resident in the Hijaz was Raḥmat-Allāh Sindhī – author of *al-Manāsik aṣ-ṣaghīr*, a considerable work on Sunnī jurisprudence – as well as other divines from the Deccan and Gujarat. An emigré from the court of Akbar, Shayk Jamāl-ad-dīn, spent twelve years in the Hijaz, having refused to sign the so-called 'infallibility' decree enlarging the ruler's religious powers.[29]

ʿAbd-al-Ḥaqq Dihlawī (1551–1642) was also making a spiritual escape from the court of Akbar when he went to the Hijaz in 1587. He then returned to India where he started the movement to rehabilitate orthodox Islam in India, and to re-establish, in the face of Alfī heresies, the central position of the Prophet of Islam through critical study and interpretation of the Prophetic Tradition.[30] ʿAbd-al-Ḥaqq was essentially a theologian who had also received spiritual training in several Ṣūfī orders. He wrote on almost every theological science, and can be regarded as by far the most outstanding Muslim theologian before Shāh Walī-Allāh in the eighteenth century. His three works on Qur'ānic exegesis include a commentary on Bayḍāwī. In his main field, the study of *ḥadīth*, he relied especially on the authority of the *Mishkāt* and commented heavily upon it.[31] In other works he emphasized the Sunnī doctrinal position as a check against the speculative and rationalist trends in sixteenth-century Indian Islam. He subjected his Ṣūfī training completely to the strong tenets of orthodoxy,[32] and thus began, in India, the movement of absorbing Ṣūfism integrally into theology, which culminated in Shāh Walī-Allāh.

In the seventeenth century, emphasis shifted to jurisprudence with the writings of Rukn-ad-dīn Nāgorī and Muḥibb-Allāh Bihārī (d. 1707); the latter's *Musallam ath-Thubūt* is perhaps the most outstanding work in India on the principles of Ḥanafī jurisprudence. In other fields of theological studies the exegesis of Muḥibb-Allāh Allāhabādī (d. 1648) interpreted the Qur'ān in the light of Ibn-al-ʿArabī's monism. The Qur'ānic exegesis of Mullā Jiwān (d. 1717) was more orthodox, and concentrated principally on points of canon law. The glosses of ʿAbd-al-Ḥakīm Siyālkotī (d. 1657) on the exegesis of Bayḍāwī, and his other work on theology and logic, won recognition in India and abroad.[33]

3. Fundamentalism and Orthodoxy since the Eighteenth Century

Fakhr-ad-dīn Zarrādī (d. 1326) shows the earliest traces of fundamentalism in Indian Sunnī Islam. A scholar of *ḥadīth* himself, he believed in the Qur'ān and the *sunna* as the ultimate sources of law, and minimized the importance of the juristic schools. He also interpreted *ijmāʿ* (consensus) as a source of law in a much broader sense than merely the consensus of the ulema.[34]

As the Mughal empire began to decline, after the death of Awrangzīb (1707), and Indian Muslim society to disintegrate at the beginning of the eighteenth century, the religio-intellectual leadership of Muslim India passed for the first time into the hands of a theologian, in the person of Shāh Walī-Allāh (1703–62). His aim was to reach the erudite public throughout the Muslim world, and he wrote in Arabic as well as Persian. He revived the study of *ḥadīth* – already rehabilitated in India in the sixteenth century by ʿAbd-al-Ḥaqq Dihlawī; related it to the study of Mālikī jurisprudence; developed an inter-juristic eclecticism recommending that on any point of doctrine or ritual a Muslim could follow the rulings of any one of the four principal juristic schools; reconciled the monistic trends of Ṣūfism with religious ideology; translated the Qur'ān into Persian; and, what is of principal importance, founded a tradition of religious scholarship and a school which was to influence religious thought in Muslim India, fundamentalist and traditional as well as modernistic, for the next three centuries.

During his years of study in the Hijaz he must have had the same teachers as his other great fundamentalist contemporary, Muḥammad ibn-ʿAbd-al-Wahhāb; but there is no evidence that they ever met or influenced one another.

Walī-Allāh's fundamentalism is based on a firm rejection of polytheistic 'association' (*shirk*). God is unique and none of his attributes can be attributed to prophets or saints; these may be considered intercessors but cannot be called upon or invoked for help. No one should be worshipped, in a direct or oblique form, except God. The basis of all religious dogma is the Qur'ān and the *ḥadīth*; all other sources of belief and law are subsidiary and subject to investigation.[35] Islamic theology needed re-examination and re-assessment and had to be presented in a new style.[36] The prescriptions and prohibitions of religious law have a three-fold aim: the cultivation of self, the propagation of religious life and the service of humanity.[37] He follows Ibn-Taymiyya in considering that *ijtihād* (use of individual reasoning) was permissible at all times and could be defined as an exhaustive endeavour to understand the derivative principles of canon law.[38] His concept of the structure of Muslim society is based on the revival of the theory of a universal caliphate.[39]

Broadly speaking, in the eighteenth and nineteenth centuries, Walī-Allāh's school in Delhi specialized in the study of exegesis and *ḥadīth*, and that of Farangī Maḥall, at Lucknow, in jurisprudence (*fiqh*).[40] Walī-Allāh's school continued to flourish under his son Shāh ʿAbd-al-ʿAzīz, a scholar with remarkable insight, though representative also, in his blurred view of history, of the decadence of Indian Islam at that stage.[41] His reaction to the suppression of Ḥanafī law by the Anglo-Muhammadan Law under the East India Company was one of sharp denunciation.[42]

A remarkable disciple of ʿAbd-al-ʿAzīz's was Sayyid Aḥmad Barēlwī, whose movement is generally known as that of the Mujāhidīn (holy warriors), and is erroneously described in the British Indian Government records as Wahhābī. It was a movement of holy war directed primarily against the Sikhs and possibly secondarily against the British. This movement marks the crystallization of Walī-Allāh's fundamentalist ideas into a practical programme. One of its objectives was to eliminate syncretistic elements borrowed into Islam from Hinduism. Its fundamentalism generally rejected the peripheral, the eclectic and the heterodox elements in religious belief. In its rejection of polytheistic associationism, it outlined more rigidly and clearly the views preached by Walī-Allāh. Its stress was on absolute monotheism. It developed into a *jamāʿa* or religio-political organization with a network of centres for the propagation and purification of Islam; villages being the basic units. It was the first agitation in the history of Indian Islam to become a popular mass movement.[43]

Unconnected with it, though parallel to it, and possibly bearing some influence of the Wahhābī movement of Nejd, was the Farā'iḍī movement of Bengal led by Ḥājjī Sharīʿat-Allāh (1764–1840) – who had lived long in the Hijaz – and his son Muḥsin, known popularly as Dhūdhū Miyān. The Farā'iḍī movement preached the achievement of a fundamentalist society, like that of the first four Orthodox Caliphs, though juristically the movement was Ḥanafī. It aimed also at the economic relief of Muslim peasants who were being exploited by Hindu landlords appointed under the revenue reorganization, which was known as the Permanent Settlement of 1793 and was introduced by Lord Cornwallis and Sir John Shore. Its followers were mainly among the peasantry, who were exhorted to resist paying taxes and even to squat on Government lands. Dhūdhū Miyān formed almost a parallel government in some villages of Bengal. The movement was unmystical and to some extent anti-Shīʿī and regarded India under the British as *dār al-ḥarb* (enemy territory).[44]

A similar fundamentalist peasant movement in Bengal, led by Tītū Mīr, was connected with that of the Mujāhidīn and not with the Farā'iḍīs. Its programme was more militant, and for a time Tītū Mīr controlled three districts of Bengal, but he was finally overpowered and slain by a British military expedition in 1831.

Fundamentalism, especially when it was imbued with Wahhābī ideas, was subjected to polemical attacks by more orthodox theologians. Karāmat ʿAlī Jawnpūrī, who had been associated with the Mujāhidīn earlier and became a modernist in his later writings, wrote virulently against the Farā'iḍīs. Several works were written in the later nineteenth century against the Wahhābis from the view point of conformity (*taqlīd*), and there were even refutations of the classics of the *mujāhidūn.*[45]

Under the influence of Wahhābism and the theologians of Nejd and the Hijaz, the Ahl-i Ḥadīth movement[46] developed in the nineteenth century. Its chief representatives were Ṣiddīq Ḥasan Khān (d. 1890) and Naẓīr Ḥusayn (d. 1902) who based their faith and creed on the classical corpus of the Prophetic Traditions. They did not consider themselves bound in conformity (*taqlīd*) to any of the four juristic schools and were consequently also called *ghayr-muqallid* (non-conformists). Their view of *ijtihād* (individual reasoning) was that every Muslim of sufficient ability can draw his own conclusions from the Qur'ān and the *ḥadīth*. They did not consider the consensus of classical jurists binding. In Walī-Allāh's tradition they re-asserted the doctrine of the absolute Unity of God and de-nounced polytheistic associationism in all forms. They regarded innovations (*bidaʿ*) as borrowed or invented accretions and as the very antithesis of the *sunna* or the Prophet's work and word. The movement of the Ahl-i Ḥadīth still survives in West Pakistan.

At the beginning of the twentieth century members of a splinter-group of the Ahl-i Ḥadīth formed themselves into another fundamentalist community, Ahl al-Qur'ān, basing their doctrine exclusively on the Qur'ān, to the exclusion even of the Prophetic Tradition as a source of law.

The most recent fundamentalist movement in the sub-continent, especially in Pakistan, is that of Abū-l-Aʿlā Maw-dūdī's Jamāʿat-i Islāmī.[47] Mawdūdī's fundamentalism conceives Islamic and indeed all human society as properly governed only by a single code, that of the immutable, everlasting, infallible, divine law of the Qur'ānic revelation. 'Islam signifies nothing but obedience and submission to Allāh.'[48] God is the only ruler and legislator of human society. Though Mawdūdī's theology is based exclusively on the Qur'ān, he often compromises with the Sunnī theologians in paying tribute to the founders of the four juristic schools and in recognizing the importance of classical *ḥadīth* as a basic source of law.[49] His political party, the Jamāʿat-i Islāmī, has a dual objective in Pakistan: to bring about a revivalistic, pietistic and conservative revolu-tion in the religious and social life of the Muslim community, and to participate actively in exercising pressure to convert Pakistan into a theocracy, or, as Mawdūdī calls it, a 'theo-democracy'.[50]

During the nineteenth century, and since, there has been an

enthusiastic revival of traditional orthodoxy under the influence of the ulema. The nineteenth century produced some great scholars of Qur'ānic exegesis, *ḥadīth*, 'rational' science, scholasticism and Ṣūfism.

The religious seminary of Deoband founded by Muḥammad Qāsim Nānotawī in 1867 became the outstanding centre of theological studies, developing its own tradition of classical scholarship. Students came to Deoband from as far as Russian and Chinese Turkestan, from Persia and Afghanistan, and its graduates included some great luminaries of Islamic learning in India. The most distinguished of these luminaries of Deoband was its leader between 1880 and 1920, Maḥmūd al-Ḥasan, a political and theological personality of outstanding vitality who planned to establish a chain of theological schools in the north-western frontier area.[51]

Nadwat al-ʿulamā', another Muslim theological school, was founded in 1894, and had as objectives the advancement and reform of Islamic scholarship, the suppression of controversial quibbles among the ulema, social reform without involvement in active politics, the propagation of the Islamic faith and the establishment of a department of theological legislation (*iftā'*).[52]

A religious movement to propagate conformity was initiated by Muḥammad Ilyās, and developed into missionary activity not only in the subcontinent, but as far away as Japan, Indonesia and the United States of America.[53]

Active participation of the ulema in the subcontinent's freedom-movement was a heritage of the Walī-Allāhī religio-political tradition, re-orientated and modernized in the seminary of Deoband. Following the lead of Maḥmūd al-Ḥasan, most of the ulema of Deoband, and those of Nadwat al-ʿulamā' and Farangī Maḥall, participated in the movement for political freedom, and in 1919 formed their organization, Jamʿiyyat al-ʿulamā'-i Hind, which played an active role in Indian politics. The Deobandī element of Jamʿiyyat al-ʿulamā'-i Hind was more inclined towards the Indian nationalist viewpoint, because of the influence of Abū-l-Kalām Āzād, and generally opposed Muslim political trends of self-determination. A splinter-group of the ulema under Shabbīr Aḥmad ʿUthmānī, also a Deobandi seceded from Jamʿiyyat al-ʿulamā'-i Hind and founded another organization, Jam'iyyat al-'ulamā'-i Islām, which supported the demand for Pakistan.

4. Modernism

Indian Islam, like Islam elsewhere, felt the impact of the West, especially after 1857, and since then three generations of modernist thinkers have tried to incorporate certain Western values into their interpretation of their religion, by processes of rationalization, re-orientation and apologetics.[54]

The modernist movement was initiated in India by Sayyid Aḥmad Khān (d. 1898), whose creed was based on the principle that between the word of God (scripture) and the work of God (nature) there can be no contradiction, and that one had to be interpreted in the light of the other.[55] His creed asserts the omnipotence of God, the prophethood of Muḥammad and other prophets and the authenticity of *waḥy* (revelation); it is immaterial whether the words of revelation were conveyed to Muḥammad by an archangel or whether the sense as well as the words were received directly by his prophetic intuition. The creed goes on to assert that the Qur'ān contains nothing which could be wrong or anti-historical, that the attributes of God exist only in their essence and are identical with His Self. These eternal attributes can have no limitation; but God, in His freedom, has created the laws of nature and maintains them as the discipline of existence. Therefore there can be nothing in the scripture contrary to the laws of nature. Qur'ānic eschatology, angelology, demonology and cosmology cannot be contrary to scientific thought. The Qur'ān contains the outlines of social mores and of possibilities for the development of human society, which can be studied and thought out.[56]

Of the four sources of law, according to Sunnī jurisprudence, Sayyid Aḥmad Khān relied almost entirely on the Qur'ān, of which he offered a rationalistic exegesis. He and his associate, Chirāgh 'Alī, doubted the authenticity of much of even classical *ḥadīth* and regarded it as apocryphal. They therefore recommended a thorough scientific and rationalistic investigation of the existing corpus of *ḥadīth* before it was relied upon as a source of law. Sayyid Aḥmad Khān rejected the principle of *ijmā'* (consensus) as a source of law, meaning by this the consensus of the classical jurists; but his contemporary Amīr 'Alī and his successor Iqbāl saw in a modernized concept of *ijmāʿ* the principle of the consensus of common Muslims and the Muslim élite, and thus the modern principle of democracy. *Ijtihād* (individual reasoning) as a substitute for *qiyās* (analogy) was regarded by the Indo-Muslim modernists as the right of every thinking Muslim.[57] Chirāgh ʿAlī and Amīr ʿAlī were Shīʿīs but they developed their religious thought within the framework of Sunnism.

There was considerable opposition to the views of Sayyid Aḥmad Khān and the modernist group, especially among the traditional theologians of Deoband and other schools. Traditional orthodoxy insisted that rationalist doubts and misgivings were an illness of the mind and should be treated as such. It argued that the incomprehensible was not necessarily impossible, and pointed out that rational dialectics was out of its depth in dealing with the recorded data of the scripture, which has to be accepted with a willing suspension of disbelief.[58]

The modernist theological speculation of Iqbāl (1875–1938) is much more subdued and closer to orthodoxy than that of Sayyid Aḥmad Khān. His exegetical approach to the Qur'ān is also highly speculative, but his theology is rooted firmly in the Ashʿarite tradition. He does not raise the question of the authenticity of *ḥadīth*, but he regards *ijtihād* as the principle of legal advance in Islam: a principle to which the Muslim élite – not necessarily identified with the ulema – has a right in every age and clime. He defines *ijmāʿ* as a consensus, arrived at through a parliamentary system of government in an Islamic state, though he also conservatively recommends associating the ulema with the system of parliamentary democracy.[59]

Islam in Pakistan has been facing, since 1947, the dilemma of a struggle between modernism and orthodoxy. Sayyid Aḥmad Khān's ideas were never accepted totally by any considerable section of the Muslim élite and were rejected by all in details, but his rationalism and general liberal approach, like that of Iqbāl, made a considerable impact on the general religious thinking of Westernized intelligentsia. This intelligentsia worked for, and achieved, the state of Pakistan, which it has been trying to run on liberal secularized principles, but yielding ground constantly to the orthodox and conformist pressures of the lower middle classes, who have greater influence among the masses and are led by the ulema and the fundamentalists, especially Mawdūdī. A Council of Islamic Ideology advises the National and Provincial Assemblies of Pakistan, as well as the Federal and Provincial Governments, on questions where the law of the land, inherited from the British Indian legal and executive institutions, does not conform to traditional Islamic jurisprudence.

The situation is confused because the Western intelligentsia is as ignorant of Islamic religion and history as the ulema and the conservatives are of the pressures, stresses and challenges of the modern highly technological civilization. Both the modernists and the conservatives talk glibly about Islam as the ideal way of life, as the form of the ideal state, but they have widely different concepts of it. The modernists think of the Islamic state under the orthodox caliphate in terms of an idealized modern social democracy. For the conservatives the modern Islamic state should be today what the Islamic state actually was under the orthodox caliphate. It is difficult to say what the final position of religion will be in Pakistan.[60]

Islam in India since 1947 has had a slightly different development from that in Pakistan.[61] Fundamentalist groups like the Jamā'at-i Islāmī and the Bhopālī movement tend to keep aloof from the secular order professed, though not actually practised, by the Indian state and concentrate on purging Muslim society of accretions borrowed from Hindu or Western influences.[62] The ulema in India, because of their alliance with the ruling party, the Indian National Congress, are in a position of special political responsibility, in fact much more so than in Pakistan. But in actual fact this has led to stagnant conservatism. Whereas family law has been thoroughly revised and polygamy forbidden for the rest of the Indian people, these family laws have not been applied to Muslims, because of the pressure of orthodox theologians. Urdu is being liquidated from schools in India and there is growing up a new generation of Indian Muslims unable to read or write that language which contains all the religious heritage of Indian Islam. The future of Islam as a religion in India is therefore bleak. No doubt some regional languages like Gujarati have some Islamic, and considerable Ismā'īlī literature, but in the great northern plains the Islamic heritage is coming to a visible end. Modernists in India try to ally themselves with the officially proclaimed secular order, but most of them, Indian nationalists of old standing like ʿĀbid Ḥusayn are expressing their discontent vocally even with the optimistic assertion: 'though there was confusion in their [the Indian Muslims'] minds and frustration and resentment in their hearts, their religious faith never wavered'.[63]

TWO

SHĪʿĪ SECTS

1. The Twelvers

Outside Iran the largest community of Shīʿīs is found in the Indo-Pakistan subcontinent. According to the census report of 1921 they were a little less than ten per cent of the total Muslim population. Their exact number cannot be easily calculated, as in recent census counts in both South Asian countries sectarian categories have been discouraged by the Muslims.[1]

Not much is known about the number or location of the Shīʿīs in India under the Delhi Sultanate. They possibly concealed their identity, practising the doctrine of *taqiyya* (concealment). We know only that there was a rising of the Ismāʿīlis under Raḍiyya (1236–40), and that Fīrūz Tughluq (1351–88) mentions their missionary activities and the steps he took to suppress them.[2] On the other hand substantial records are available about the position and influence of the Shīʿī sect in the Deccan. From the outset the Bahmanids had Shīʿī proclivities. Though officially most of them were Sunnīs, their Sunnism was tinged with the doctrine of *tafḍīliyya* (or the superiority of ʿAlī and the subsequent *imāms* to the first three Orthodox Caliphs).[3] In 1429 Aḥmad Shāh Walī Bahmanī (1422–36) was overtly converted to Shīʿism. The two political factions at the Bahmanid court, the *āfāqī* (foreigners) and the local *Dakanī*, showed sectarian as well as racial rivalry.[4]

Of the successor states of the Bahmanids, Bijapur and Golconda were ruled by Shīʿī dynasties from the beginning, and the dynasty at Ahmadnagar was converted to Shīʿism in the second generation.

Yūsuf ʿĀdil Shāh (1489–1510), the founder of the kingdom of Bijapur, was encouraged by the example of the Ṣafavids to give a Shīʿī tinge to the ritual of public worship in his territory;

though he did not interfere with the practice of Sunnī law in courts, and prudently discouraged the cursing of the first three caliphs. His caution suggests that then, as now, the majority of the Muslim population in that area was Sunnī. Under his son Ismāʿīl ʿĀdil Shāh (1510–34) Shīʿism was more firmly entrenched in administration, and the name of the Ṣafavid shāh was mentioned in the Friday *khuṭba* (sermon). Shīʿism received a setback in Bijapur under Ibrāhīm I (1534–58) who was a Sunnī, but it was revived to the point of polemical virulence under his successor ʿAlī I (1558–80). A more liberal *modus vivendi* between the Shīʿīs and the Sunnīs was evolved under Ibrāhīm II (1580–1627).[5]

Qulī Quṭb Shāh (1512–43) founded the kingdom of Golconda as a Shīʿī state, in which *khuṭba* was read in the name of the twelve Shīʿī *imāms*. Golconda developed a Shīʿī civilization, nourished by Persian noblemen like Mīr Muḥammad Mū'min and Mīr Jumla.

Burhān I (1509–53), the second ruler of Ahmadnagar, was converted to Shīʿism by his pious minister Shāh Ṭāhir. Shīʿism was more virulent in Ahmadnagar than in other states of the Deccan; the practice of cursing the earlier caliphs was introduced, but abandoned in the face of a Sunnī revolt.

Dynastically the Great Mughals were, and remained, Sunnīs. Bābur (1526–30) and Humāyūn (1530–56), who had sought Persian help, paid lip service to Shīʿism under Ṣafavid pressure, but actually they remained good Sunnīs. Akbar's guardian, Bayrām Khān, his first *shaykh al-Islām*, Gadā'ī, and his tutor, ʿAbd-al-Laṭīf, were either Shīʿīs or *tafḍīlīs*; and there are certain esoteric extreme Shīʿī elements in the ritual and belief of Akbar's imperial heresy, the *Dīn-i Ilāhī*. Some of the distinguished Shīʿī élite in Akbar's court influenced his religious ideas to some extent. These included the versatile and erudite Ḥakīm Abū-l-Fat'ḥ Gīlānī and Mullā Muḥammad Yaz[illegible].

Jahāngīr and Shāh Jahān were staunch Sunnīs, but owing to the influence of Nūr-Jahān – Jahāngīr's beautiful and accomplished Persian queen – of her powerful family, and of the Persian faction of the court in general, Shīʿism entrenched itself as a spiritual and cultural variant among the Muslim élite of northern India. Awrangzīb's Sunnism was fanatical to the point of distaste for Shīʿism and, though his conquest – and absorption into the Mughal empire – of the Shīʿī kingdoms of Golconda and Bijapur was not officially designated a *jihād*, it was no doubt considered by him as a meritorious act.

It was under Akbar that the most distinguished Twelver Shīʿī divine, Nūr-Allāh Shustarī, migrated to India in 1587. Introduced to the Emperor by the Shīʿī *amīrs* of the court, he was appointed the chief *qāḍī* of Lahore, where he gave his rulings according to the Sunnī law. His Shīʿī bias was discovered in Jahāngīr's reign and he was executed in 1604. He is regarded by the Shīʿīs of India as *Shahīd-i thālith* or the third Martyr.[6] His famous hagiological work, *Majālis al-mu'minīn*, is highly polemical and brings forth Shīʿī accusations against Sunnism in the context of historical Islam.[7]

During the period of Mughal decline, the only ruler who can be said to have had *tafḍīlī* tendencies was Bahādur Shāh I (1707–12), whose introduction of a Shīʿī formula in the *khuṭba*, led to widespread unrest. Owing to the weakness of the later Mughals, the two principal political factions, *Irānī* and *Tūrānī*, which were Shīʿī and Sunnī respectively, swerved apart. Dynamic leadership of the Shīʿī faction was provided by the indigenous Sayyids of Bārha, led by the brothers ʿAbd-Allāh Khān and Ḥusayn ʿAlī Khān who became king-makers and placed several puppet Mughal emperors on the throne, or removed them, until their power was broken by a strong Sunnī coalition under Muḥammad Shāh (1719–48).

The rise of the Bārha Sayyids and, later, of the Shīʿī dynasty of the Nawwāb-wazīrs of Oudh (Awadh) led to bitter feuds between Sunnīs and Shīʿīs. Popular riots had their counterpart in the theological writings of the period. Anti-Shīʿī works were written by Walī-Allāh and his son ʿAbd-al-ʿAzīz.[8]

The Shīʿism of Oudh with its cultural capital at Lucknow is the link between the Mughal empire and the Indian Shīʿism of today.[9] Next to Lucknow, Rampur, until recently the capital of a small Shīʿī principality, has been a centre of Shīʿism.

The Nawwāb-wazīrs of Oudh became rulers of the autonomous principality of Oudh; at the same time some of them served as prime ministers of the puppet Mughal emperors during the eighteenth century. In 1815, under British encouragement, the Nawwāb-wazīr claimed a royal title. Under the dynasty, a refined, though slightly effeminate, Shīʿī culture developed in Lucknow and its environs, an area which still remains the heartland of Shīʿism in India. Shīʿī themes and values are expressed in Urdu poetry written in the region and in the architecture of the *imāmbāṛas*. In Oudh Shīʿī law replaced Ḥanafī law in the law-courts during the reign of Amjad ʿAlī (1842–7). Lucknow produced some fine scholars including Tafaḍḍul Ḥusayn Khān who also knew some Latin.[10] In 1856 the principality of Oudh was absorbed into British India; but Shīʿī culture continued to flourish in Lucknow. There has been functioning for some time a Shīʿī school for the training of preachers. The All-India Shīʿa Conference, organized in 1907 for the social and educational advancement of the Shīʿīs, established a Shīʿa College at Lucknow. There was special provision for the teaching of Shīʿī theology in the MAO College founded by Sayyid Aḥmad Khān at Aligarh.

The Shīʿīs in India observe piously the Muḥarram, mourning the assassination of the Prophet's grandson and the third *Imām*, Ḥusayn ibn-ʿAlī, at Kerbela in 680. As the martyrdom occurred on the tenth of Muḥarram, the first ten days of that month are devoted to passionate mourning which takes the form of assemblies (*majālis*) for the recital in prose and verse of the events of the battle of Kerbela followed by *mātam*, which takes the form of passionate self-infliction of blows on the chest. Miniature replicas of Ḥusayn's tomb, called *taʿziyas*, and *ʿalams* (standards) representing the standard of his brother ʿAbbās, are kept in specially consecrated halls called the *imāmbāṛas*; they are taken out in a procession on the tenth of Muḥarram, and the *taʿziyas* are sunk in a stream or well, known as local Kerbelas and representing the battle-field. The passion of Ḥusayn has a strong emotional effect on women, who break their glass bangles in mourning, do not comb their hair, do not wear any jewellery, avoid bright colours in dress, and suppress laughter or any other expression of joy during the period of mourning. This mourning sometimes continues until the fortieth day of the assassination of Ḥusayn, called *Chihillum*. Some of the practices of the Shīʿī passion of Muḥarram have been influenced by Hindu rituals in India.

In the syncretistic atmosphere of India, Sunnism has tried to compromise with Shīʿism; the doctrine of *tafḍīliyya* is accepted by a small section of the Sunnī élite, and the Umayyads are generally held in abhorrence. This trend has received a recent set-back in areas of Shīʿī density, like Lucknow, because of the Shīʿī practice of openly cursing the first three caliphs. It has led to the counter demonstration of *mad'ḥ-i ṣaḥāba*, or public recital of the praise of these caliphs, and has stirred up sectarian riots. Temporary contractual marriage (*mutʿa*), though permitted in Shīʿī jurisprudence, is frowned upon by the Westernized Shīʿī élite and rarely practised.

With the late nineteenth-century growth of modernism, there has been a self-identification of Shīʿī modernists with Sunnī Islam, though in varying degrees. There was also curiously enough a recognition of the Ottoman claim to the caliphate, crystallized into a theory by Amīr ʿAlī, who distinguishes between the 'apostolic' *imāmate* and the 'pontifical' caliphate. The first president of the republic of Pakistan, Iskandar Mirzā, was a Shīʿī; and the two constitutions of Pakistan, promulgated respectively in 1956 and 1962, while emphasizing their conformity to the Qur'ān and the *sunna*, explain that the *sunna* is applicable to each Muslim sect according to its own interpretation of it.

2. Ismāʿīlis[11]

Carmathian (Qarmatian) influence reached Sind fairly early. Multan was seized by the Carmathian ʿAbd-Allāh about 900. The Arab geographer, al-Maqdisī, who visited Multan in 985, records that by that time the people of that city had been converted to Ismāʿīlism. The chief *dāʿī* (missionary) of Multan was in correspondence with the Fāṭimid, al-Muʿizz (953–75). The power of the Ismāʿīlis was established in Multan by Jalam ibn-Shaybān in 983 when he acknowledged the suzerainty of the Fāṭimids, which lasted, though only nominally, for over a century. In 1005, and again in 1010, Maḥmūd of Ghazna defeated Abū-l-Fat'ḥ Dā'ūd the Carmathian ruler of Multan, and occupied that city. It was however a temporary occupation. The Sumra rulers of Sind, before their reconversion to Hinduism, passed through an intermediate phase of Ismāʿīlism; and one of the Sumra rājahs received an epistle from the Druze leader Bahā'-ad-dīn in 1032. The correspondence of al-Mustanṣir (1036–94) mentions administrative problems regarding the *dāʿis* in India.[12]

In 1175 Muḥammad ibn-Sām Ghūrī conquered Multan and brought the Ismāʿīlī hold there to an end. He was assassinated either by the Ismāʿīlis or the Khokkars.[13] There was a major rising of the Ismāʿīlis during the reign of Sulṭāna Raḍiyya under the leadership of Nūr Turk, who regarded Sunnis as Nāṣibīs and enemies of ʿAlī and whose followers had converged probably from Sind and Gujarat.[14] One may disregard Menant's theory,[15] identifying Nūr Turk with the khoja leader Nūr Satgur, as being highly speculative, and may also neglect hagiographical records exonerating Nūr Turk from the charge of Ismāʿīlism.[16] Nūr Turk's rising was suppressed quickly by the state. Under Fīrūz Tughluq, the Ismāʿīlī religious propaganda was still active, and he took steps to suppress it.

The two principal Ismāʿīlī sects of India are Bohras and Khojas. The cleavage between them goes back to 1094 when al-Mustaʿlī (1094–1101), instead of his brother Nizār, succeeded al-Mustanṣir as the Fāṭimid caliph in Egypt. The Bohras trace the line of their *imāms* to al-Mustaʿlī. On the other hand the claim that Nizār's *imāmate* was the real one was taken up by Ḥasan-i Ṣabbāḥ and, in the wake of the Nizārīs of Alamūt, by the Khojas of India, who regard the Āghā Khān as their living *imām*. Both these commercial communities of Gujarat as well as the Sunnī Memons were converted from Hinduism during the eleventh and twelfth centuries.[17]

3. Bohras[18]

Bohras are either named after a syncretistic Hindu community Vohra, or else derive their name from the Gujaratī word *vohuru* meaning trade, which is their occupation. There are two distinct sub-sects of the Bohras, the Sulaymānīs, or followers of Sulaymān ibn-Ḥasan, who are found in Gujarat, Bombay and the Deccan; and the Dā'ūdīs, who are followers of Dā'ūd ibn-ʿAjab Shāh (d. 1589), and have links with the Yemenite Ismāʿīlism. The two sub-sects revere two different lines of supreme missionaries. There is also a small minority of Sunnī Bohras called Jaʿfarīs, who are agriculturists and do not concern us here. There are also other minor and unimportant sub-sects of the Bohras, for example, the ʿAliyya, the Nagōshiya and the Hiptia.

The Sulaymānī *dāʿī muṭlaq* (supreme missionary), Yaḥyā

ibn-Sulaymān, transferred his headquarters from the Yemen to India in 1539.[19] Administration of the community is authoritarian. At the apex is the *dā'ī muṭlaq* who is the uncontested leader and administrator of the community. Under him are a *ma'dhūn* and a *mukāsir*, whose offices are a remnant of the old Ismā'īlī hierarchy. Next come eighteen *mashā'ikh* trained at *Sayfī dars*, the Bohra seminary at Surat. Next come *'āmils*, or agents, appointed in towns with a significant Bohra population in order to lead congregational prayers and perform marriages and other services. At the bottom of the hierarchy are the *mullas* who work as teachers in Bohra schools.[20] The seat of the *Sulaymānī da'wat* is at Baroda in Gujarat, and Muḥammad Burhān-ad-din is the present *dā'ī muṭlaq* who is representative of the alive and concealed (*ghā'ib*) *imām*. A covenantal oath of loyalty to the *imām* and of secrecy is administered to every Bohra convert.

The Bohra community lives in an exclusive quarter of a city, has its own mosques and congregation halls (*jamā'at khānas*). The Bohras do not mix much with other people, and they marry among themselves. Their women do not observe purdah.[21] The cosmogony and esoteric interpretations of the Bohras are derived from the Fāṭimid Ismā'īlī literature.[22] The Bohra calendar is two days ahead of the common Muslim calendar. The Bohras follow the Twelvers in certain ritual matters, such as the formula of the *adhān* (call to prayers) and the celebration of the *'Id al-Ghadīr* commemorating the alleged nomination of 'Alī to the caliphate by Muḥammad.

Many Hindu heritages still survive among the Bohras, for example, in their marriage and other customs, in the laws of inheritance which deprive a woman of her share in property, in their calendar, in giving and taking interest on loans, and in beginning their fiscal year like the Hindus on the Hindu lamp-festival (*dīpāwalī*).[23]

The Bohra community is well-disciplined, closely-knit, enterprising, prosperous, quiet and tidy. Their social welfare enterprise takes care of the poor among them. Though influenced by Hinduism, like other Shī'īs they will not eat or drink from the hands of Hindus or other non-Muslims. If their clothes are washed by a Hindu they ritually sprinkle water on them to purify them before use.

4. Khojas[24]

Etymologically the name Khoja is derived from *khwāja*, which has connotations of commerce and business. The Khojas are a well-knit, prosperous community. Many of its members in East Africa and the Indo-Pakistan subcontinent are very rich.

The Khojas regard Nūr Satgur (or Satgar), who arrived from Alamūt probably in the twelfth century, as their first missionary in India. He soon incorporated certain Hindu practices, such as *samādhī* or the mystic contemplative seance, into his mystic teaching.[25]

The religious books of the Khojas are known as *Ginans*, and one of these, *Das Avatār* (Ten Incarnations), written by Ṣadr-ad-dīn in the fifteenth century, is the most important. It contains ten chapters, each describing one of the incarnations of the Hindu god Vishnu, of whom ʿAlī is regarded as the most important. The Khoja personal law also derives largely from Hindu law, though Āghā Khān I tried to free it from that source in 1847.[26]

The Āghā Khāns are the living and present (*ḥāḍir*) *imāms* of the Khojas and have divinity attributed to them. The first of the Āghā Khāns to migrate to India was Ḥasan ʿAlī Shāh who arrived in Sind in 1840, aided the British against the Amīrs there and received the title of His Highness and the status of a ruling prince without any territory. Every Khoja pays from one-tenth to one-eighth of his income as a *dassondh* (literally one-tenth) offering to the Āghā Khān. Salvation for him lies in recognizing the *imām*, failing which he has to pass through a cycle of eighty-four rebirths.[27] Under the Āghā Khān there is a Supreme Council for India, a Central Committee of five called the *Panjebhā'i*, and a central treasurer. These institutions are repeated at the provincial and regional levels and in the Khoja communities outside India. *Ḥajj* (pilgrimage) for the Khojas is a visit to see the Āghā Khān and not the usual pilgrimage to Mecca. But they visit Najaf and Kerbela, the burial places of ʿAlī and his son Ḥusayn respectively. *Dassondh* replaces *zakāt* (obligatory charity), and *jihād* (holy war) is interpreted as the struggle against one's own vile instincts.

Members of a sub-sect of the Khojas, the Shamsīs, followers of Shams-ad-dīn (c. 1500), are found in West Pakistan. They also venerate the Āghā Khān as an incarnation of the deity, but are a syncretistic sect even more deeply influenced by Hinduism; they call the corpus of their religious books *Atharv Vedh*, use Hindu caste names, and associate the Prophet as well as their *imāms* with the Hindu supreme god Brahma.[28]

Though the Khoja religion is highly coloured by Hinduism, it is remarkable that Āghā Khān III (Sulṭān Muḥammad Shāh) was, from 1908 onwards, one of the outstanding leaders of Muslim separatism in Indian politics; while Muḥammad ʿAlī Jinnāḥ, the founder of Pakistan, was originally a Khoja.

The Khojas do not have mosques. They pray three times a day in their congregation halls (*jamāʿat khānas*). These prayers do not even remotely resemble the Sunnī or orthodox Shīʿī *ṣalāt*, but are in fact devout homage to the Āghā Khān, tinged with some Hindu features. On the other hand the Khojas offer the two *ʿīd* prayers, with Sunnīs or orthodox Shīʿīs, in the great congregational mosques of a city; and in the ritual *ṣalāt* they follow the physical movements of the members of the majority communities.

A reformist faction – called the Bārbhāi – which has reservations about accepting the Āghā Khān's claim to divinity and absolute leadership rose among the Khojas in 1840; its members, who tend to be inclined either towards Sunnism or Twelver Shīʿism, were excommunicated during the 1850s by the Āghā Khān, who won the undisputed leadership of the community in a case against them in the Bombay High Court in 1866.

Another Khoja group, Pīra'ī, localized in Sind, does not acknowledge the authority of the Āghā Khān and is close to Hinduism in its rituals of life and death.

5. Minor Ismāʿīlī Sects

After the death of the Khoja missionary, Imām Shāh, in 1512 some of his followers developed the Imāmshāhī schism. Their syncretism drifted back into Hinduism and they are disclaimed by Muslims and Hindus alike. They regard *Panjtan* (Muḥammad, ʿAlī, Fāṭima, Ḥasan and Ḥusayn) as divine, and Muḥammad's daughter Fāṭima as a Hindu goddess. *Ṣalāt* is unknown among them. They cremate their dead like the Hindus, but bury their bones.[29]

Another very Hinduized group of Khojas are the Swāmī Narāyan Panthis. Yet another group is known as Guptīs, who believe in God, in the Prophet, and in 'Alī as an incarnation of the Hindu god Krishna; they regard the founder of this sect Imām-ad-dīn as 'Alī's deputy. The Guptīs conceal their religious beliefs, abstain from meat like Hindus, and observe neither *ṣalāt* nor fast. When a Guptī openly professes Islam, he is excommunicated and called Parghātī (from the other mountain-range).

The Mominas are a Shī'ī group within the generally Sunnī, Memon commercial community of Bombay and Gujarat. They are Hinduized to some extent.[31]

Nūr Bakhshiyya were the Kashmīrī followers of the Ismā'īlī missionary Shams-ad-dīn 'Irāqī (c. 1486), who is regarded by his followers as the Mahdī.[32] This sect was suppressed by the Tīmūrid prince and historian, Mirzā Ḥaydar Dughlat, in 1541.

'Alī Ilāhī, an extremist Shī'ī sect, is found in northern Kashmir and in Hyderabad (the Deccan). Their chief tenet is a belief in the divinity of 'Alī. They believe in metempsychosis, and are vegetarian. They regard 'Alī as the manifestation of God and His *jism* (body) or garment (*libās*). 'Alī is also identified with the sun. The 'Alī Ilāhis reject the Qur'ān as partly a forgery. They consider Muḥammad to be a prophet sent by 'Alī, the God who later 'assumed the human form for the purpose of assisting the Prophet'.[33] The 'Alī Ilāhis do not have mosques; they do not observe ritual cleanliness; they eat pork and drink wine. They are monogamous and do not permit divorce; and their women have a certain measure of freedom.[34]

THREE

MESSIANIC MOVEMENTS

1. The Mahdawiyya

The first recorded messianic heresy in Islamic India was that of Rukn, who claimed to be the Mahdī in the fourteenth century and who seems to have had certain esoteric notions akin to those of the Ḥurūfīs. He was executed for apostasy during the reign of Fīrūz Tughluq.[1]

In the fifteenth century, nearly a thousand lunar years after the advent of the Prophet, a group of heresies made their appearance in northern India and were designated as Alfī (millennial) by Blochmann.[2] Three of these stand out as of some significance, the Mahdawiyya of Sayyid Muḥammad, Mahdī of Jawnpur, the Dīn-i Ilāhī of Akbar, and the Rawshaniyya which developed in the north-western frontier region.

The messianism of Sayyid Muḥammad (1443–1504) may have been influenced by the fall of Jawnpur and the end of the Sharqī Shāhs in 1477; he may have read in that event the sign of the approaching end of the world. He was a selfless preacher who believed in his own messianic mission and had no ambition for worldly power. Therefore his messianism was very different from that of the African Mahdīs. He went on a pilgrimage to Mecca in 1495, and it was there that he made his first *da'wa* (claim of being the Mahdī or the leader who was to restore Islam to its pristine purity before the end of the world). He reasserted this claim on his return to Ahmadabad in India in 1499 and incurred the hostility of the ulema, including the traditionist 'Alī Muttaqī.[3] Hunted by the theologians from place to place, he revived the doctrine of *hijra* or emigration as an act of piety. Nevertheless his mission had some limited success among the nobility of Gujarat, and the Sultans of Gujarat (Maḥmūd Shāh Begrā) and Ahmadnagar (Aḥmad Shāh Baḥrī) held him in esteem. His wanderings ended at Faraḥ, in modern Afghanistan, where he died in 1504.

His message was one of human love and fellow-feeling. People left their belongings to follow him. His preaching was to some extent synthetic and fundamentalist, trying to bridge over juristic differences between the Sunnī schools of law. He commanded the respect of the Sunnī élite, which did not follow him or believe in him as Mahdī, but respected his piety.[4] The Mahdawiyya upheld other-worldliness, aimed at the company of the righteous, practised asceticism, believed in resignation (*tawakkul*) to the will of God, aspired to the Beatific Vision – which it believed might be had by mortal eyes, expected an individual to distribute one-tenth of his income as charity, and spent considerable time in liturgical recitation (*dhikr*).[5] Education and scholarship were not considered necessary for faith or works. Disciples of the Mahdī were advised to earn sufficient only for the barest subsistence. Like orthodox Ṣūfis they lived on *futūḥ* (income received gratuitously) and did not accumulate any wealth.[6]

The Mahdawiyya regarded Sayyid Muḥammad of Jawnpur as a follower of the Prophet, but claimed that he had an equal rank with him and that the Mahdī and the prophet were identical and differed only in title. They believed only in that part of the *ḥadīth* which was in conformity with the preachings of their Mahdī.[7]

The Mahdawī camps, temporary or semi-permanent, were called *dā'iras*, and often consisted of hutments made of mud walls and thatched roofs on the outskirts of a town.[8]

Muḥammad Mahdī's chief lieutenants in north India were ʿAbd-Allāh Niyāzī and Shaykh ʿAlā'ī who were persecuted by Makhdūm-al-Mūlk, a narrow-minded theologian who was Shaykh al-Islam under Islām Shāh Sūrī (1545–54) and under Akbar. Of these two prominent Mahdawīs, Niyāzī renounced his faith under the lash, and ʿAlā'ī died under it. The last eminent propagator of the Mahdawiyya was Miyān Muṣṭafā (d. 1575), after whom the movement disintegrated in the north. In southern India it lost its other-worldly character in the hands of adventurers like Jamāl Khān who, as a king-maker, raised Ismāʿīl Niẓām Shāh (1589–91) to the throne of Ahmadnagar and converted him to Mahdawī faith. Within two years Jamāl Khān's power collapsed and Ahmadnagar reverted to Shī'ism. Mahdawī communities still survive in the Deccan and Gujarat.

As a branch of the Mahdawī sect in Baluchistan, the Dhikrī (liturgists) or Dā'irewāla (of the circle) pray on the *laylat al-qadr* in Ramaḍān within a circle of stones. Another Dā'irewāla sub-sect is found in the Deccan; it reveres Sayyid Aḥmad (1444–1504), who turned away from the Mahdawiyya to assert that he himself was the Mahdī.[9]

2. The Dīn-i Ilāhī[10]

The Mughal emperor Akbar (1556–1605) had received little formal education, since he was raised indifferently when his father's fortune was at the lowest ebb. But he had an alive and inquisitive mind. He began as a good Muslim with a reverence for Chishtī Ṣūfism, and observed conformity in religion. In due course he was revolted by the petty-mindedness and worldliness of the religious dignitaries of his court, especially Makhdūm-al-Mulk, the shaykh al-Islām, and 'Abd-an-Nabī, the Ṣadr-as-ṣudūr. About the same time he came under the influence of an ex-Mahdawī rationalist Shaykh Mubārak and his gifted son Abū-l-Faḍl. The power of the theologians was badly curtailed when, in 1579, Shaykh Mubārak manœuvred them to sign a *fatwā* – wrongly called an 'infallibility decree' by some European historians – by which they invested the Emperor with the power to legislate in accordance with the *sharī'a* if, on any question, there was a dispute or a difference of opinion among the theologians. Soon a hall, called '*ibādat khāna*' (place of worship), intended originally for ritual or mystical worship, was converted into a chamber where religious debates were held between representatives, first, of the Muslim sects, and later, of other religions. During these debates, Akbar's and Abū-l-Faḍl's eclecticism grew deeper. Akbar became a vegetarian, developed a veneration for sun and light verging almost on a solar monotheism, came to believe in an inter-religional ethics, and finally, in 1581, founded his own heretical messianic sect the Dīn-i Ilāhī. The sect was really a palace club, to which membership was not encouraged, and no effort was made to propagate it publicly. It centred round the person of the Emperor in an ambiguous way, attributing something like prophethood or even a shade of divinity to him, but on the whole it remained within Islam and was closer to it, than, for instance, the Khoja sect.

The Dīn-i Ilāhī prohibited sensuality, lust, misappropriation, deceit, slander, oppression, intimidation and pride. It frowned upon animal slaughter and extolled celibacy. Nine of the ten values it enjoined were derived directly from the Qur'ān, and indeed from the scriptures of other religions as well. These were liberality, forbearance, abstinence, avoidance of 'violent material pursuits', piety, devotion, prudence, gentleness and kindness. To these was added the Ṣūfistic aim of the purification of the soul by yearning for God. The Dīn-i Ilāhī did not claim to possess a revealed text, and did not develop a priest-craft.

The sect had nineteen members and only one of them was a Hindu. Its preoccupation with light and sun suggests Zoroastrian and Hindu as well as *Ishrāqī Ṣūfī* influences. Its ritual prayer telescoped Zoroastrian practices into the Muslim *ṣalāt*. It is difficult to believe that any of its members, least of all Akbar himself, seriously believed in it. It was therefore largely a spiritual hobby. It slowly died out during the last years of Akbar's reign, when some of its members died and Akbar became preoccupied with other problems.

3. The Rawshaniyya[11]

Another Alfī heresy was started in the sixteenth century by Bāyazīd b. 'Abd-Allāh Anṣarī (1525–72), a Pathān who came early under the influence of Sulaymān, an Ismā'īlī, to whom can be traced certain of his religious precepts like the emphasis on the *pīr-i kāmil* (the perfect preceptor), the use of *ta'wīl* (metaphorical interpretation) in explaining the five pillars of faith and the injunctions of ritual purity. He associated early in his life with Hindu yogis from whom he must have learnt the doctrine of the transmigration of souls. He claimed to be a Mahdī, organized his own theology and came to be called Pīr Rawshan (Enlightened Preceptor) by his followers, and Pīr Tārīk (Saint of Darkness) by his opponents.

The central doctrine of Bāyāzīd is based on the gnosis of God, to which creaturely obedience, worship and charity are made subordinate; it can be attained through following the

Preceptor, i.e., Bāyāzīd. His followers began their spiritual career with repentance (*tawba*), performed ascetic exercises, including quadragesimal fasts, in cells and finally reached a spiritual state where they were considered free from the obligations of the ritual of the *sharīʿa*.

Bāyāzīd claimed to be directly in communication with God without the intermediacy of Gabriel. He introduced changes in the Muslim attestation of faith (*kalima*). His ethics was strongly tinged with Ṣūfism and based on a distinction between esoteric and exoteric acts of piety. His followers could offer their prayers in any direction they chose, regarding God as omnipresent. *Wuḍū* (ritual ablution) was dispensed with, and air was regarded an element as purifying as water. A number of works in various languages have been attributed to him.[12]

After some initial opposition, his mission thrived among certain frontier tribes. He and his followers lived as free-booters but kept one-fifth of the booty in a *bayt al-māl*, which went to help those in want. Punitive expeditions were taken against him and his successors by Akbar, which resulted in their suppression. His followers have almost disappeared through orthodox pressures as well as internal tensions.

4. The Aḥmadiyya[13]

The Alfī heterodoxies of the fifteenth and sixteenth centuries are very different from the Aḥmadiyya, which rose in the Punjab towards the close of the nineteenth century, partly as an aggressive syncretism against the challenge of Āryā Samāj and Christian missionary activities,[14] and partly as a compromise between a messianic concept of Islam and modernistic trends.

Its founder, Mirzā Ghulām Aḥmad of Qādiyān (1839–1908), led a life of religious study and meditation, and at an early age 'heard voices'. In 1880 he began publishing a periodical *Burhān-i Aḥmadiyya* which was generally well received. In 1889 he claimed to be Masīḥ (Messiah) and Mahdī, and this led to the opposition of orthodox Muslims. In 1904 he claimed to be an incarnation of the Hindu god Krishna as well as Jesus returned to earth, and at the same time the *burūz* (re-manifestation) of Muḥammad.

Ghulām Aḥmad's doctrines differ from orthodox Islam on three cardinal points. First and foremost was his denial, at least to some extent, of the finality of Muḥammad's prophethood,[15] since he attributed to himself a minor prophethood without a scripture of his own. He distinguished between primary and secondary (Mahdistic) prophethood. In contradiction of this theory he asserted that he received revelation directly from God. Ghulām Aḥmad's claim to minor prophethood led to very strong Sunnī and Shī'ī opposition. This remained confined to written and preached polemics during British rule, but in Pakistan in 1953 took the form of a dangerous riot which the state had to suppress by imposing martial law in Lahore. The second controversial point was his Christology which runs counter to the Christologies of Christianity and Islam alike, for he created a mythology of Christ's sojourn and burial in Kashmir and approximated himself to the role of a resurrected Jesus. The third point was his 'loyalist' theory of *jihād* which he equated with proselytization or missionary work.

Like the Khārijites and the Mu'tazila, the Aḥmadīs believe in the Qur'ān as created.[16] They practise ritual separatism and do not offer congregational prayers with the orthodox Sunnīs. Wherever there is a sufficient number of Aḥmadīs, as in some cities in the West and in Africa, they have their own mosques.

Even Aḥmadī modernism, which is generally close to other modernistic trends in Indian Islam, is to some extent 'hidden behind the mist of medieval mysticism and theology'.[17] On the question of the freedom of women and of family life the Aḥmadīs have remained strongly conservative. They adhere strictly to polygamy, *purdah* (veiling of women) and the classical rules of divorce. Aḥmadī political theory strongly advocates support of the established political order. Under British rule they were consequently accused of subservient loyalism. This political quietism is reflected in their theory of *jihād*. In Pakistan they have continued the policy of loyalty to the state.

Aḥmadīs are polemically called Qādiyānīs or Mirzā'īs by their opponents. Half the community lives in Pakistan; the other half in diaspora in India and the rest of the world. They total about half a million. The members of the community pay point four per cent of their income to a religious fund and may make further contributions to it. The organization of the community is strong and centralized. It operates its own *qaḍā'* (judicial system). The headquarters of the community had been at Qādiyān, which became part of India in the partition of the subcontinent in 1947. The headquarters were then shifted to Rabwah in West Pakistan, where the *khalīfa* of Ghulam Aḥmad resides and runs the spiritual and material affairs of the community with the help of an elected advisory council and a central secretariat.

A split occurred in the Aḥmadiyya under its first *khalīfa*, Nūr-ad-dīn, in 1914. A faction, based in Lahore, led by Khwāja, Kamāl-ad-dīn and Muhammad ʿAlī, seceded from the main group. This Lāhōrī group regards Ghulām Aḥmad as a reformer (*mujaddid*) and not a prophet, and is generally very close to Sunnī Islam. Its principal stand has been that the community should be guided by a secular committee rather than a *khalīfa*.[18]

The main Aḥmadī (Qādiyānī) group and the Lāhōrī group have both produced an extensive missionary literature in various languages, including English. Both have foreign missions in the West, in countries of Asia, and especially in Africa where they, particularly the main Aḥmadī group, have met with considerable success.

FOUR

ORTHODOX ṢŪFISM

1. Ṣūfism in India

Ṣūfism made its appearance in India quite early. One of the earliest Indian mystics was Abū-ʿAlī as-Sindī who met Abū-Yazīd al-Bisṭāmī in 777, and it is controversial what sort of influence he exercised on him.[1] Another Ṣūfī, Shaykh Ismāʿīl, arrived in Lahore from Bukhara in 1005 when it was still under Hindu rule. Shaykh Ṣafī-ad-dīn Gāzrūnī (962–1007) seems to have lived under the Ismāʿīlīs of Multan at Uch. Sayyid Aḥmad, popularly known as Sulṭān Sakhī Sarwar (d. *c.* 1181), exercised some influence also on the Hindus. The most eminent of the Ṣūfīs in Ghaznavid Lahore was ʿAlī ibn-ʿUthmān al-Jullābī al-Hujwīrī, the author of the earliest Persian classic on Ṣūfī doctrine and practice, *Kashf al-maḥjūb*.[2]

Ṣūfī literature in India falls into four categories: treatises on doctrine, a category in which hardly any work of universal significance was written, except that of al-Hujwīrī; *malfūẓāt* or dicta of a shaykh compiled by one of his disciples and in most cases 'vetted' by the shaykh himself and containing his mystical, religious and ethical maxims; *maktūbāt* or the letters written by a shaykh to his preceptor, his disciples, and other contemporaries, touching upon doctrinal questions and sometimes on religion and politics in general; and the *tadhkiras* or Ṣūfī hagiographies which follow the Central Asian tradition of ʿAttār, Jāmī and Wāʿiẓ al-Kāshifī. In addition to these there were commentaries on Ṣūfī classics, especially the *ʿAwārif al-maʿārif* of Shihāb-ad-dīn Suhrawardī and *Fuṣūṣ al-ḥikam* of Ibn-al-ʿArabī. Ṣūfī hagiography is parallel, and sometimes contrary, in approach to historiography from the thirteenth to the sixteenth century, when historians like Abū-l-Faḍl and, after him, Firishta began to make use of Ṣūfī sources and came to be quoted in turn in Ṣūfī hagiographical literature.[3]

Ṣūfīs in India regarded themselves as responsible for the spiritual welfare of the people; and considered themselves entrusted with spiritual government, parallel to the political government exercised by the Sultans and their *amīrs*. The Ṣūfī hierarchy (of *abdāl* etc.) divided the area of a state by regions. Each *walī* (saint) had a *wilāyat* in a spiritual as well as a territorial sense.[4] The founder of the Chishtī order, Mu'īn-ad-dīn Sijzī, 'assigned the territory of Delhi' to his disciple Bakhtiyār Kākī.[5] Amīr Khusraw used regal imagery in describing his preceptor Niẓām-ad-dīn Awliyā (d. 1323).[6]

This led to a chequered pattern of relationships between the Ṣūfīs and the Sultans and made the former suspect under the Khaljīs. Matters came to a head under the Tughluqs when Muḥammad ibn-Tughluq humiliated and dispersed the Chishtī Ṣūfīs.[7] Under the Sultanate there was also considerable rivalry between the ulema and the Ṣūfīs, focussed most often on the question of listening to music (*samā'*). The attitude of the ulema changed in the seventeenth century when there was a reconciliation of the religious law (*sharī'a*) and the mystic path (*ṭarīqa*). The traditionist, 'Abd-al-Ḥaqq Dihlawī, had been initiated into several mystic orders; and Mullā Niẓām-ad-dīn, the compiler of the famous Niẓāmiyya syllabus, had for his preceptor, 'Abd-ar-Razzāq of Bansa, a mystic who was inferior to him in scholarship.

Medieval Ṣūfis earned their livelihood by two means: *iḥyā'*, or cultivation of unproductive land, and *futūḥ*, or unsolicited charity other than gifts of immovable property and regular payments. Gifts received were not hoarded but given away in charity almost immediately.[8] *Shughl*, or earning one's livelihood in the state service, was permitted in some orders, but by the Chishtīs only to their fringe disciples. It was, however, considered an obstacle in the gnostic's path.[9] In the Chishtī order, in an advanced stage of discipleship, a mystic wore the cup of four-fold renunciation (*kulāh-i chahār tarkī*) signifying the renunciation of this world and of the next, of food and sleep, except the necessary minimum, and of one's base ego.[10]

The life of the mystics was organized in hospices which were of three catagories: *khānqāhs* or larger Ṣūfī hostels with separate accommodation for every inmate or visitor; *jamā'at khānas* (not to be confused with the Ismā'īlī houses of worship) or large halls where some disciples lived; and *zāwiyas* or smaller houses where mystics lived in seclusion from the world.[11] The medieval *khānqāh* was not an institution of asceticism. The life lived in it was what the Catholics describe as the 'mixed' life, a step beyond the 'life active' and the 'life contemplative'. Its social basis was the principle of contact – intimate contact between the disciples of the same shaykh, and humanitarian contact in relation to guests, visitors and the surrounding populace in general. The residents of a hospice were divided into three categories: attendants, companions and the elect. Residential life was subject to strict and elaborate rules. Travellers were received as guests and could stay for three days or, as attendants, even longer.[12] Some hospices, especially those of the Suhrawardīs, were supported by endowments (*awqāf*). Social institutions at a hospice included performances of spiritual music (*samā'*), celebrating the anniversary (*'urs*) of a dead saint, and a *langar* or open table for any one who wished to come and partake of a meal. The life of the *khānqāh* revolved round the shaykh and the routine of worship and mystical exercise he prescribed. Visitors to a hospice included not only Muslims but also yogis or Hindus of lower castes. People came often to confide their problems to the shaykh and ask for his blessing.[13] It was in these hospices that the Ṣufīs acted as missionaries of Islam in India.

The two principal emblems of initiation into a mystical order were the wearing of the patched cloak (*khirqa*) and the shaving of the head.[14] A shaykh's cloak, his prayer-rug, sandals, rosary and walking stick were the insignia of his holiness and were assigned by him towards the end of his life to his principal successor (*khalīfa*).[15] A certificate of succession (*khilāfatnāma*) was issued by a shaykh to his most pious disciples who had attained an advanced mystical stage. It constituted the permission to propagate the *silsila* (order) in their own rights. Instructions given in the *khilāfat nāma* were activist and anti-eremitical. The recipient was advised to open a centre in some region, far or near, and to lead a life of self-denial and piety, but to abstain from the idle seclusion of asceticism.[16]

The two dominant Ṣūfī *silsilas* (orders) under the Sultanate were the Chishtī and the Suhrawardī. Both of these declined during the fourteenth and fifteenth centuries. Two other orders rose in prominence during the Mughal period, the Naqshbandī and the Qādirī.

2. Chishtiyya[17]

Some Chishtīs trace their origin to Ḥasan al-Baṣrī. Actually the order derives its name from Chisht, a village near Herat where the founder of the order, Khwāja Abū-Is'ḥāq resided for some time in the twelfth century.[18] It was introduced into India by Mu'īn-ad-dīn Sijzī (d. 1236), who was a disciple of 'Uthmān Harwānī and who, it is claimed, had met the founders of the Qādirī, the Kubrāwī and the Suhrawardī orders during his extensive wanderings.[19] He arrived in India shortly before the conquests of Muḥammad ibn-Sām Ghūrī (commencing 1192) and chose Ajmer, in the very heart of war-like Hindu Rajput territory, as the location for his hospice. On the whole he was tolerated there, but it is probable that his missionary activity flourished only after the Muslim conquest.

Two other Chishtī centres were established by his disciples; at Delhi by Bakhtiyār Kākī (d. 1236), and at Nagor by Ḥamīd-ad-dīn. The former was closer to Islamic culture in general, while the latter adopted itself to some extent to rural Hindu ways of life, including vegetarianism.[20] Another centre, with an austere ascetic discipline, was established at Ajodhan by Kākī's disciple, Farīd-ad-dīn, hagiographically known as Ganj-i Shakar (1175–1265).[21] One of his disciples, 'Alī ibn- Aḥmad Ṣābir, founded the Ṣābiriyya sub-order.

The most eminent of the Delhi Chishtīs was Farīd-ad-dīn's disciple Niẓām-ad-dīn Awliyā (d. 1323). He seems to have exercised a powerful pietistic influence over the Muslim society of his age, which held him in great esteem; and the historiographical tradition is at one with the hagiographical in attributing to his influence the development of interest in mysticism, pietistic conformity, other-worldliness, and a high ethical tone, during the late Khaljī and early Tughluq periods.[22] His choice of the environs of Delhi for his hospice was regarded by him as an anti-ascetic and a pietistic challenge.[23] Some of the Khaljī sultans were apprehensive of his influence, according to the hagiographical tradition, but all of them except Quṭb-ad-dīn Mubārak held him in respect.[24] Some tension developed between him and the first Tughluq sultan.[25] Niẓām-ad-dīn advised his successor Naṣīr-ad-dīn, known as Chirāgh-i Dihlī (d. 1367),[26] to face similarly the challenge of residence in Delhi[27]; this he did and suffered considerable indignities at the hands of Muḥammad ibn Tughluq (1325–51), who exercised pressure on a number of Chishtī shaykhs to emigrate to the provinces and devote themselves there to missionary work and to the service of external and political Islam.[28] It may therefore be said that the principal phase of the centralized activity of the Chishtiyya order ended about 1325 when its dispersal into the provinces began.

Shaykh Sirāj-ad-dīn (d. 1357) introduced the order into Bengal. Prominent among his disciples was Ashraf Jahāngīr Simnānī (d. 1405) who propagated the order in the middle Ganges valley. The Chishtī order was introduced into the Deccan by Burhān-ad-dīn Gharīb (d. 1340). Another prominent Chishtī in the Deccan was Muḥammad Gīsūdarāz (d. 1422) author of several interesting works on Ṣūfism. The Ṣābiriyya sub-order was propagated by Aḥmad ʿAbd-al-Ḥaqq in the valley of the Ganges in the fifteenth century. In the sixteenth century a Chishtī, Shaykh Salīm, was held in great esteem by Akbar. In the eighteenth century there was a revival of the Chishtiyya in its Niẓāmiyya sub-order, mainly through the efforts of Shāh Kalīm-Allāh (d. 1729).

The sheet-anchor of the Chishtī order was the doctrine of ontological monism (*waḥdat al-wujūd*) which explains the influence on it of Ibn-al-ʿArabī's almost pantheistic ideas. Its mystical practices were the same as those of other orders, and included liturgy (*dhikr*), regulation of the breath, which was probably an Indian influence, concentrated seance (*murāqiba*) and an Indian practice, namely, secluded worship (*chilla*) for forty days. An extravagant form of this last practice was *chilla-i maʿkūs*, in which a Ṣūfī was suspended upside down in a well for forty days, an exercise of undoubted yogic origin. The Chishtīs held assemblies devoted to spiritual music (*majālis as-samāʿ*), wore coloured garments, preferably light almond, tolerated non-Muslims in their midst and had a taste for literature.

The earlier Chishtīs refused to accept land grants or stipends offered by the sultans; though they accepted unsolicited gifts as *futūḥ* but without storing them.[29] Some of them cultivated unproductive land to gain a meagre sustenance; others followed the example of Hindu or Buddhist monks in passing around a begging bowl (*zanbīl*) from house to house.[30] After their dispersal into the provinces the Chishtīs became less ascetic and accepted favours from rulers or nobles.

3. Suhrawardiyya[31]

The Suhrawardiyya order was founded by Shaykh Najīb-ad-dīn 'Abd-al-Qāhir Suhrawardī (d. 1169), and developed by his nephew, Shihāb-ad-dīn Suhrawardī (d. 1234), in Iraq. A number of his disciples took refuge in India from disturbed conditions in Persia and Iraq, and one of them, an Indian, Bahā'-ad-dīn Zakariyyā, established the order in Multan in the thirteenth century. Another, Jalāl-ad-din Tabrīzī, introduced the order in Bengal.

Zakariyyā maintained his hospice in Multan in wealth and affluence, and established good relations with Iletmish, who appointed another disciple of Suhrawardī Nūr-ad-dīn Mubārak Ghaznavī as his *shaykh al-Islam*.[32] The Suhrawardīs remained on cordial terms with the sultans of Delhi, the one exception being Zakariyyā's son and successor at Multan, Ṣadr-ad-dīn 'Ārif (d. 1285), who preferred, like the Chishtīs, a life of ascetic poverty.[33] His son Rukn-ad-dīn (d. 1335) reverted to the earlier Suhrawardī tradition of affluent living and close ties with the rulers. He was on good terms with the later Khaljis and early Tughluqs, and owing to Muḥammad ibn-Tughluq's policy of using mystics for political ends his hospice fell considerably under the influence of the state.[34] The Suhrawardīs argued that their association with the rulers was to exercise a moral and spiritual influence over them. But this led in turn to a moral decline in the main Suhrawardī branch of Multan and resulted in the execution of the last considerable shaykh of that branch, Hūd, by Muḥammad ibn-Tughluq.

The Uch branch of the Suhrawardī order was founded by Jalāl-ad-dīn Surkh Bukhārī, generally known as Makhdūm-i Jahāniyān, who combined other-worldliness and good relations with the Tughluq sultans.[35] His younger brother, popularly known as Rājū Qattāl, passed into syncretistic mysticism and folklore.

In 1443 a Multanī Suhrawardī, Shaykh Yūsuf, was even elected king of Multan and northern Sind, but his reign was short-lived. The Suhrawardī order broke up in Northern India during the political chaos that followed Tīmūr's invasion. It, however, thrived regionally in Gujarat, where Quṭb 'Ālam (d. 1453) and his son, Shāh 'Alām, enjoyed considerable prestige in the courts of the kings of Gujarat. With the Mughal conquest of that region the Suhrawardī order declined there too.

The Indian Suhrawardīs were staunch Ḥanafīs and stressed the importance of ritual prayer.

4. Naqshbandiyya

In intellectual calibre, and because of the influence it radiated from India into the Muslim world, the Naqshbandī is the most outstanding of the Ṣūfī orders of India. It originated in Central Asia and was at the beginning influenced by certain Mahāyāna Buddhist features although it was a Sunnī movement aiming at the integration of external ritual with inner spirituality. It has been suggested that it was a reaction of the Iranian civilization against the Turco-Mongol paganism.[36] Its foundation is attributed to Aḥmad 'Aṭā Yaswī (d. 1116).[37] It was developed by Bahā'-ad-dīn. Apocryphally it traced its discipline through Abū-Yazīd Bisṭāmī to the first orthodox caliph, Abū-Bakr. The Naqshbandīs received the patronage of Bābur, which may have helped the establishment of the order in India by Muḥammad Bāqī bi-llāh (1563–1603) in the reign of Akbar.

The principal doctrine of the order is *Waḥdat ash-shuhūd* (phenomenological monism or 'unity of witness', translated by Massignon as 'Monisme testimonial'), which has been defined by Massignon and Gardet as a belief in 'God witnessing to Himself in the heart of His votary (*'ābid*). This union with God (*jam'*) leads to a unification (*ittiḥād*) which is not a unification of substance, but operates through the act of faith and of Love.'[38] The doctrine is traceable to al-Ḥallāj. In the Naqshbandiyya order it was evolved in Central Asia by 'Alā'-ad-dawla Simnānī (d. 1336)[39] and fully developed by the great Indian Naqshbandī mystic, Shaykh Aḥmad Sirhindī, in the seventeenth century.[40]

A champion of Ibn-al-'Arabī's doctrine of *waḥdat al-wujūd*

(ontological monism or unity of being) in India was Ashraf Jahāngīr Simnānī (d. 1346), who refused the thesis of 'Alā'-ad-dawla Simnānī and corresponded on the point with the theologian Shihāb-ad-dīn Dawlatabādī, who was also attacking Ibn-al-'Arabī's doctrine from the viewpoint of the *sharī'a*.[41]

Shaykh Aḥmad Sirhindī's severe attack on Ibn-al-Arabī's pantheistic monism changed the mystical moorings in Muslim India. He argued that the doctrine of ontological monism was in conflict with religion as well as reason in its denial of all existence except that of God. Phenomenological monism on the other hand believed in simple unitarianism: God exists and is unique (*yagāna*), and no created object can be a part of him in any way. Therefore it will be wrong to say: 'All is God'; it will be more correct to say: 'All is from him'. Thus in Sirhindī, phenomenological monism took a very different shape from the one initially given to it by Ḥallāj. In seceding from pantheistic ontological monism Sirhindī worked out a close integration between Ṣūfism and theology.

Some of the Naqshbandīs still continued to follow Ibn-al-'Arabī in the seventeenth century and, later, a dialectic compromise between the doctrines of phenomenological and ontological monism was worked out by Walī-Allāh. But Sirhindī's influence was largely predominant. Awrangzīb is reputed to have been under this influence to some extent though he was on the whole an externalist.

The next outstanding figure in Naqshbandī Ṣūfism is the poet Maẓ'har Jān-i Jānān (1699–1780). The order, which had been aggressively anti-Hindu under Sirhindī, became tolerant and even eclectic under Jān-i Janān. But Hindu mysticism, isolated as it was from the faith of Islam, was regarded by him as incomplete and defective.[42] He and his successor, Ghulām 'Alī, attracted disciples from abroad, the most eminent of them being Khālid al-Kurdī, who transplanted the order to the Ottoman Empire. Earlier, Sirhindī's influence had reached Central Asia. The order suffered an eclipse in the nineteenth century but it has been revived in recent years in the Punjab and in Kashmir.

Apart from the doctrine of phenomenological monism and close adherence to the *Sharī'a*, the principal features of the order were concentration on the intellectual image of the preceptor (*taṣawwur-i shaykh*), and rejection of music as a spiritual stimulant.

5. Qādiriyya

This order, the most widespread in the subcontinent in modern times, was founded in Iraq by a Ḥanbalī mystic, ʿAbd-al-Qādir al-Jīlānī (1077–1166). It was first introduced into India by Muḥammad Ghawth, who established a hospice at Uch in 1482. It was, however, established in India much later, under the Mughals, by Shāh Niʿmat-Allāh and Makhdūm Muḥammad Jīlānī.[43]

In the sixteenth century the chief representatives of the order were Shaykh Dā'ūd, whose hospice also carried on missionary work among the Hindus, and Shaykh Muḥammad Ḥasan (d. 1537), who was more preoccupied in other-worldly monism.[44]

In India it rose to prominence in the early seventeenth century with Muḥammad Mīr (1550–1635), popularly known as Miyān Mīr, the preceptor of Shāh Jahān's son, Dārā Shukoh, and daughter, Jahān Ārā. Miyān Mīr was an ontological monist deeply under the influence of Ibn-al-ʿArabī, and held significant discussions with the prominent theologian of the age ʿAbd-al-Ḥakīm Siyālkotī.[45] Also under the influence of Ibn-al-ʿArabī were the other prominent Qādirīs of the eighteenth century, Mullā Shāh and the erudite Muḥibb-Allāh Allāhābādī. The Qādirīs were generally tolerant of the non-Muslims, and this attitude must have been one of the formative influences on the syncretistic thinking of Dārā Shukoh. The order suffered a temporary eclipse under Awrangzīb, but it remained on the whole the most popular. Indian Muslims hold its founder, ʿAbd-al-Qādir al-Jīlānī, in great esteem and, because of his tomb, regard Baghdad as one of their holy cities. The order adheres strictly to the *sharīʿa*.[46]

6. Other Orders

Twelve Ṣūfī sects have been mentioned by Hujwīrī: Ḥulūlī, Ḥallājī, Ṭayfūrī, Quṣṣārī, Kharrāzī, Khafīfī, Sayyārī, Muḥāsibī, Ṭustarī, Ḥakīmī, Nūrī and Junaydī.[47] It is possible that followers of some of these early orders found their way into the Ghaznavid Punjab. A number of other orders, most of them orthodox, were mentioned by Abū-l-Faḍl in the sixteenth

1. *Mughal miniature* c. 1630. *Shāh Jahān and Dārā Shukoh*

2. *Atala Mosque, Jawnpur,* 1408

century.[48] These included the Ḥabībī (followers of Ḥasan al-Baṣrī), Kubrāwī, Karkhī, Saqaṭī (which included Jews and Christians in its ranks), Ṭayfūrī, Ad'hamī and Kāzarūnī (followers of Abū-Is'ḥāq b. Shahriyār). None of these orders was widespread with the exception of the Kubrāwiyya, founded by Najm-ad-dīn al-Kubrā and introduced into Kashmir by Sayyid ʿAlī Hamadānī, who was a strict Shāfiʿī but believed in ʿAlī as a fountainhead of spiritual manliness (*futuwwa*).[49] The Kubrāwiyya remained confined to the valley of Kashmir.

Another order which had a regional success in Bihar was Firdawsiyya, founded by Sayf-ad-dīn Bākharzī in Central Asia and introduced by his disciple Badr-ad-dīn Samarqandī into India.[50] Its principal propagator in India was Aḥmad ibn-Yaḥyā Mānerī (d. 1371) who spent several years in ascetic exercises[51] and possibly absorbed some Indian influences. He was treated with respect by the Tughluqs, and carried on an extensive correspondence with some of his contemporaries on mystical and religious points. He believed in a latitudinarian application of theological law, and regarded ethics and human welfare as incomparably more important than mere ritual.[52]

The Shaṭṭārī order had a regional success in the sixteenth century. Compared with all the orthodox orders in India it absorbed much basic Hindu influence into its liturgy, ascetic exercises and general mystical outlook.[53] It traced its origin to Abū-Yazīd al-Bisṭāmī and may have some link with the Ṭayfūriyya.[54] It was introduced into India (Jawnpur and Malwa) by Shaykh ʿAbd-Allāh (d. 1485). The order displayed opulence, its adherents had a prescribed uniform and carried flags.[55] Most eminent of the Shaṭṭārī shaykhs was Muḥammad Ghawth of Gwalior (d. 1563), who combined extreme ascetism with affluence and who established contacts with Bābur, Humāyūn and Akbar successively.[56] For a time he lived in Gujarat, where the ulema criticized some of his ascetic practices which they regarded as heterodox.

FIVE

FOLK-BELIEFS

1. Bī-sharʿ (Irreligious) Ṣūfism

At the popular level Indian Islam represents a mosaic of demotic, superstitious and syncretistic beliefs, which movements of mass reform like that of the Mujāhidīn in the nineteenth century and the Jamāʿat-i Islāmī in the twentieth have tried to erase, but not with complete success.

Ṣūfīs were responsible more than any other religious or cultural group, for the conversion, in India, of masses of Hindus to Islam. But at the popular level Ṣūfism itself became distorted, and even orthodox orders developed irreligious (*bī-sharʿ*) off-shoots, and most of them absorbed at that level *malāmī* (blameworthy) features. A heterodox off-shoot of the Junaydī order is the Rifāʿī, popularly known as Gurzmār, for its followers carry maces and inflict wounds upon themselves with them. Allied to them are the Rasūl Shāhīs, known generally as Mastān (intoxicated ones), of Gujarat whose sub-order developed in the eighteenth century. The Chishtīs, whose hospices were often situated among dense Hindu populations, absorbed certain Hindu practices such as the collection of food in a begging bowl (*zanbīl*) and upside-down suspension in a well for forty days or nights (*chilla-i maʿkūs*) which was probably borrowed from the ritual of the Urdhamukhtī sādhūs.[1] A heterodox off-shoot of the Suhrawardiyya was the Jalālī order, who took hashish and ate snakes and scorpions; their leader had the right of sexual intercourse with any woman of the sub-order he liked.[2] Heterodox off-shoots of the Qādiriyya are the Bīnawā and Nawshāhī orders; the heterodoxy of the latter consists in mixing up music and dancing with the orthodox ritual.[3]

In northern India the term *qalandar* underwent a lowering of meaning, and now denotes a wandering mendicant, who sometimes earns his subsistence by showing the tricks of a bear or a monkey which he leads. It also means, sometimes, an ordinary beggar. As a *bī-sharʿ* order, the *qalandars* were noted in India as early as the thirteenth century or soon after, and though its eponymous founder in Indian tradition is a local saint, Abū-ʿAlī Qalandar, it was probably imported from Iran where it was founded by Sawījī. Some of the indigenous *qalandars* represented the vulgarized decadence of an element of an orthodox order. Shaykh Ḥusayn, a *qalandar* of the fourteenth century who refused to offer ritual prayer, was the disciple of a disciple of Niẓām-ad-dīn Awliyā. A variety of the *qalandar* was *majdhūb* (the saturated one), whose spirituality was almost indistinguishable from mental disease. During its development abroad, and subsequently in India, the Qalandariyya seems to have accepted a number of Indian influences including the use of intoxicants. The *qalandars* shaved their heads and all hair on their faces, and went about wrapped in blankets. Others roamed about naked like Hindu yogis or wandered in forests.[4] The poet Sarmad, a protégé of Dārā Shukoh who was executed by Awrangzīb on charges of heterodoxy, went about naked in mystic ecstasy. Another *malāmī* order was that of the Ḥaydaris, whose bizarre practices included adorning themselves with iron necklaces and bracelets and wearing a ring attached to a lead bar piercing their sexual organs in order to eliminate any chance of sexual intercourse.[5]

Most wide-spread of the heterodox orders was that of the Madārīs founded by a former Syrian Jew, Shāh Madār, who emigrated to India in the fifteenth century. Though claiming some affinity to the Chishtīs, it was essentially a *bī-sharʿ* order, with syncretistic features borrowed from Hindu yogism as well as from Christianity and Judaism, such as using hashish, 'knowing neither fasting nor prayer', rubbing ashes on their bodies like Hindu Sanyāsis, and occasionally going about naked.[6] The order survived well into the nineteenth century and was known as Daflis by reason of a small drum its members carried with them.[7]

A number of practices, which from the fundamentalist vie[illegible] point appear heterodox, were common even among the [illegible] dox Ṣūfīs and some of them were of extra-Indian Islam[illegible] Amulets, (*taʿwīdh*) containing verses of the Qu[illegible] pious formulae, were prepared and distributed in the Ṣūfī hospices. Shāh Walī-Allāh and Shāh ʿAbd-al-ʿAzīz deal with them in their writings with pious credulity. Amulets are still very much in use in India, as indeed in other parts of the Muslim world. A written verse or prayer or blessing is enclosed in a little metal case or sewn in cloth and hung by a thread round the neck as a charm against misfortune or disease. By the end of the eighteenth century there was an extensive variety of these amulets suitable for almost every conceivable calamity and misfortune.[8] A Shīʿī form of amulet in use by all the Muslim sects in India is *imām ḍāmin*; it consists of one or more coins sewn in a cloth arm-band which is tied round the arm before the commencement of a journey to plead the protection of the Imām Mahdī. When there is blight in Kashmir peasants hang amulets in their fields.[9]

Animism in Islam, as in other religions throughout the world, is to some extent rooted in popular beliefs. In India it may have been influenced to some uncertain extent by Hinduism. The veneration in which *Ḥawḍ-i Shamsī*, a pool built by Iletmish, was held by ordinary people as well as some mystics shows a semi-animistic pattern. It was connected mystically with the water-saint Khiḍr and with *jinn*; it was also used by orthodox mystics for certain rituals.[10] Even the great Ṣūfīs of the thirteenth and fourteenth centuries believed in magic and witchcraft as a cause of illness, and those suspected of practising either were sometimes prosecuted by the state.[11]

Ṣūfīs, orthodox or eponymous, have been credited in popular belief with supernatural powers. Farīd-ad-dīn Ganj-i Shakar is supposed to have possessed the *dast-i ghayb* ('hidden hand'), or the magical bag of folklore which gave him anything he wanted.[12] ʿAbū-ʿAlī Qalandar is imagined as riding about on a wall. An apocryphal saint, Mūsā Suhāg, has five tombs in Gujarat. There are several 'headless' saints who were beheaded fighting the Hindus, but who kept on fighting without their heads.[13] 'Nawgazē pīrs' are imaginary pseudo-saints, nine yards tall, and huge graves have been built to denote their burial places. It might have shocked Niẓām-ad-dīn Awliyā to know that he was revered as a patron-saint by the Thugs, the robbers and murderous bands of the eighteenth century.[14]

Tombs of orthodox Ṣūfīs were, and are, held in veneration

by mystics, the élite and the common people. On the anniversary of the death of particular saints there are celebrations at their mausoleums, accompanied by elaborate fairs and musical assemblies. Earth taken from the graves of Muslim saints is valued as a remedy. More bizarre is the festival of Sālār Masʿūd Ghāzī, who died a bachelor, for annually there is a celebration of his marriage to a woman bedecked in bridal array who is probably seduced by one of the attendants at his tomb.[15] Phērū, the Indian personification of whirlwind, identified by some Hindu communities with the deified monkey Hanūmān, is regarded by common Muslims, in certain areas, as a disciple of the popular saint Sakhī Sarwar.[16] This Phērū is identical with Bhairon, who started his career probably as the deified dog of the cowherds, and was later worshipped in popular Hinduism as a godling of earth. Hanging rags on trees to ward off disease is a popular Hindu practice, which corresponds to the Muslim custom in certain rural areas, especially in Sind, of hanging similar rags on the tomb of an obscure saint.[17] Muslim *siflī ʿamal* (earthly or vicious magic), corresponds to the popular Hindu magical practice of eating dirt or filth or using filth in some other way to gain power over an enemy or an evil spirit.[18]

2. Popular and Syncretistic Beliefs

The life of sections of the uneducated Muslim masses, from the cradle to the grave, is full of folk-beliefs, some of them syncretistic in origin. Common to Muslims and Hindus is a dread of the effect of the eclipse of the sun or moon on a pregnant woman, and she must lie quietly for the duration of the eclipse lest her child be born deformed; the deformity is related in nature to the work she would be doing during that inauspicious hour.[19] Certain days, especially Wednesday, were considered unfortunate for the birth of a child.[20] The *Chhattī*, or the celebration of the sixth day after the birth of a child, when the mother takes the bath of purification, actually represents deliverance from the dread of a Hindu godling, Chhattī, who personifies the septicaemia which often follows childbirth in unhygienic conditions.[21]

Muslim women in Lucknow drink water exposed to moonlight as a cure for palpitation of the heart. The practice is connected with the Hindu moon-cult and the symbolic drinking of *soma*.[22] The fear of the evil eye is a superstition common to many peoples of the world. Its Indo-Muslim form *naẓar* is partly a residual form of the superstition imported from abroad and partly its indigenous counterpart. The evil eye of a deformed or mutilated person is especially feared. The prosperous fear the evil eye of the indigent. One of the antidotes against it is the concealment or multiplication of names. The Mughal emperors were sometimes given as many as three names, and Akbar was given a new name at his circumcision.[23] Lemon is considered a protection against the evil eye, an antidote presumably borrowed from the practice of the Hindus.

'Sweeping and blessing' (*jhār phūnk*), or waving, over the person possessed by an evil spirit, a winnowing fan or branch of a tree, while the exorcist blows upon him, has either been borrowed from the Hindus or imported from other parts of the Muslim world. In any case the Muslim formula in the ritual of exorcism is to recite verses of the Qur'ān or some other revered text. The Hindu scapegoat rite of sacrificing or setting free an animal or chicken has been accepted in popular Indian Islam and telescoped with the ritual charity (*ṣadaqa*) enjoined in Islamic law.[24]

Shāh Walī-Allāh regards the commemoration by the Shī'īs of the marriage of 'Alī and Fāṭima on the twelfth of Rajab as a replica of the Hindu celebration of the marriage of Krishna and Rādhā. He also regards the *panja* and *'alam* taken out by the Shī'īs in Muḥarram processions as of Hindu origin.[25] The *panja* is a five-pointed symbol of the Panjtan (the Prophet, 'Alī, Fāṭima, Ḥasan and Ḥusayn). It seems to have a curious ancestry. It is probably adopted from the Hindu practice of impressing, on the outside of a house near the entrance, the mark of the hand with fingers outspread as a protective charm. This is in turn a practice allied to the equilateral triangle drawn on paper and hung round children's necks in some Hindu communities. Among the Semites the hand was a euphemistic symbol of the phallus.[26]

The mystic number five also forms the basis of Pānch-pīrīya, a group of five syncretistic saints venerated by the peasantry of northern India. The group includes two Hindu figures Bhairon, the old earth godling, and Āmina, a Muslim woman identified with a Hindu, self-immolating widow (*satī*) Kālika, as well as three nondescript, Muslim characters ʿAjab Sālār, Hatīlē Pīr and Rajab Sālar. Closely linked with this quintet is the cultus of a Muslim pseudo-saint, Ghāzī Miyān, identified with one, Sālār Masʿūd, who is said to have died fighting the Hindus at Bahrā'ich in 1034, but is revered by both communities.[27]

Originally a snake godling, who was given a Muslim name, is Zahriya Pīr (the poisonous saint), later transformed metathetically into Ẓāhir Pīr (the saint apparent), and given a legendary historicity as a martyr who died fighting the Rājpūt hero Prithvī Rāj in 1192. He still retains characteristics of a snake-godling; and Hindu as well as Muslim beggars carry his standard (*chharī*), begging alms in the rainy season when the snakes are most dreaded.[28]

Khiḍr, the water-saint revered by Muslims all over the world, connected generally with sea, rivers and water, and related obliquely to Noah, is synthesized in parts of the subcontinent with local Hindu godlings, and bears various names including those of Pīr Badr (Saint Full-Moon) in Bengal, and Daryā Pīr (River Saint) in Sind. His special vehicle is a fish, and he is propitiated during the dangers of flood or drought. His *bērā* (fleet) is a raft on which burning lamps, and bouquets of flowers, and fruit are floated. In the Punjab the cultus of Khiḍr was assimilated with rituals of maternity.[29] Muslim fishermen in Bengal, like low-caste Hindus, revere a patron Hindu godling, Devtā Mahārāj, and his attendant Hadā, represented by a number of symbols including a fishing net and a hook.[30]

Small Muslim communities which are strikingly syncretistic are embedded among the millions of the subcontinent. Thus in Purnea in Bengal some village Muslims worship God as well as the Hindu death-goddess Kālī, and a part of the marriage ceremony is performed in the temple of the Hindu goddess Bhāgwatī.[31] Muslim Mīrdhas in villages near Indore in Central India have Hindu names, live like Hindus and venerate Bhawānī and other Hindu deities.[32] Various small communities in Gujarat have retained Hindu customary and ritual practices despite their conversion to Islam. In the Central Provinces in the district of Nīmar, a sect known as Pīrzādas, followers of Shāh Dūlla, believe in the tenth incarnation of Vishnu.[33]

A malevolent saint, probably of purely Muslim origin, is Muḥyī-d-dīn, known as Shaykh Ṣaddū to women who propitiate him. As early as the thirteenth century, a mosque at Amroha was converted into Ṣaddū's hospice where, we are told, all sorts of superstitious abominations were practised.[34] Depression, hypochondria and hysteria in women is attributed to seizure by him; and he is propitiated by women in a special seance (*baythak*) when they stimulate themselves into an ecstatic hysteria. Goats or kids are slaughtered to propitiate him and to protect women and children from his malevolent influence. It is possible that he was originally a fertility figure.[35]

In the Indian province of Maharashtra Sītla, the Hindu goddess of small-pox has become syncretistic. While she represents epidemic small-pox, the disease in its endemic form is supposed to be in charge of her male twin who has a Muslim name, Sayyid Kākā (Lord paternal uncle), and both are propitiated by the Muslim Mominas.[36] A curious case of syncretistic demonology is Hawwā, the Prakrit form of the Sanskrit Humma, a malignant spirit who, in the sixteenth century, came to be identified with the soul of the Mughal emperor Humāyūn. Another Hindu malignant figure, Māno (the cat), is transfigured into a respectable Muslim spirit, Nīkī Bībī (Lady Virtue).[37]

Hindu dread of the departed wandering soul, *prēt*, is to some extent accepted in popular Indian Islam. So is *bhūt*, or the malignant soul of the victim of a violent death. Most notorious of this category of ghosts is the female *churēl*, the woman who died while pregnant; her feet are turned backwards and she feeds on the livers of human beings.[38] Lonā Chamārin, a Hindu witch of the low shoe-maker caste, is also dreaded syncretistically; she has a twin with a Muslim name, Ismāʿīl Yogī.[39]

In medieval and pre-modern India, belief in astrology and magic was quite common among Muslims. Astrologers thrived even under the pious and puritan Awrangzīb. In the early nineteenth century, Tīpū Sulṭān, otherwise an orthodox Muslim, had recourse to esoteric practices prescribed by Hindu astrologers.

Among the unorthodox folk-beliefs listed by Shāh Walī-Allāh's grandson, Shāh Ismāʿīl, in the 1820s, were animal sacrifices and gun-firing at a child's birth to inject courage into him, placing an arrow and the Qur'ān at the pillow of the new mother after child-birth, tying a bracelet of hair around an uncircumcised child's wrist or making him hold a bar of iron—both presumably charms for future virility—painting the doors, like the Hindus, with magical marks in indigo, and regarding certain days of the week and certain dates of the month as inauspicious.[40]

These folk-beliefs should be viewed in their proper perspective and should not be over-emphasized or over-rated. They are specific to microscopic Muslim communities and are generally the exception rather than the rule. They were challenged by the fundamentalist, orthodox and modernist movements alike in the nineteenth and twentieth centuries. They have completely ceased to exist in the Westernized upper class, and nearly so in the orthodox lower middle classes. In the predominantly Muslim regions which now constitute West Pakistan their hold was not very strong even in the lower classes, and fundamentalism is now rooting them out. In the lower classes of East Pakistan, some folk-beliefs still persist despite the fundamentalist Farā'iḍī movement's success in the nineteenth century, and the Jamaʿat-i Islāmī's growing influence on religious life today.

In the Republic of India the situation is potentially different. Orthodoxy, in the form of the political influence of the ulema, is still powerful, but the extent of its influence is confined to economically retrogressing and numerically dwindling middle classes, which, in India, are no longer able to play the role of a creative minority by providing leadership for the vast masses of Indian Muslims. These masses, especially in the rural areas, are yielding to popular Hinduism's pull of absorption, largely through folk-beliefs and through participation in Hindu festivals.[41]

SIX

EDUCATION

1. Medieval

The pattern of education in medieval Muslim India was the same as in the rest of *Dār al-Islām*. Its chief beneficiary was the élite, although, through mosque schools, it was within reach of the children of the common people, if circumstances permitted.

Under Maḥmūd, a school and a library were attached to a mosque in Ghazna; the poet 'Unṣurī taught at that school. Under his successor, Mas'ūd, several such schools were opened. When Lahore became the secondary – and later the main – capital of the Ghaznavid state, mosque schools were opened there.[1]

With the advent of the Delhi Sultanate, education came to be organized there, and historians inform us of two famous schools under the 'Slave' Sulṭans, the Shamsiyya and the Nāṣiriyya. As the Mongols overran the heartlands of Islam, scholars flocked into Delhi from Central Asia and Persia, and the general level of learning rose considerably. Religious schools, where these immigrants taught, served a practical purpose, that of producing *qāḍīs* and *muftīs* for the judicial and ecclesiastical departments of the state.

This tradition of learning continued under the Khaljīs, though 'Alā'-ad-dīn Khaljī was himself uneducated, and his neglect of the education of his sons had disastrous consequences for the future of his dynasty. Delhi, however, continued to be a great centre of learning and a hub of scholars and writers. Under the influence of Niẓām-ad-dīn Awliyā, religious and mystical literature was much in demand. 'Alā'-ad-dīn's chief minister Shams-al-Mulk was a liberal patron of learning, so were the Sayyids of Gardīz and Bayana among the élite.

Scholarship in history, jurisprudence (*fiqh*), theology, linguistic sciences and the exegesis (*tafsīr*) of the Qur'ān flourished. Attention was paid from this period onwards to the study of Graeco-Arab medicine. Among the famous physicians of the Khaljī age were Badr-ad-dīn Dimashqī and Juwaynī Ṭabīb.[2]

The first three rulers of the Tughluq dynasty were themselves distinguished scholars. Ghiyāth-ad-din Tughluq's learning was generally pietistic but that of his son Muḥammad ibn-Tughluq was almost encyclopaedic and he had an insatiable thirst for knowledge. He was also well-versed in the rational (philosophical) as well as the theological sciences, and even his worst critics pay homage to his high intellectual calibre. Although Delhi was ruined for a time by his temporary transfer of the capital to Dawlatabad in the south, it still remained, during his reign, one of the great centres of learning in the Muslim world. Al-Qalqashandī quotes *Masālik al-abṣār* in stating that there were one thousand schools in Delhi at that time.[3] His cousin and successor Fīrūz Tughluq, under whom two great works of jurisprudence were compiled, was a theological scholar, and also the author of a brief memoir of his own reign, the *Futūḥāt-i Fīrūz Shāhī*. He encouraged scholars to spread out in various parts of the sultanate where they imparted instruction to the people. He rebuilt several schools and constructed new ones. One of these at Firuzabad was of an exquisite architectural beauty. To a greater extent than his predecessors, he assigned endowments (*awqāf*) for the expenses of these schools, which had residential quarters for both the teachers and the students, and personal contact between them was encouraged as a matter of educational policy.[4] Works from Sanskrit were translated by a number of scholars, including A'azz-ad-dīn Khāliq Khānī, at the command of Fīrūz Tughluq.

The last two rulers of the Sayyid dynasty (1434–51) lived in Bada'un, a town about a hundred miles from Delhi. Under them, Bada'un became an educational and intellectual centre with a large number of schools. This town was to produce in later generations several scholars of distinction.

The reign of Sikandar Lōdī (1489–1517) is a landmark in the history of medieval Indian education, mainly because of two administrative steps that he took. One was an insistence on a certain educational level for all his civil and military officers. The other was his famous decree substituting Persian for Hindi as the language of the lower administration, a step which forced the administrative Hindu communities to learn Persian and for that purpose to attend schools of this type which were not attached to mosques. This in turn led to the secularization of a stream of education, a development which reached its culmination under Akbar. Another important feature of the educational policy of Sikandar Lōdī was the growing emphasis on rational sciences (*maʿqūlāt*), although the chief preoccupations of a Muslim scholar were still largely the traditional sciences (*manqūlāt*). He himself occasionally attended the courses of a scholar, ʿAbd-Allāh Tulanbī. He established new schools in several parts of his kingdom and invited scholars from other parts of the Muslim world.[5]

This educational policy was continued by the Mughals. During the few years of Bābur's reign the Department of Public Affairs (*Shuhrat-i ʿāmm*) was entrusted with the construction of schools and colleges.[6] During Humāyūn's disturbed reign no great advance could be made in public education, although he had a large library and an observatory constructed for his own use. Humāyūn is credited with the invention of an astrolabe, known as the *Usṭūrlāb-i Humāyūnī*.[7] A school which became famous was attached to his tomb – built by Akbar.

Akbar's educational policy was based on eclecticism and provided for the instruction of Hindus as well as Muslims. Under him the school seems to have gained a position for itself outside the mosque, of which it had hitherto been an appendage. Studies began in primary and secondary schools with a training in Persian. At a higher level, sciences were taught in the following order: ethics, mathematics, agriculture, geometry, astronomy, physics, logic, natural philosophy, theology and history.[8] Akbar's educational policy was shaped by his minister, Fat'ḥ-Allāh Shīrāzī (d. 1588), himself a scholar of the rationalist sciences and well-versed in Arabic literature and theological studies. Fat'ḥ-Allāh Shīrāzī introduced into the curriculum works of Dawānī, Mullā Ṣadra and Mīrzā Jān. Rationalist trends in education were strengthened by the influx of teachers from Central Asia, who found Transoxiana under ʿAbd-Allāh Khān Ūzbek unfavourable for rationalist disciplines.[9] The number of educational institutions increased under Akbar. A

3. *Shāh Jahān Mosque, Thatta, mid-17th century*

4. *Pearl Mosque, Agra, built inside the Red Fort,* 1648

college was founded at the new capital Fat'ḥpur Sikri. Some of these schools were residential, others non-residential. Schools were also founded by the ladies of the harem. One such school was that founded in Delhi by Akbar's wet-nurse, Māham Anga, and noted for its architectural beauty.

Jahāngīr issued an edict stating that the property of a well-to-do person or rich traveller who died without heirs would escheat to the state and the monies utilized for the building and repair of schools and colleges. During his reign a number of colleges which had closed down or fallen into ruin were repaired and revived.[10] Under Shāh Jahān an imperial college was attached to the cathedral mosque in Delhi – built in 1650, and several other colleges were restored. During his reign Sialkot became a great centre of learning. There, ʻAbd-al-Ḥakīm Siyālkotī's school, famous for the study of medieval rational sciences, attracted scholars from all over India and from abroad.[11]

Awrangzīb established a large number of schools and colleges; the foundations of the great religious seminary of Farangī Maḥall at Lucknow were laid during his reign. Later in his reign, a school was inaugurated at Delhi by Shāh Walī-Allāh's father, ʻAbd-ar-Raḥīm. This Madrasa-i Raḥīmiyya later became the great seminary of the tradition of Walī-Allāh. Under Awrangzīb, all students of theology, when they attained a certain standard, were given stipends. Efforts were also made to spread theological education among communities under Hindu influence, like the Bohras.[12] Education seems to have been thriving in Awrangzīb's reign, and a famous speech attributed to him by Bernier, lamenting the inadequacy of traditional education, is presumably a fabrication of the French traveller's fertile imagination.[13]

In the anarchy which accompanied the decline of the Mughal Empire after Awrangzīb, educational institutions suffered. The responsibility for maintaining them passed to the successor states, but in the Muslim successor states, like Oudh and Rohilkhand, educational standards were maintained. In the valley of the Ganges certain educational centres rose to prominence in their own right, like Bilgram, Allahabad and Sahali.

In the outlying provinces of India, schools had been constructed by the successor states of the Delhi Sultanate at a much earlier date. There were such schools in Bengal, the Deccan and in Gujarat. The most eminent was the one built at Bidar by the Bahmanid minister, Maḥmūd Gāwān, in the fifteenth century. Architecturally it was a palatial building with two minarets and rooms for teachers and students. The provincial schools were financed by *awqāf* as well as by direct grants from the state.

The development of the medieval educational curricula can be divided into three periods. In the first period – that of the Sultanate and its successor states in the provinces until 1500 – the subjects taught were theology, jurisprudence (*fiqh*) and its principles (*uṣūl*), exegesis, *ḥadīth*, Ṣūfism, grammar, rhetoric and logic. The chief emphasis was on the study of the principles of jurisprudence and their application. The second period ranges from the reign of Sikandar Lōdī to the early period of the reign of Akbar, from 1500 to 1575. This is the phase of growing emphasis on the medieval rational sciences, logic, mathematics, medicine and astronomy. The third phase begins with the age of Akbar, when there was even greater emphasis on rationalism, though this process was reversed to some extent under Awrangzīb. Ethics seems to have been the chief area of concentration in this period, with the inclusion of *Fürstenspiegel* literature ('Mirrors for Princes').

Mosque architecture in Delhi, Agra, Lahore, Jawnpur and Ahmadabad shows a common pattern of small rooms built on the sides, which were meant for teachers' and students' residences. Ṣūfī hospices had also rooms, or sections reserved for theological education, which was not necessarily Ṣūfistic. Income from the rent of shops around a mosque was earmarked for the expenses of the mosque as well as the school attached to it. In some cases teachers received pensions from the state. From Akbar's time onwards state grants were given to Hindu schools and Muslim schools unattached to mosques, without any discrimination.[14]

School hours were from morning to noon; then from early afternoon to evening. All elementary education preparatory to entrance to a theological school was imparted in Persian. The syllabus of Persian studies included literature, *inshā'*, didactic studies, history and ethics.[15] In an advanced school the syllabus was distributed over a number of years according to the length of the texts, which were divided into three categories, short, medium and long. After completing their studies, scholars were categorized according to the area of specialization. A *fāḍil* was one who had specialized in rationalist (*maʿqūlāt*) sciences, an *ʿālim* in theological studies, and a *qābil* in literature and grammar.

Apart from the teaching in schools, learned men of means on occasion held classes in their own homes and, in certain cases, supplied their students with board and lodging. This type of teaching was especially suitable for fine arts, like music and painting, which were not taught in mosque schools or public schools.[16]

Despite seclusion the women of the upper and middle classes received some general, but mainly religious, education. School mistresses were appointed for the instruction of princesses and girls of the ruling élite. In Akbar's palace at Fat'ḥpur Sikri a special quarter was used as a girls' school.[17] Sultana Raḍiyya was highly accomplished. Some of the Mughal princesses received a high standard of education and were very talented.

2. Modern

Education in modern Muslim India has been flowing in two streams. There is a conservative stream which has preserved the medieval tradition and much of the medieval syllabus. It has been fighting a losing battle with the other stream, that of modern, Westernized education.

The oldest of the conservative schools is that of Farangī Maḥall at Lucknow founded in the late seventeenth century by Muḥammad Sahālawī, on a property allotted by Awrangzīb. One of its early professors, Mullā Niẓām-ad-dīn, evolved a syllabus, known after him as the *dars-i Niẓāmiyya*, which came to be taught in the majority of conservative schools. This syllabus included Arabic grammar and syntax, philosophy, mathematics, rhetoric, jurisprudence and its principles, scholasticism, exegesis (*tafsīr*), traditions (*ḥadīth*) and the principles and history of Ṣūfism. In this syllabus there was less emphasis on the traditional theological sciences compared with medieval rationalism and mysticism, and for this reason it was criticized by some orthodox ulema.[18]

These ulema, Muḥammad Qāsim Nānotawī and Rashīd

Aḥmad Gangohī, who had been deeply influenced by the teachings of Shāh Walī-Allāh's school, founded a more orthodox school at Deoband in 1867.[19] The founders of the school were strict Ḥanafīs. In dogma they followed the Ash'arite and Māturīdīte theology. These theologians had taken some part in the Mutiny of 1857 and had seen the rapid disintegration of the Muslim élite of northern India, and their school had as its principal aim the rehabilitation of theological sciences in Muslim India. Its course of studies excluded modern sciences, though it taught, with far less emphasis than at Farangī Maḥall, the medieval rationalist sciences, conceding that these were a bridge between the old intellectual world and the new. Its syllabus gave the chief place to jurisprudence (*fiqh*), exegesis and *ḥadīth*; but also included scholastic theology, dialectics, medieval geometry and astronomy, logic, the history of Islam, Arabic and Persian grammar, prosody and literature. The courses were originally spread over a period of ten years, but were later reduced to six. The entire syllabus consisted of 106 texts, and the students were classed by the books they studied rather than the year of their study.

The second generation of professors at Deoband had as their head the illustrious Maḥmūd al-Ḥasan (1850–1921), under whose direction Deoband achieved an international reputation in the world of Islam, next only to that of al-Aẓ'har with which it forged links. It attracted students from all over the subcontinent and from South Africa, Malaya, Central Asia and Iran and especially Afghanistan. Maḥmūd al-Ḥasan also encouraged the foundation in the north-west frontier areas of a large number of primary theological schools, leading to Deoband. He tried to bridge the gulf between Deoband and the modernist Muhammadan Anglo-Oriental College at Aligarh through the exchange of scholars. We are not concerned here with his activities in the Hijaz during the First World War, where he established contacts with the Turkish leaders Jamāl and Enver, and was, as a result, interned for several years by the British Government.

The third major theological school was Nadwat al-'ulamā' founded by a group of middle-of-the-road scholars in 1894 at Lucknow.[20] Its prime mover was 'Abd-al-Ghafūr, a Deputy Collector in the British government service. Other founders included the exegete ʿAbd-al-Ḥaqq Ḥaqqānī and the historian Shiblī Nuʿmānī, who remained actively associated with it and in control of it from 1904 to 1913.

The manifesto of the Nadwat al-ʿulamā' aimed at the advancement of theological studies, the development of a consensus of theological opinion, the minimization of differences in theological views, the rehabilitation of ethics and a general reform of Muslim society, without any involvement in politics. Rashīd Riḍā was invited to visit the school, and since then it remained sensitive to the intellectual speculations of the *al-Manār* group in Egypt. The school was conceived as having a middle position between the extreme conservatism of Deoband and the modernity of Aligarh, but soon it developed conservative contours of its own and its product became generally indistinguishable from that of Deoband in theological and intellectual outlook. One of the outgrowths of the Nadwat al-ʿulamā', the research and publication institute called *Dār al-muṣannifīn* of Aʿzamgarh, has made valuable contributions towards the enlightenment of Islamic studies in India.

A number of minor theological schools were opened all over the subcontinent in the later nineteenth and early twentieth century. One of these, Maẓāhir al-ʿulūm, at Saharanpur was modelled on Deoband. Similar schools came to be founded at Muradabad and Darbhanga. A theological school was run by the neo-traditionalist Ahl-i ḥadīth at Benares. Other theological schools were opened at Calcutta, Patna, Hyderabad and Madras. Shīʿī theological schools were founded at Lucknow. The Madrasa-i Iṣlāḥ, at Sarai Mir, a middle-of-the-road school, modelled on the Nadwat al-ʿulamā', was founded in 1909 and concentrated on Qur'ānic fundamentalism.

A school for the preservation of Yunānī, actually Graeco-Arab medicine, was started at the close of the nineteenth century by Ḥakīm ʿAbd-al-Majīd Khān in Delhi. A woman's section – an unusually progressive element – was added to it by the physician and politician Ḥakīm Ajmal Khān.

Oriental schools which touched the fringe of modernity were first established for Muslims in Bengal. Warren Hastings took the first step in this direction by establishing the Calcutta Madrasa which soon became famous. Ḥājī Muḥsin, a Muslim merchant of Calcutta, gave a substantial grant to the East India

Company in the early nineteenth century, for the general advancement of Muslim education and for financing schools like the Madrasa ʿĀliya of Calcutta.

The most outstanding of the semi-Westernized schools was the Delhi College, founded in 1792.[21] It began to receive aid from the East India Company in 1825; an Englishman, J. H. Taylor, was appointed its principal with a staff of *mawlawis*. In 1828 English was introduced as one of the subjects of instruction; but because of conservative pressure English classes were kept separate from the oriental section. By 1831 three hundred students were studying English.

The remarkable feature of the Delhi College was that Urdu was its medium of instruction and it continued as such in, and after, 1835 when all government-sponsored and government-aided institutions were substituting English for Persian by decision of the governor-general, Bentinck. In 1844 the Western (English) and Oriental (Urdu) sections were amalgamated to achieve a uniform standard of education for all students in physical and social sciences. Simultaneously a programme was introduced to translate scientific works from English into Urdu. From 1846 the East India Company participated directly in arranging the higher curricula and examinations in such subjects as history, English, Arabic and Sanskrit; while examinations in law and ethics and some other subjects continued to be organized by the College itself. In 1854 there were 333 students in the College of whom 112 were Muslims. The teachers of its oriental section included Mamlūk al-ʿAlī of the Walī-Allāhī school, as well as a Shīʿī savant Jaʿfar ʿAlī. There were separate theological courses for Sunnī and Shīʿī students. During the principalship of the orientalist Sprenger, from 1845 to 1848, teaching methods in Arabic and Persian were considerably improved. A local committee ran the administration of the College until 1843, when it was taken over by the Lieutenant-Governor of the North-West Provinces who made its policy similar to that of other government colleges.

The humanism of the nineteenth-century north-Indian Muslim élite, which forged a place for itself in Urdu literature, is traceable in large measure to the Delhi College, where a number of Sayyid Aḥmad Khān's associates were educated.

These included the historian Zakā-Allāh, the novelist Nadhīr Aḥmad, the stylist Muḥammad Ḥusayn Āzād and the poet Alṭāf Ḥusayn Ḥālī.

Delhi College was sacked, its library burnt, and its English principal killed by the mutineers, during the Indian Mutiny of 1857. Rather unjustly the College became a casualty of the Mutiny and was closed after it. It had a temporary revival from 1864 to 1877, but in this secondary stage it was a different institution. Urdu was no longer its medium of instruction and its 'personality' was no longer moulded on Islamic culture.

The pioneer of modern Muslim education in India, as of Muslim free-thinking and modern Muslim politics, was Sayyid Aḥmad Khān. The educational programme he initiated in 1859 and pushed forward in subsequent years until his death in 1898, changed the intellectual, political and economic destiny of Indian Muslims, and formed the main bridge of intellectual transition from medievalism to modernism. From the outset he realized the necessity of using English as the medium of instruction, on the one hand, and of developing Urdu on the other, through the translation into it of basic works of social and physical sciences. In 1864 he founded a Scientific Society[22] for the introduction of Western sciences. It embarked upon the translation of scientific works into Urdu and published a bilingual journal. In 1864 he founded a modern school at Ghazipur, primarily with a view to educating local Muslims. This led a little later to the formation of a number of educational committees in several districts of the North-West Provinces.

In 1869–70 Sayyid Aḥmad Khān visited England, and studied the educational system at Cambridge University, with a view to laying the foundations of an educational institution for Muslims, which might later develop into a University. In 1874 he finalized the scheme of his Muhammadan Anglo-Oriental (MAO) College at Aligarh. School classes were opened in 1875, and college classes in 1878. The college assumed a personality of its own as it grew, and showed hardly any influence of the original Cambridge model. It was meant, as its name suggests, primarily for Muslims, but was open also to Hindu and other non-Muslim students. Because of the unpopularity of his own radical and modernist religious views Sayyid Aḥmad Khān allowed the department of theology to be controlled by his orthodox critics, who provided religious courses for Sunnīs and Shīʿīs separately.

The MAO College, which became the Muslim University three decades after Sayyid Aḥmad Khān's death, developed into the most significant educational institution in Muslim India. It aimed at a liberalization of outlook, a broad humanism and a scientific world-view. In religious ideas its curriculum covered a wide spectrum, ranging from enlightened orthodoxy to agnosticism. In politics it trained its students in adjustment to the British ruling power, and to be wary of the Hindu political stance. Most of the intellectual and political leaders of Muslim India in the last decades of the nineteenth and the first half of the twentieth century were educated at Aligarh. They played a prominent part in the Khilāfat movement of the 1920s and the Pakistan movement of the 1940s. After the partition of the subcontinent in 1947 Aligarh was placed, by the government of independent India, under the control of the nationalist, Zākir Ḥusayn, whose aim, and that of his successors appointed by the Indian government, was to wean it away from Muslim nationalism to a composite Indian nationalism. Since 1947 the personality of the Muslim University at Aligarh has been gradually altered. In 1966 the education minister, M. C. Chagla, attempted to change its name to Aligarh University, thus depriving it of its specifically Muslim character and making it conform to the general pattern of Indian educational institutions.

In 1886 Sayyid Aḥmad Khān founded the Anglo-Muhammadan Educational Conference for the general advancement of Western education in Muslim India.[23] The Conference championed the use of English as the medium of instruction but also exercised pressure for the acceptance of Urdu as the secondary language in government schools in northern India, and broadened the Scientific Society's project of translating scientific classics into Urdu. It also had a vague programme for the development of female education among Muslims.

A number of other Muslim educational institutions developed during the late nineteenth and early twentieth century all over the subcontinent. A religious welfare association, Anjuman-i Ḥimāyat-i Islām, did pioneer educational work in the north-west and founded the Islamia Colleges at Lahore and Peshawar as well as a number of intermediate colleges elsewhere. An Anglo-Arabic College developed in Delhi.

One of the most remarkable educational experiments in modern, Muslim India was the foundation of the Osmania (ʿUthmāniyya) University at Hyderabad in 1917 with Urdu as the medium of instruction. A Translation Bureau (*Dār at-tarjuma*) was set up to translate – on an extensive scale – works of physical and social sciences into Urdu from English and other European languages as well as from Arabic and Persian, and to publish original textbooks. The Osmania University established pragmatically the thesis that Urdu or an Indian vernacular could be as successful a medium of instruction as a Western language. The Osmania University still survives, but the medium of instruction was changed to English after the Indian occupation of Hyderabad in 1948. There is a movement in Pakistan to develop a university there with Urdu as the medium of instruction.

The Jāmiʿa Milliyya Islāmiyya was founded at Aligarh, at the height of the Khilāfat disturbances, in 1920, by Mawlānā Muḥammad ʿAlī and other Khilāfat leaders, who regarded Aligarh's loyalism as reactionary. It was inaugurated by Maḥmūd al-Ḥasan of Deoband, but in its syllabus and educational policy it had nothing in common with that theological seminary. It followed the Osmania University in using Urdu as the medium of instruction. But it modelled itself primarily on the self-sacrificing idealism of certain Hindu educational institutions where teachers received minimal wages and imparted instruction of high intellectual calibre. Soon the Jāmiʿa Milliyya Islāmiyya came under the influence of pro-Congress Muslim leaders like Abū-l-Kalām Āzād, Mukhtār Aḥmad Anṣārī and Ḥakīm Ajmal Khān. The institution was developed and brought to maturity by Zākir Ḥusayn, who, later, rose to be the President of the Republic of India. It developed especially the disciplines of history and sociology.

In Pakistan the educational structure and policy was a heritage of the British government of undivided India. A national educational policy was worked out by the Education Commission of Pakistan which was appointed by the Martial Law Regime (1958–62) and submitted its report in 1959.[24] The report covers all aspects of academic, technical and vocational education, but its primary emphasis is on higher, i.e. university education and research. It realizes the necessity of professional and technical education for the developing society of Pakistan. It recommends compulsory primary education, but that is unrealizable owing to the lack of financial resources. Its recommendations for the improvement of secondary education are, in comparison, more practical. On female education, the Commission's view is that 'women need education just as Pakistan needs educated women'. It recommends a special programme for girls at the primary stage, but at the secondary and the university stages a similar pattern of education for boys and girls. It does not specify whether there should be separate or mixed educational institutions for men and women.

The most interesting part of the Commission's Report is the short chapter which deals with religion.[25] The Commission starts from the premiss: 'As education aims at the integrated and balanced development of the whole man – body, mind and spirit – it must create an appreciation of the fundamental and spiritual values that constitute the foundations of civilization, towards which all human endeavour should be directed. In performing this task a system of education must benefit from the humanizing influence of religion, which broadens sympathies, inculcates tolerance, self-sacrifice and social service, and removes artificial distinctions between man and man. Reverence for God and the Prophets has an enobling effect on the soul and opens the mind to an appreciation of the unity of mankind.' The Commission, however, keeps in check any tendency towards obscurantism in religious education. It stipulates that such education should do nothing which would impair social and political unity in the country. It warns that religion 'is not to be presented as a dogma, superstition or ritual'. It specifically states that not merely Islam, but several religious faiths are professed and practised in Pakistan and that the teaching of them should be confined to those who profess them.[26] Religious teaching is divided into three stages. For the Muslim students, teaching of *Islāmiyyāt* should be compulsory from classes I to VIII; it should be optional in classes IX and X of the secondary school and in the University; but the Universities should develop institutes of Islamic research 'capable of interpreting Islam and presenting it as a body of thought that can meet the challenge of modern times and fulfil the requirements of a modern scientific society'. Turning to the vestiges of the medieval heritage of education – the *madrasas* and *maktabs* or old conservative religious schools – the Commission recommends that vocational and professional courses may be introduced in them side by side with religious instruction, and that the latter in its turn may be revolutionized to present 'Islam as a dynamic and progressive movement which can endure through changing times'. On the question of the medium of instruction, the Commission feels that Urdu and Bengali should gradually replace English in West and East Pakistan respectively, but English should be taught as the compulsory language from Class VI onwards through the degree level. The Commission does not straightaway recommend the use of Roman script for Urdu and Bengali, but recommends the formation of committees to consider this question as well as that of orthographic reform of Bengali and Urdu.

Some of these recommendations have already been applied to educational development in Pakistan, and a few more universities have been opened in East and West Pakistan. But considering the vast population of the country primary, secondary and higher educational institutions are few and inadequate, and Pakistan has one of the lowest rates of literacy in the world.

Whereas some effort towards educational revival and educational reform is being made in Pakistan, the prospects for Muslims in India since 1947 have been much bleaker. Before independence, lower middle-class Muslims usually sent their children to schools and colleges, but owing to adverse political and economic decisions taken by the Indian central government, and especially the state governments, they can no longer afford to do so. To quote an Indian nationalist Muslim educationist, 'Ābid Ḥusayn: '... many Muslims stopped sending their children to schools and as they could make no private arrangements for teaching them, they remained practically illiterate. With respect to secondary and higher education their condition was even more deplorable, partly because the medium of instruction was Hindi, but largely because educated Muslim families could not generally afford to bear the expenses of educating their children.'[27]

SEVEN

LITERATURE IN ARABIC, PERSIAN AND TURKISH

1. Arabic

The cultural expression of Islamic India is best reflected in its literature, which is written in several languages. At first the classical languages of the Islamic world, Arabic and especially Persian and even Turkish, were used for literary composition. Then Urdu was evolved and developed. Simultaneously in various areas where there was a concentration of Muslim population a popular regional literature also developed.

Arabic was used sparingly and mainly as a language of religious scholarship.[1] The tradition of Arabic writing in India was the same as elsewhere in the Muslim world and without any specifically Indian features. Only in Arab Sind under the Umayyads and ʻAbbāsids and possibly under the Ṣaffārids was Arabic the language of administration. It was there that the first history of Muslim Sind, *Minhāj al-masālik*, was written. The original is now lost, but its Persian version, *Chach Nāma*, prepared in 1216 by ʻAlī ibn-Ḥāmid Abū-Bakr al-Kūfī,[2] survives, and constitutes one of the earliest sources of the history of Sind. *Ḥadīth* flourished as a discipline in Sind. Most remarkable was the effort of the Sindhī scholars in translating Sanskrit scientific works into Arabic for the ʻAbbāsids and Barmakids. Almost all of these works mentioned by Ibn-an-Nadīm[3] have been lost. Belles-lettres in Arab Sind are represented by the poet Abū-ʻAṭā' as-Sindī.[4]

At Ghazna, under the patronage of Maḥmūd and Masʻūd in the early eleventh century, Arabic writing flourished. It was here that Abū-Rayḥān al-Bīrūnī wrote, among other works on various sciences, his monumental *Taḥqīq mā li-l-Hind*, the first and foremost Indological study written by a Muslim.[5] This work, which evaluates with erudition and objectivity Hindu religion, philosophy, geography, metrology, cosmography, astronomy, chronology and literature as well as manners and customs, still remains an indispensable classic for the study of ancient Hindu civilization. At the Ghaznavid court al-ʿUtbī's[6] history, written in 1020–1, furthered the important transfusion into Persian of elements of the Arabic historiographical tradition, a process which had already begun under the Samānids. When the Ghaznavid capital moved from Ghazna to Lahore, on the soil of subcontinental India, the tradition of Arabic scholarly writing failed to take root there, and Persian supplanted it.

The revival of Arabic writing in the Delhi Sultanate seems connected with the relations between Baghdad and Delhi. Under the Delhi Sultanate the Mongol onslaught against the heartlands of Islam brought an influx of Arabic-speaking refugee scholars from Iraq after the sack of Baghdad by Hülagü in 1258. It cannot be considered as mere coincidence that the first outstanding author in Arabic in India, Raḍī-ad-dīn Ḥasan ibn-Muḥammad aṣ-Ṣaghānī, was also a special envoy of Caliph an-Nāṣir to the court of Iletmish in 1219–20.[7] After his return from Baghdad and during his subsequent stay in Delhi, Saghānī, who was an Indian by birth, probably compiled his major work, *Mashāriq al-anwār* – a selection of Prophetic traditions – and wrote the *Risāla fī-l-aḥadīth al-mawḍūʿa*, one of the earliest treatises on *hadīth*-criticism to appear in India. His lexicographical work, *Kitāb al-ʿubāb*, which was praised by Jalāl-ad-dīn as-Suyūṭī, shows that interest in the Arabic language was already well entrenched in the Delhi sultanate by the early decades of the thirteenth century.[8]

During the reign of ʿAlā'-ad-dīn Khaljī (1296–1316) a famous Egyptian theologian Shams-ad-dīn visited India. Eminent among the ulema of his reign was Ḥusām-ad-dīn Surkh, a scholar of jurisprudence and Arabic language, who taught in Delhi.[9] Among the Arabic scholars of the Khaljī period was Abū-Bakr Is'ḥāq (d. 1335), better known as Ibn-Tāj, who wrote in Arabic on a variety of subjects, including Qur'ānic exegesis, theology and Ṣūfism. The *khuṭba*, composed by Niẓām-ad-dīn Awliyā in this period, was read in mosques throughout India and is still read.[10] Amīr Khusraw, though he had no pretensions to scholarship in Arabic, occasionally composed verses in it. The Chishtī mystic, Naṣīr-ad-dīn 'Chirāgh-i Dihlī', and his disciple, 'Abd-al-Muqtadir (d. 1388), also occasionally composed in Arabic.[11] Much of this poetry accepts unquestioningly the figures of speech and the conventions of classical Arabic verse.

Shihāb-ad-dīn Multānī was a well-known scholar and a teacher of the principles of jurisprudence as well as of the Arabic language and literature in the late Khaljī and early Tughluq period.[12] To the latter period belongs Sirāj-ad-dīn 'Umar ibn-Is'ḥāq āl-Hindī (1314–72) who achieved fame not only in India but also in Egypt where he was appointed *qāḍī* at Cairo, and who wrote on theological and mystical themes.

Sayyid Muḥammad al-Ḥusaynī (d. 1422), better known as 'Gīsūdarāz', a famous Chishtī mystic who emigrated to the Bahmanid successor state in the Deccan, wrote in Arabic as well as in Persian and early Urdu. 'Alī ibn-Aḥmad Mahā'imī (d. 1471) wrote on jurisprudence and mysticism. Zayn-ad-dīn Abū-Yaḥyā ibn-'Alī al-Ma'barī (1468–1521) achieved fame through his mystical as well as poetical work in Arabic, since it received recognition outside India and was commented upon by scholars in the Hijaz and in Java.

Qāḍī Shihāb-ad-dīn Dawlatābādī, who wrote principally in Persian, is also the author of several works in Arabic on a variety of subjects, including jurisprudence, grammar and rhetoric. During the fourteenth century Mu'īn-ad-dīn 'Umrānī wrote commentaries on classical theological works in Arabic. Sayyid Yūsuf Multānī (d. 1388) also wrote commentaries on works of jurisprudence and scholasticism.

In 1417 Badr-ad-dīn Muḥammad, better known as Ibn-ad-Damāmīnī, migrated from Egypt to Gujarat and wrote on a variety of theological and literary subjects. Later he attached himself to the court of the Bahmanids in the Deccan.

Once the hegemony of Portuguese navigation had been established, after the defeat of the indigenous and Turkish fleets in the Indian Ocean in the sixteenth century, voyages between the Hijaz and India became safe. A number of Indians visited the Hijaz, and some even migrated there for the study of classical theological sciences. Prominent among these scholar-migrants to the Hijaz are Sayyid ʿAlī al-Muttaqī and his disciple, ʿAbd-al-Wahhāb al-Muttaqī. Both of them were outstanding scholars of *ḥadīth*, both wrote in Arabic, and from their teachings and writings there sprang the revival of the discipline of *ḥadīth* in Muslim India.

It was actually ʿAbd-al-Wahhāb al-Muttaqī's famous disciple, ʿAbd-al-Ḥaqq Dihlawī, who re-established the study of *ḥadīth* in India. He wrote mainly in Persian, but some of his works are in Arabic, including *Lumʿāt at-tanqīḥ*, a commentary on the classical *ḥadīth* collection *Mishkāt al-maṣābīḥ*. On the science of biography, (*ʿilm asmāʾ ar-rijāl*) pertinent to *ḥadīth*, he wrote two books.[13] On Ḥanafī jurisprudence he wrote a treatise, *Fatʾḥ al-mannān fī taʾīd an-Nuʿmān*,[14] and two other works. He also wrote in Arabic on Ṣūfism and ethics.

Arabic writings by ʿAbd-al-Ḥaqq Dihlawī and a number of other writers in the Mughal period were balanced by a contrary trend: that of translations from Arabic into Persian, which developed in the court of Akbar and under his patronage. This trend is explained by Akbar's policy of the secularization of education, but it was not conducive to the encouragement of original writing in Arabic. All the same, a significant number of theologians continued to write in Arabic under the Mughals.[15] By far the most outstanding of these was ʿAbd-al-Ḥakīm Siyālkotī (d. 1656), who wrote commentaries on the exegetical work of al-Bayḍāwī and on the *ʿAqāʾid* of at-Taftāzānī and also wrote a large number of works on various classical disciplines including the rationalistic sciences. Arabic Studies occupied the central position in his school at Sialkot.

Like ʿAbd-al-Ḥaqq Dihlawī, Shāh Walī-Allāh (1703–62) received his formative education in the Hijaz, where he studied *ḥadīth* with Shaykh Abū-Ṭāhir Muḥammad ibn-Ibrāhīm al-Kurdī, and Mālikī jurisprudence under a North-African scholar, Shaykh Sulaymān al-Maghribī. Also among his teachers were Shaykh as-Sanāwī and Tāj-ad-dīn Ḥanafī.[16] When he returned to India he wrote his chief works in Arabic, probably because he was aiming at a learned readership both abroad and in India, and because Persian was already losing ground as the language of the élite, with the decline of the Mughal Empire and with the use of Urdu as the language of poetry and ordinary life.

Walī-Allāh's *Ḥujjat Allāh al-bāligha*[17] is the most outstanding theological work written in India. It introduces an explanation of theology scholastically and uses an approach to religious problems which may be defined as that of pre-modernist fundamentalism. It discusses dialectically both metaphysics and the psychology of religion. In its sociological chapters it takes an evolutionist view of human history. It concerns itself with individual morality as much as with social organization, and especially with the elucidation of the problems of Islamic society and the position in it of the institution of the caliphate, kingship and feudal nobility. Its religious argument is based principally on the Qur'ān and the corpus of *ḥadīth*, while in relation to law and jurisprudence it recommends a course of selection from, or synthesis of, the rulings of the four Sunnī juristic schools. Its one defect is that its organization of the subject-matter is atomistic.

Other works by Shāh Walī-Allāh written in Arabic include: *Ṭā'wīl al-aḥādīth*, on the interpretation of Prophetic traditions; *al-Musawwa'*, a commentary on the *al-Muwaṭṭā'* of Mālik ibn Anas; *at-Tafhīmāt al-Ilāhiyya*, which is partly in Arabic and deals with Ṣūfism, as does also his *Khayr al-kathīr*; and *'Iqd al-jīd fī aḥkām al-ijtihād wa-t-taqlīd*, which deals with the problems of *ijtihād* (use of individual reasoning) and *taqlīd* (conformity), and was used as an indispensable source-book by nineteenth-century theologians, fundamentalist and modernist alike.[18] His *Fuyūḍ al-Ḥaramayn* is a memoir of actual and spiritual experiences during his stay in the Hijāz from 1731 to 1732. Shāh Walī-Allāh also composed Arabic poetry, and is the author of a collection of devotional panegyrics on the Prophet.

The famous writer of *tadhkiras* (biographical dictionaries), Ghulām 'Alī Āzād Bilgrāmī (d. 1785), also composed poetry in Arabic. His compatriot and contemporary, Murtaḍā 'Alī Zabīdī Bilgrāmī (d. 1790), is another eminent writer in Arabic. Zabīdī was a disciple of Walī-Allāh; later he travelled to the Yemen, where he was admitted to the 'Idrūsī order, and to Egypt, where he won fame as a lexicographer. His *Tāj al-'arūs* is a voluminous lexicographical commentary on the famous *Qāmūs* of Majd-ad-dīn Fīrūzabādī. Zabīdī was consulted as an authority on *ḥadīth* by 'Abd-al-Ḥamīd I and his grand wazīr,

5. *Fat'ḥpur Sikri, near Agra. Built by Akbar* 1569 – 72

Rāghib Pāsha.[19] Another lexicographer of the eighteenth century was Muḥammad ʿAlī Tahānawī, author of *Kashshāf iṣṭilāḥāt al-funūn*, a dictionary of technical scientific terms.

During the later nineteenth and early twentieth century, some Indo-Muslim scholars made an effort to reach a readership in the Arab world. Ṣiddīq Ḥasan Khān, ʿAbd-al-Ḥayy of Farangī Maḥall (d. 1886) and Ashraf ʿAlī Tahānawī (d. 1943) wrote in Arabic as well as in Urdu.

Some Arabic periodicals were published in India during the nineteenth and twentieth century, three of them from Lucknow: *al-Bayān*, *al-Jāmiʿa*, which was edited by Abū-l-Kalām Āzād, and *aḍ-Ḍiya*, the organ of the Nadwat al-ʿulamāʾ. The Government of Pakistan publishes a general cultural monthly, *al-Waʿī*, which contains articles by Arab as well as Pakistani writers.

In recent years some theologians have arranged for translations of their Urdu works into Arabic. Most of the major writing of Abū-l-Aʿlā Mawdūdī is available in Arabic. Some of Abū-l-Ḥasan ʿAlī Nadwī's writing is also in Arabic and has made considerable impact.[20]

Bohra ulema have consistently used Arabic and not Persian or Urdu for their religious writings.

2. Persian[21]

The Ghaznavids, with whom the continued process of the Muslim conquest of India began, were Turks, but their cultural language was Persian. Under them Lahore became the secondary capital and then the main capital of the kingdom. Even when the seat of power was at Ghazna, Lahore was referred to as the 'little Ghazna' (*Ghaznīn-i khurd*). It was here that Persian established itself as the language of the Muslim élite. Ghazna, under Maḥmūd (998–1030), had inherited from the Samānids the patronage of Persian letters, especially Persian poetry. It was under Mahmūd's patronage that Firdawsī composed his monumental epic, *Shāh Nāma*, and other poets, Manūchihrī, ʿAsjadī and ʿUnṣurī developed Rudakī's style of the *ghazal* (rhymed song, elegy of love) and transferred the tradition of Khurasan's school of poetry (*sabk-i Khurāsānī*) to the frontiers of India. Lahore followed the example of Ghazna. Two of the eminent Ghaznavid administrators stationed in Lahore, Niẓām-ad-dīn Abū-Naṣr and Zarīr Shaybānī, were

6. *MS painting from the* Ḥamza Nāma, c. 1575

patrons of poets and it was under their patronage that the tradition of Persian poetry took root at Lahore. The first Persian poet in Lahore was Abū-ʿAbd-Allāh Rūzbih ibn-ʿAbd-Allāh an-Nakatī (or *Nakhatī*), writing panegyrics in praise of the Ghaznavid Masʿūd (1030–1040).[22] Al-Hujwīrī (d. 1071), the eminent author of the Ṣūfī work *Kashf al-maḥjūb*, was also a poet, and internal evidence indicates that some of the verses attributed to him are probably genuine. Abū-l-Faraj ibn-Masʿūd ar-Rūni (d. 1091?), the court poet of Ibrāhīm ibn-Masʿūd (1059–99), was a native of Lahore.[23] He is the first great poet of the subcontinent whose *dīwān* (collection of *ghazals*) has survived. His style was imitated by the famous Persian panegyrist Anwarī.

More outstanding than Rūnī was his younger contemporary and rival Masʿūd Saʿd Salmān (1046–1121), whose verse, some of it written in prison, shows emotional depth and has a sincere musical quality.[24] Rūnī and Salmān are the two prominent figures of Ghaznavid Lahore and their eminence shows that in the later eleventh century there were also a number of lesser luminaries whose work has not reached us, but whose names and odd verses have been recorded by the biographer ʿAwfī. After the sack and burning of Ghazna by the Ghūrid ʿAlā'-ad-dīn Jahānsūz (World-Burner) in 1151, Lahore became the principal intellectual centre of the Ghaznavid kingdom and increased its importance when it became the capital of the kingdom under Khusraw Malik (1160–86). His court poets included the panegyrists Yūsuf ibn-Naṣr al-Kātib and Shihāb-ad-dīn Muḥammad ibn-Rashīd (d. 1201), whose verse is distinguished by fanciful and ornate imagery.[25]

When the expanding Ghūrid empire in 1186 absorbed the Ghaznavid kingdom and rapidly spread over practically the whole of northern India, a number of Ghaznavid poets of Lahore attached themselves first to Muḥammad ibn-Sām Ghūrī and then after his death to the courts of his slaves and successors Quṭb-ad-dīn Aybak (1206–10) at Delhi, and Nāṣir-ad-dīn Qubācha at Multan. Among these poets were ʿAbd-ar-Rāfiʿ Harawi and Abū-Bakr Khusrawī.[26]

During the brief reign of Qubācha in the southern Punjab and Sind, his capital Multan and another town Uch became centres of Persian learning, a development which followed the

Ghūrid occupation of Lahore and was greatly accentuated after the Mongol sack of that city. In a school which Qubācha founded at Uch, ʿAwfī and the historian Minhāj-as-Sirāj al-Jūzjānī began their careers as instructors. Qubācha's minister ʿAyn-al-Mulk was also an active patron of poets, including Faḍlī Multānī, Ḍiyā'-ad-dīn Sijzī and Shams Balkhī whose names and some of whose verses have survived in ʿAwfī's notices.[27] ʿAwfī was himself a poet of considerable merit.

When Qubācha perished (1228) in his struggle with Iletmish (1211–36), poets and scholars of his entourage, including ʿAwfī and Jūzjānī, turned to Delhi for patronage. From then until the beginning of the eighteenth century Delhi remained the principal centre of Persian poetry in the subcontinent. The first remarkable poet writing in Delhi at the court of Iletmish was Tāj-ad-dīn Sangrīza; he and his younger contemporary, Shihāb-ad-dīn Mahmara, were of Indian origin.[28] Very little of the work of either has survived. A later poet, some of whose panegyrics have reached us, was ʿAmīd Sannāmī, attached to the entourage of Nāṣir-ad-dīn Maḥmūd (1246–66) and of Balban's (1266–87) son Muḥammad at Multan.

Among the Ṣūfī poets of the early Delhi Sultanate was Jamāl-ad-dīn Hānsawī (d. 1259), whose verses combine mysticism with a pious attention to the externalities of ritual. He wrote a moving elegy on the death of Iletmish, who was regarded by most mystics as a very pious sultan. A heterodox mystic poet of that age is the almost semi-legendary Abū-ʿAlī Qalandar (d. 1323). It is difficult to ascertain the genuineness, or otherwise, of the ecstatic esoteric verses attributed to him whereas the work attributed to Hānsawī is probably genuine.

Amīr Khusraw[29] (1253–1325), by far the most eminent Indo-Persian poet, was attached to the courts of Prince Muḥammad, the Khaljī sultans and the first two Tughluqs. Mystically, he was one of the prominent disciples of Niẓām-ad-dīn Awliyā. A great deal of apocryphal material surrounds his personality and work, but from what can be ascertained to be genuinely his, one can assess the magnitude and versatility of his genius. His poetical writing falls into two broad categories; lyrical, with the *ghazal* as the principal form, and having a musical quality emphasized by the sensitive ear of an accomplished musician; and narrative, consisting of a number of *mathnawis* (narrative poems composed of distichs corresponding in measure and each having a pair of rhymes) of both the courtly (*bazmiyya*) and the epical (*razmiyya*) varieties. He has five collections of *ghazals*: one of juvenile verse, the *Tuḥfat aṣ-ṣighar*; a later one, showing greater maturity, the *wasṭ al-ḥayāt*; the third, the *Ghurrat al-kamāl*, showing his genius and craftsmanship at its perfection, has a long, illuminating prose introduction (*dībācha*); the fourth, *Bāqiya nāqiya*, supplements the third; and the last, *Nihāyāt al-kamāl*, contains the verse of his old age.

Khusraw's courtly narratives are modelled on Niẓāmī, and similarly, five of them constitute his *khamsa*, which includes the mystical and allegorical *Maṭla' al-anwār*, the pre-Islamic Persian romance, *Shīrīn wa-Khusraw*, the Arab romance, *Layla wa-Majnūn*, the Alexander romance, *A'īna-i Sikandarī*, and another old Persian tale, *Hasht Bihisht*. Also courtly in theme is his '*Āshiqa*, the story of the love of 'Alā'-ad-dīn Khaljī's son, Khiḍr Khān, for the Hindu princess Dewal Rānī, composed in 1315. His epic narratives include *Qirān as-sa'dayn* on the reconciliation of the last 'slave' sultan, Mu'izz-ad-dīn Kayqubād (1287–90), with his father, Bughrā Khān, an event by which a dynastic civil war was averted. More mature is his *Miftāḥ al-futūḥ*, celebrating four victories of Jalāl-ad-dīn Khaljī (1290–1296). The *Nuh siphir* combines epic content with fanciful virtuosity of structure and style; and finally there is the *Tughluq Nāma*, an epic of considerable documentary value celebrating the organization and success of the Tughluq Revolution (1320).

Khusraw's historical epics began a tradition which reached its apex in the succeeding generation with 'Iṣāmī's *Futuḥ as-salāṭīn*,[30] a rhymed history of the Muslim conquest and rule in India, modelled on Firdawsī's *Shāh Nāma*.

A contemporary of Khusraw, and like him a disciple of Niẓām-ad-dīn Awliyā, was Ḥasan Sijzī Dihlawī (1257–1336) whose lyrical verse is impregnated with mystical fervour.[31] Other outstanding Persian poets of the age of 'Alā'-ad-dīn Khaljī (1296–1316) were Shihāb al-dīn Ṣadr-nashīn, 'Ubayd Ḥakīm, and others, whose works have not survived.

The Tughluq era forms a watershed in the growth of Persian poetry in India. The straightforward, gently lyrical tradition of Mas'ūd Sa'd Salmān and Amīr Khusraw came to an end, and new poets either turned inward towards a greater intellectualization of style, or sought inspiration from unfamiliar sources of narrative work. The two trends are best represented by Badr-ad-dīn Muḥammad, popularly known as Badr-i Chāch, who came from Chāch or Shāsh (modern Tashkent), and Ḍiyā'-ad-dīn Nakhshabī, who was the first Muslim poet writing in the subcontinent to turn to Hindu lore in search of narrative themes.

Badr-i Chāch[32] is the most difficult of Indo-Persian poets, with a style which thrives on almost incomprehensible conceit and undecipherable enigma. The challenge of his genius seems to have attracted the intense intellectuality of his patron Muḥammad ibn-Tughluq (1325–51), whose military expeditions Badr-i Chāch celebrated in an epic, the *Shāh Nāma*. Another poet close to Muḥammad ibn-Tughluq, and like him a rationalist, was ʿUbayd, who is mentioned in chronicles, but whose work has been lost.

Ḍiyā'-ad-dīn Nakhshabī (d. 1350) was a poet of a very different order. His lyrical verse is simple, but he is known chiefly for his *Ṭūṭī Nāma*, which is based on a Sanskrit original and consists of a series of stories told by a loyal parrot to the potentially unfaithful wife of his master, a merchant who is away on a journey, in order to keep her mind occupied night after night and save her from adultery. The *Ṭūṭī Nāma* was later translated into several languages, including Turkish, and formed the basis of several Urdu narrative poems.

Other poets of the later Tughluq period were the didactic Muṭahhar (c. 1350), and the Ṣūfīs Masʿūd Bek (d. 1397) and Sayyid Muḥammad al-Ḥusaynī Gīsūdarāz, some of whose verses also treat frankly of profane love.

Ḥāmid ibn-Faḍl-Allāh Jamālī (d. 1536),[33] a protégé of Sikandar Lōdī (1480–1517) was a gifted poet as well as a respected Ṣūfī hagiographer. The chief quality of his mystical poetry is its closeness to the soil. He travelled abroad and met Jāmī in Herat, but it is difficult to trace the latter's influence in his verse.

The Persian poetry of the Mughal period began with an influx of fresh influences, first, from Central Asia, and, later, from Persia. The Central Asian poets Fārighī, Nādir Samarqandī and Ṭāhir Khwāndī accompanied Bābur to India. Persian poetry rose to great heights in the age of Akbar with ʿUrfi Shīrāzī (1556–91), whose genius was characterized by a lyrical dynamism, and the more indigenous Fayḍī (1574–95) a free-thinking intellectual whose inspiration was controlled by ingenious artifice. Another poet of remarkable talent, Naẓīrī Nīshāpūrī (d. 1613), was attached to the entourage of ʿAbd-ar-Raḥīm Khān-i Khānān, one of Akbar's chief administrators. ʿUrfī, Fayḍī and Naẓīrī made the age of Akbar the golden age of Persian poetry in India. One of their contemporaries further south, in the court of Bijapur, was Nūr-ad-dīn Ẓuhūrī, a consummate stylist in verse as in prose. Ṭālib Āmulī (d. 1626) and Ṣā'ib Tabrīzī were later poets, both from Persia. Ṭālib was poet laureate of Jahāngīr (1605–27); but Ṣā'ib's was more profoundly philosophical in expression.

Compared with these Persian émigrés, Munīr Lāhōrī's (1609–45) work was comparatively mediocre. His more famous contemporary, Qudsī Mashhadī (d. 1646), had a versatile and felicitous style. Shāh Jahān's poet-laureate, Abū-Ṭālib Kalīm (d. 1651), had the startling quality of being able to analyse minute nuances of emotion in an intellectualized but spontaneous style.

Sarmad (d. 1660), a heterodox Ṣūfī and a friend of Prince Dārā Shukoh, who, though principally a student of comparative religion and a hagiographer, was also a poet, wrote quatrains of ecstatic and unorthodox mystic lore. Ghanī Kashmīrī (d. 1661) experimented with illustrative symbolism in his verse. Their contemporary was the first outstanding Hindu poet in Persian, Chandra Bhān Brahman (d. 1662), who was also a prose stylist of quality.

In the puritanical age of Awrangzīb (1658–1707) no official patronage was extended to poets, and Persian poetry would have declined but for the individual genius of Mirzā ʿAbd-al-Qādir Bīdil (d. 1721),[34] the most challenging of Indo-Persian poets, whose content and diction are marked by an extreme effort at the intellectualization of thought and imagery. The work of his contemporaries was very different; Ghanīmat Kunjāhī (d. 1695), whose narrative verse, especially, reflects unmistakable signs of Mughal decadence, and Nāṣir ʿAlī Sirhindī (1697), whose artificiality sometimes borders on the ridiculous.

In the eighteenth century some of the Urdu poets, such as Ārzū (1689–1755), and the Naqshbandī mystic, Maẓ'har Jān-i Jānān, wrote also in Persian.

Equally important both in Persian and Urdu was the verse of Ghālib (1797–1869), although he personally regarded his Persian output as superior. The tradition of Bīdil finds its culmination and its dissolution in the Persian verse of Ghālib.[35] Ghālib's style has an impetuous force and vitality and is an integral vehicle for the subtlety of his fanciful thought.

The last great poet who chose to write in Persian as well as in Urdu was Muḥammad Iqbāl (1875–1938). Iqbāl chose Persian especially for his more philosophical, speculative and meditative poetry and used the form of *mathnawī*. His first two narrative poems in Persian, *Asrār-i khudī*[36] and *Rumūz-i Bīkhudī*,[37] expound his theory of human Self and its relation to society. *Jāwīd Nāma*[38] is an eschatological poem inspired by Dante's *Divina Commedia*. Two other narrative poems, *Musāfir* (Traveller) and *Pas chi bāyad kard ay aqwām-i sharq*, are broadly political. Iqbāl also wrote lyrical, reflective and political verse in Persian in the form of *ghazals*, and modern poems consisting of two collections *Payām-i Mashriq*[39] and *Zabūr-i ʿAjam*.[40]

The style of Persian poetry in the subcontinent, especially a particular stream of it in the seventeenth and eighteenth century, is known as the *sabk-i Hindī* (Indian style).[41] It is generally argued that it began with the transplantation of Fighānī Shīrāzī's (d. 1519) highly complex style by ʿUrfī Shīrāzī in the age of Akbar. East-European and Soviet Central-Asian scholars trace this style to the influence of ʿAlī Shīr Nawā'ī and Jāmī, which reached India early in the sixteenth century with Bābur.

The present writer is of the view that elements of this particular style are to be found from the very outset in Persian poetry written in the subcontinent. Elements, which are the components of this highly symbolical, fanciful and complex style, can be traced as early as the beginning of the eleventh century in certain poems of Abū-ʿAbd-Allāh Rūzbih an-Nakatī. Masʿūd Saʿd Salmān, writing in Ghaznavid Lahore, has two distinct styles. One of these is the simple, straightforward 'Khurāsānī'. but the other one is closer to the later intellectualized 'Indian style' in its efforts to create difficulties of expression for itself.

A later Ghaznavid poet, Abū-Bakr ar-Rūḥānī, who wrote in the early twelfth century, has recourse to fanciful enigma; and experiments in complexity of style are made by his contemporary Muḥammad al-Yamīnī.

The next landmark in the development of the particular 'Indian style' is the highly enigmatic verse of Badr-i Chāch, which has all the difficulty of a crossword puzzle. Badr-i Chāch's *qaṣīdas* (panegyrics) were a part of the school curriculum probably from the late fifteenth century, but his actual influence in the late development of the 'Indian style' is hard to assess, because his verse was too difficult to be easily imitable.

Persian poets of Bābur's entourage had close affinities with the school of Turkish and Persian poetry developed in Herat at the court of Sulṭān Ḥusayn Bayqara by Nawā'ī and Jāmī. There is substance in the argument of Soviet and East European scholars that Nawā'ī's was certainly a formative influence on the 'Indian style', though it must be added that it was neither the first nor the only one. Then in the age of Akbar the complex and highly intellectual-lyrical style of Fighānī was transplanted to India by ʿUrfī, and during the seventeenth century this style, which is the core of the 'Indian style', reached its apex. It is clearly distinguishable from the purely indigenous one, the best representative of which in the late sixteenth and early seventeenth century was ʿUrfī's contemporary, the poet-laureate Fayḍī.

The Fighānian style flourished in India in the next two generations with the works of poets who were émigrés from Persia, chiefly Ṭālib Āmulī and Ṣā'ib, whose verse has a philosophical charm, and Kalīm Hamdānī, who could masterfully crystallize nuances of emotional experience in spontaneous though unusual expression. The 'Indian style' reached its climax in the explosively intellectualized verse of Bīdil, whose subjectivity seems to burst through the stylistic fetters he creates for himself. Ghālib inherited Bīdil's style and used it in his early Persian verse, but, later, he freed himself from it. It is in Ghālib that the 'Indian style' finally dissolves itself.

Persian prose of the subcontinent is best represented by the tradition of historiography, which had its beginnings under the Sāmānids in Central Asia with al-Balʿamī's abridged translation of aṭ-Ṭabarī's history. This tradition was developed under the patronage of Maḥmūd and Mas'ūd in Ghazna where an outstanding history, *Ta'rīkh-i Mas'ūdī*, was compiled by Abū-l-Faḍl Muḥammad ibn-Ḥusayn Bayhaqī,[42] which is a graphic account of some of the events of the reign of these two, especially the latter monarch, and incorporates valuable documentation. More concise and less ambitious is Abū-Sa'īd Gardīzī's *Zayn al-akhbār*,[43] composed a little earlier, and dealing briefly with the political history of the Ṭāhirids, the Ṣaffārids, the Sāmānids, the Ghaznavids and the early Seljūqs.

It is surprising that the historiographical tradition of Ghazna was not continued in Lahore. Muḥammad 'Awfī's (d. 1232) *Jawāmi' al-ḥikāyāt*, composed under Qubācha in Multan and the early Slave sultans in Delhi, has some historical interest, but is largely anecdotal. His contemporary, Fakhr Mudabbir, wrote three works which touch the fringe of historical writing. The first of these, *Shajarat al-ansāb*[44], as P. Hardy has shrewdly observed, 'epitomized the state of Muslim historiography in the outside Muslim world at that time'.[45] This compilation of genealogical tables has a lengthy introduction which, among other material, also describes briefly the process of the Muslim conquest of northern India and the accession of Quṭb-ad-dīn Aybak. Some of the material of the book is in the genre of *Fürstenspiegel*, and this is well represented. There is a theory of the Muslim treatment of non-Muslims in the newly conquered lands in his *Ādāb al-mulūk*.[46] This work continues the tradition of Niẓām-al-Mulk's *Siyāsat Nāma*, and precedes such classical 'mirrors for princes' as the ethical works of Naṣīr-ad-dīn Ṭūsī, Dawānī and Wā'iẓ al-Kāshifī, though it is doubtful whether it had any direct influence on them. Fakhr Mudabbir's third work, *Ādāb al-ḥarb wa-sh-shujā'a*, continues the same theme and is also a manual of the art of war.[47]

Regular Persian historiography began in the subcontinent with a remarkable universal history, Minhāj-as-Sirāj al-Jūzjānī's *Ṭabaqāt-i Nāṣirī*,[48] which deals with Islamic history and pre-Islamic Iranian history in general, and with Ghūrids and the early Slave sultans in particular. The author, a *qāḍī*, professor and orator, was one of the pioneer organizers of the Indo-Muslim intellectual tradition, and he brings to his history a valuable sense of the assessment of historical detail, and an eloquent, forceful style. It serves as the solid foundation on which future generations of historians built the structure of Indo-Muslim historiography.

A lesser contemporary of Jūzjānī was Ḥasan Niẓāmī whose *Tāj al-ma'āthir*,[49] dealing with the reign of Quṭb-ad-dīn Aybak and briefly with those of his predecessor and successor, has little historical value and is better known for its florid, highly artificial style. '. . . In the second half we have images derived from mirrors, pens and chess each running on for many pages. . . . Here also we are introduced to new conceits, where whole sentences and pages are made to consist of nothing but sibilants and labials.'[50]

Ḥasan Niẓāmī's style was imitated by Amīr Khursaw in his account of ʿAlā' ad-dīn Khaljī's conquests in the Deccan, the *Khaẓā'in al-futūḥ*,[51] which has greater historical value as a contemporary record.

In the mainstream of historical writing in the Tughluq period,[52] Jūzjānī's tradition was continued by Ḍiyā'-ad-dīn Baranī in his *Ta'rīkh-i Fīrūẓ Shāhī*,[53] which begins, where Jūzjānī left off, with the reign of Balban. This work concerns itself exclusively with Indo-Muslim history, and thus removes from the central historiographical tradition which developed in India the pattern of universal or international history. Baranī's indispensable work is a thorough documentation of the Khaljī and early Tughluq period; its style has an eloquent velocity which yet brings the minutest details into relief, but it suffers from one glaring fault, a subjectivity which often takes the form of inventive dramatization of his historical characters to project his own ideas.[54] These lapses into exercises in *Fürstenspiegel* reflect his views on the nature of the state, on the duties of a Muslim monarch and on the control and humiliation of non-Muslim subjects, views which are expressed in more detail in his *Fātāwā-i Jahāndārī*,[55] which follows the tradition of Fakhr Mudabbir's *Ādāb al-mulūk*.

Having the same title as Baranī's work, Shams Sirāj ʿAfīf's *Ta'rīkh-i Fīrūẓ Shāhī*[56] is of a very different order and deals exclusively with the political and administrative history of the long reign of Fīrūz Tughluq (1351–88) who was also the first Muslim monarch in the subcontinent to compose memoirs outlining the principal features of his administrative policy.[57]

The historiography of the Delhi Sultanate at its zenith was contemporaneous with Īl-Khānid historiography in Persia, though there was hardly any mutual influence. No Indian historian shows any knowledge of the works of al-Juwaynī or Rashīd-ad-dīn Faḍl-Allāh; and no Īl-Khānid historian showed any Indian influence until we come to Waṣṣāf.[58]

ʿIṣāmī's epic, *Futūḥ as-salaṭīn*,[59] has as significant a position in historical literature, as it has in belles-lettres. It helps considerably in establishing a comparative perspective of the political events of the Delhi Sultanate under the Khaljis and the Tughluqs. But the author's aim was epic rather than purely historical. There are therefore instances of the careless use of such sources as Jūzjānī.

Yaḥyā ibn-Aḥmad Sirhindī's *Ta'rīkh-i Mubārak Shāhī*[60] covers the same period as a secondary source and is valuable because of its last chapters, dealing with the Sayyid dynasty. Sayyids and Lodīs are also dealt with in Muḥammad Bihmad Khānī's *Ta'rīkh-i Muḥammadī*,[61] which is intended as a universal history but is of indifferent value.

Only the fringe of the creativity of Tīmūrid historiography touched India. Presumably the Indian sections of ʿAbd-ar-Razzāq's *Maṭlaʿ as-saʿdayn*[62] were written on Indian soil when he was Shāh Rukh's ambassador at the court of the Rāja of Vijyanagar. Shaykh Āzarī, a poet connected with Shāh Rukh's court, came to India and took service under Aḥmad Shāh I Bahmanī (1422–36) and composed *Bahman Nāma*, a versified history of the Bahmanid dynasty. He, later, returned to Transoxiana. Mirzā Ḥaydar Dughlat, Bābur's cousin and the conqueror of Kashmir, probably wrote his history in that region and it does not deal with events in the subcontinent.[63] A central Asian historian at Bābur's court was Zayn-ad-dīn Khawāfī, the author of *Wāqiʿāt-i Bāburī*;[64] it is also debatable whether Ibrāhīm ibn-Ḥarīrī's *Ta'rīkh-i Ibrāhīmī (Ta'rīkh-i Humāyūnī)*[65] was compiled at the court of Humāyūn or in that of Ibrāhīm ʿĀdil Shāh at Bijapur.[66] Khwāndmīr (d. 1535), author of the great historical work, *Ḥabīb as-siyar*, whose methodology was Tīmūrid and Central Asian, had already completed his *magnum opus* before he came to India to seek the patronage of Bābur and, after him, of Humāyūn. But in India he compiled his *Qānūn-i Humāyūnī*, a short account of the court ritual and practices introduced by Humāyūn under astrological influences, with notes on some of his architectural enterprises.[67] It is probable that Yaḥyā ibn-ʿAbd-al-Laṭīf's universal history *Lubb at-tawārīkh* was composed at the court of Ṭahmāsp in Persia and not at that of Humāyūn in India. It won more fame than it deserved in Europe because of the Latin translation of Gaulmin and Galland; and because Pietro della Vale had intended to translate it into Italian.

The historiographical tradition of the sultanate and the rising school of historiography under the Mughals established a continuity with such works as Aḥmad Yādgār's *Ta'rīkh-i Shāhī*,[68] a history principally of the Afghān Lodī and Sūrī dynasties, commissioned by Humāyūn and completed early in the reign of Akbar. It has a straightforward style and deals chiefly with political events, supplemented by biographical notices. Other histories of the Afghāns are ʿAbbās Khān Sarwānī's *Ta'rīkh-i Shīr Shāhī*,[69] commissioned by Akbar, ʿAbd-Allāh's *Ta'rīkh-i Dā'ūdī*,[70] Khwāja Niʿmat-Allāh Harawī's *Ta'rīkh-i Khān Jahānī wa makhzan-i Afghānī*,[71] compiled in 1612 under the patronage of Khān Jahān Lōdī, an Afghān general of the Mughals, and Rizq-Allāh Mushtāqī's (d. 1581) *Wāqiʿāt-i Mushtāqī*,[72] which also has chapters on some kings of Malwa and Gujarat.

One of the earliest Mughal chronicles is Bāyazīd Bayāt's *Tadhkira-i Humāyūn wa-Akbar*,[73] a useful history of the reign of Humāyūn and early years of Akbar. The *Humāyūn Nāma* of Humāyūn's sister, Gulbadan Begum,[74] is a sensitive narrative of some of the eventful years of her brother's career and is distinguished by a delicate feminine touch. Even one of Humāyūn's personal attendants, Jawhar Aftābchī, tried his hand successfully at historical writing.[75]

Like their ancestors the Tīmūrids, and their eponymous ancestors the Mongols, the Indian Mughals were very conscious of their position in history. As the Mughal empire rose to eminence under Akbar, three types of historiography emerged. First, there was the official historiography based upon the records of the court diarist (*wāqiʿa-nawīs*). The second was the universal or regional history commissioned by the emperor, some instances of which we have already come across. The third was the unofficial or private historiography, where a historian described the events he had observed, or studied, with greater subjectivity, and with a religious, didactic, or even scientific motive. The principal official historical work of Akbar's reign is Abū-l-Faḍl's voluminous and monumental *Akbar Nāma*.[76] The third part of this work is *Ā'īn-i Akbarī*,[77] which is, among other things, a detailed record of life at the imperial court and a directory of the administration of the empire. The most ambitious historical work commissioned by Akbar was the *Ta'rīkh-i Alfī*, a universal history compiled by Mullā Aḥmad Tahattawī and others,[78] but a universal history devoid of any originality or insight, and of no significance except as a symbol of Akbar's claim to be a renovator of religion, a thousand years after the Prophet's death.

Of the unofficial histories of Akbar's reign the most remarkable is ʿAbd-al-Qādir Badā'ūnī's *Muntakhab at-tawārīkh*,[79] which stands in piquant contrast to Abū-l-Faḍl ʿAllāmī's official and eulogistic history, for it denounces Akbar's heresy and was obviously meant for private circulation. Badā'ūnī had a strong traditional religious bias, which amounted to prejudice, but he had a historian's acumen for the recording of details, and his historiographical treatment of events is sincere, thorough and efficient. At the end of his history, notes on the élite and the poets are a useful source of information. More formal and tactful – consequently silent on controversial issues but still a useful document – is Niẓām-ad-dīn Aḥmad Bakhshī's *Ṭabaqāt-i Akbarī*,[80] which remains a useful source for the history of Muslim India and covers the first thirty-eight years of Akbar's reign.

Minor historical writing during Akbar's reign included Fayḍī Sirhindī's *Ta'rīkh-i Humāyūn Shāhī*,[81] Shaykh ʿAbd-al-Ḥaqq Dihlawī's *Ta'rīkh-i Ḥaqqī*; and ʿAbd-al-Bāqī Nihāwandī's biographical, *Ma'āthir-i Raḥīmī*.[82]

A classical history of the regional and central dynasties of Islamic India, the *Gulshan-i Ibrāhīmī*,[83] was compiled at Bijapur by Muḥammad Abū-l-Qāsim ibn-Hindū Shāh Firishta under the patronage of Ibrāhīm ʿĀdil Shāh II (1580–1627). This is a detailed political and military history of the Muslim dynasties of the Deccan and other parts of India and it makes a worthwhile contribution to the history of the Delhi sultans and the early Mughals. At the end there are notices on saints and mystics, which use hagiographical as well as historical source material. Firishta is painstaking in his quest for historical truth and factual accuracy; and handles the subjective elements in his sources with exceptional objectivity. His style is cumbersome and monotonous owing to his preoccupation with the minute details of military undertakings.

The most prominent of the historical works of Jahāngīr's reign is the autobiography or *Tuzuk*[84] of the Emperor himself written in the tradition of the founder of the dynasty. Left incomplete by Jahāngīr, his memoirs were completed by Muḥammad Hādī.

Another valuable history of Jahāngīr's reign is Muʿtamad Khān's short work, *Iqbāl Nāma-i Jahāngīrī.*[85] Minor histories of the age include Kāmgār Khān's *Ma'āthir-i Jahāngīrī.* Two works in the *Fürstenspiegel* genre were written in Jahāngīr's reign, Bāqir Khān's *Mawʿiẓa-i Jahāngīrī*[86] and Qāḍī Nūr-ad-dīn Khāqānī's *Akhlāq-i Jahāngīrī.*[87]

The Deccan produced, about this time, another great historian, Khurshāh ibn-Qubād, who was sent as an ambassador from Ahmadnagar to the Ṣafavid court in Iran and whose *Ta'rīkh-i Ilchī-yī Niẓām Shāh* presents useful material in the history of the Deccan kingdoms, of Qarā Qoyunlū and also of the early Ṣafavids.[88]

The official documentary history of Shāh Jahān's reign was ʿAbd-al-Ḥamīd Lāhōrī's *Bādshāh Nāma*,[89] which was also rendered in verse by the poet-laureate Qudsī Mashhadī. It is matched in wealth of detail by another contemporary history of the period, Muḥammad Ṣāliḥ Kanbū's *ʿAmal-i Ṣaliḥ* or *Shāh Jahān Nāma.*[90] ʿInāyat Khān's *Shāh Jahān Nāma* is a comparatively minor work; so also is the work of Ṣādiq Khān bearing the same title.[91]

The decline of Mughal historiography begins in the reign of Awrangzīb. The official history by Muḥammad Kāẓim, *ʿĀlamgīr Nāma*,[92] was discontinued after ten years of the reign either because of financial stringency or for reasons of pietistic modesty on the part of the Emperor. The rest of the reign was covered by Sāqī Mustaʿid Khān, with concise precision, in his semi-official *Ma'āthir-i ʿĀlamgīrī.*[93] A voluminous universal history compiled in Awrangzīb's reign was Bakhtāwar Khān's *Mir'āt al-ʿālam*,[94] and there was its plagiarized version the

Mir'āt-i Jahānumā of Mīr Muḥammad Baqā'.[95] As a universal history, the *Mir'at al-'ālam* makes no original contribution; in its treatment of the first ten years of Awrangzīb's reign it draws largely on the work of Muḥammad Kāẓim, and its only contribution seems to be the biographical notices on the intellectual and artistic élite of the Mughal period.

The swan-song of the great Mughal tradition of historiography is marked by Khafī Khān's monumental work *Muntakhab al-lubāb*,[96] which combines objectivity with historical imagination, and brings to life the splendour of Shāh Jahān's court and describes the tensions during the long reign of Awrangzīb; there is also a pathetic account of the decline of the Mughal empire under his successors.

Histories written during the eighteenth century in the period of Mughal decline include *Ta'rīkh-i Irādat Khān*,[97] Khushḥāl Chand's *Ta'rīkh-i Muḥammad Shāhī Nādir az-zāmānī*,[98] Muḥammad Qāsim's *Ta'rīkh-i Bahādur Shāhī*,[99] and a large number of other minor works which emphasize the precipitous decline of Mughal historiography. Some eclectic Hindu communities which barely had an indigenous historiographical tradition of their own, mastered not only the Persian language but produced some historians of importance.[100] Chandra Bhān Brahman's *Chahār Chaman*[101] is stylistically an interesting prose chronicle compiled during the reign of Shāh Jahān. Most remarkable of the works of these Hindu historians is Sujan Rāī's *Khulāṣa-at-tawārīkh*,[102] compiled in the reign of Awrangzīb in 1695.

Regional histories of considerable calibre were written away from Delhi. These go back to *Chach Nāma*,[103] the translation of an original Arabic history of Sind. Another classical history of Sind is Sayyid Muḥammad Ma'ṣūm Bhakkarī's (d. 1583) *Ta'rīkh-i Ma'ṣūmi*.[104] A valuable history of Gujarat is Sikandar ibn-Muḥammad Manjhū's *Mir'at-i Sikandarī*.[105] A comprehensive history of Gujarat under its sultans and, later, under the Mughals and the Marāthās is 'Alī Muḥammad Khān's *Mir'at-i Aḥmadī*.[106] Numerous other regional histories were compiled in the Deccan, Bengal, Punjab and Kashmir.

The *tadhkira* (biographical dictionary) comes closest in objective treatment to historiography, and is usually alphabetical. The genre was the Persian counterpart of the Arabic discipline of *asmā' ar-rijāl* which was a by-product of the science of the investigation of the chain-links of *ḥadīth*. Curiously enough the earliest *tadhkira* which has survived is literary rather than historical: Muḥammad ʿAwfī's *Lubāb al-albāb*, written at Multan in the early thirteenth century. Political *tadhkiras* must have been written under the Sultanate, but they seem to have been lost. One of the earliest surviving is the *Dhakīra al-khawānīn* of Shaykh Farīd Bhakkarī.[107] A number of historians like Aḥmad Yādgār, Badā'ūnī and Firishta included biographical notices of the élite in their histories. The most famous *tadhkira* of the Mughal élite is Shāh Nawāz Khān's encyclopaedic *Ma'āthir al-umarā'*.[108]

Ṣūfī hagiographical *tadhkira*-writing goes back to the early fourteenth century with the *Siyar al-awliyā'* of Amīr Khurd, who was a disciple of Niẓām-ad-dīn Awliyā. Other classical Ṣūfī *tadhkiras* include Jamālī's *Siyar al-ʿĀrifīn*[109] compiled in the fifteenth century; Ghawthī Shaṭṭārī's *Gulzār-i abrār*[110] written in the sixteenth; and ʿAbd-al-Ḥaqq Dihlawī's *Akhbār al-akhyār*[111] written in the seventeenth century. In the eighteenth century Prince Dārā Shukoh wrote two hagiographical works: *Sakīnat al-awliyā'* a biography of his preceptor, the Qādirite Miyān Mīr, and *Safīnat al-awliyā'*,[112] a general *tadhkira* modelled on Jāmī's *Nafaḥat al-uns*. A number of authoritative *tadhkiras* of the Muslim élite were compiled by Ghulām ʿAlī Āzād Bilgrāmī.[113] *Tadhkiras* of Urdu poets were compiled by the poet Ghulām Hamdānī Muṣ'ḥafī.

A distinguished but very ornate genre of Persian prose was epistle-writing (*inshā'*), which was cultivated at various courts, no doubt including that of the Delhi Sultans, though of this hardly any records have survived. Epistle-writing was especially admired in the sixteenth and seventeenth centuries at the Mughal court. The chanceries of the Mughal, the Ottoman, the Ṣafavid and the Uzbek courts vied with each other in their diplomatic correspondence to cultivate elegance and eloquence in a complex, artificial style. Letters written from the Mughal court to the provincial governors and other subordinates were much simpler. The earliest surviving collection of letters of a nobleman, the *Inshā'-i Māhrū*, goes back to the Tughluq period. In the Mughal period the apex of stylistic refinement was reached in the letters composed by Akbar's secretary and

7. Quṭb Minār, Delhi. Built in 1193, *the earliest extant monument of Islamic architecture in India*

8. *Detail from the Quṭb Minār*

confidante Abū-l-Faḍl.[114] Letters written by Awrangzīb to his sons and officers are in a more straightforward and practical style.[115] To-the-point letters written by ʿAbd-Allāh Khān Quṭb-al-mulk are examples of the art of *inshā'* during the Mughal decline in the eighteenth century.[116]

A Hindu eclectic community, the Kāyasthas, specialized in epistle-writing and produced some outstanding *munshīs* in the later Mughal period. The work of Munshī Harkaran,[117] composed in the reign of Shāh Jahān, came later to be regarded as standard, and was prescribed as a textbook in schools. Other Hindu epistle-writers of the later years of the reign of Shāh Jahān were Jaswant Rāi and Chandr Bhān Brahman. In the eighteenth century, as the immigration of Persian *munshīs* ceased, due to unsettled conditions in Iran as well as in India, epistolography became almost the exclusive monopoly of the Kāyasthas in the hands of masters of style, like Mādhū Rām. Hindu *munshīs* continued to be employed in the court of the *nawwāb-waẓīrs* of Oudh and some other Muslim regional rulers.

The Ṣūfī tradition of epistolography is more pragmatic and utilitarian, with greater emphasis on content than on style. Epistles were written by shaykhs to their disciples to explain the minutiae of the mystic doctrines of their orders, and along with *dicta* took the place of the methodical works on the theory and practice of Ṣūfism written elsewhere. The entire doctrine of the Firdawsiyya order is, for instance, concentrated in the letters of Aḥmad ibn-Yaḥyā Mānerī.[118] Similarly the Naqshbandī theory of *Waḥdat ash-shuhūd* (phenomenological monism) was explained at length, and exclusively, in the letters of Shaykh Aḥmad Sirhindī.[119] Ṣūfī shaykhs also wrote political letters to Muslim nobles to give advice on what they considered major political issues. After the accession of Jahāngīr, Sirhindī wrote to Shaykh Farīd urging him to influence the new monarch in the direction of orthodoxy, and to react against the heretical and eclectic practices introduced by Akbar, which in his view had endangered the position of Islam in India. Letters of Maẓ'har Jān-i Jānān cover Ṣūfistic as well as general themes.[120] Theologians, like ʿAbd-al-Ḥaqq Dihlawī and Shāh Walī-Allāh, also wrote letters on theological, political and general themes.[121]

A speciality of Ṣūfī, Persian literature are the *malfūẓāt* (dicta) of various shaykhs. Recent research has established that several collections, supposed to be the dicta of early Chishtī mystics, are in fact spurious.[122] The earliest authentic collection is Amīr Ḥasan Sijzī's *Fawā'id al-fu'ād*, containing the dicta of Niẓām-ad-dīn Awliyā. This was followed by *Khayr al-majālis*, the dicta of Naṣīr-ad-dīn Chirāgh-i Dihlī compiled by Ḥamīd Qalandar.[123] Later, dicta of Sharaf-ad-dīn Aḥmad ibn-Yaḥyā Mānerī,[124] of Muḥammad al-Ḥusaynī Gīsūdarāz[125] and of several others were compiled.

Except for al-Hujwīrī's *Kashf al-maḥjūb*, mentioned earlier, no outstanding, sustained work on the theory and practice of Ṣūfism was compiled in the subcontinent. There were, of course, commentaries on Ṣūfī classics, especially on Muḥyī-d-dīn Ibn-al-ʿArabī's *Fuṣūṣ al-ḥikam*, and Shihāb-ad-dīn Suhrawardī's *ʿAwārif al-maʿārif*. But these deal with minute doctrinal points pietistically or polemically, and do not make any significant contribution to Ṣūfī theory, except in the letters of Shaykh Aḥmad Sirhindī, discussed earlier. Dārā Shukoh's works are interesting, but they suffer from the unscientific nature of his eclecticism.

A considerable amount of theological literature was written in Persian. But most of this is, again, doctrinaire. There were, however, important theologians in India, like Shihāb-ad-dīn Dawlatabādī, who wrote the first Persian commentary on the Qur'ān, ʿAbd-al-Ḥaqq Dihlawī and Shāh Walī-Allāh, who wrote outstanding theological works in Arabic as well as Persian concerning most disciplines. Of lesser calibre are the judicial rulings (*fatāwī*) as well as other religious and polemical writings of Walī-Allāh's son and successor, Shāh Abd-al-ʿAzīz.

Other genres transmitted in Persian included lexicography, which began in the Sultanate period and reached its culmination in the hands of Hindu, eclectic Kāyasthas, especially Anand Rāj. An instance of stylistic belles-lettres is Ẓuhūrī's *Sih nathr*, a collection of three highly rhetorical and ornate compositions.

In the eighteenth century, Urdu rapidly displaced Persian as the language of poetry. In the early nineteenth century, Urdu prose developed in the Fort William College and, by the middle of that century, came to be generally used, first, in correspondence, then, in sustained writing. During this period, however, highly stylistic Persian prose persisted in the writings of such accomplished craftsmen as Ghālib, though the final blow to Persian in India had already been dealt when, in 1835, the East India Company decided to replace it by English as the language of administration.

3. Turkish

For the brief period of one generation, Turkish was, along with Persian, a literary language in India. Bābur conquered India some years after the golden age of Chaghatāy Turkish poetry, represented by ʿAlī Shīr Nawā'ī at the court of Sulṭan Ḥusayn Bayqara in Herat. Bābur had been in correspondence with Nawā'ī and was influenced by him in his Turkish verse, but was not a mere imitator.[126] As Fuad Köprülü remarks: 'In the technique of versification Bābur was not inferior to any of the fifteenth century Chaghatāy poets, not even Nawā'ī, and he expressed his thoughts and feelings in an unaffected language and style'.[127] In his short *Dīwān*, Bābur tried his hand at various genres of short poem; and he also composed a *mathnawī Mubayyan*, which treats some religious themes as well as matters of warfare.

The most outstanding of Bābur's work, and, indeed, of Chaghatāy prose in general, was his *Tuzuk* (autobiography), also known under the title *Bābur Nāma*, which, in a straightforward and objective style, describes the main events of his stormy career. Apart from its literary value, the *Bābur Nāma* remains a valuable historical record both of the events in Central Asia at that period and of Bābur's reign in India, which was, however, very brief (1526–30). It is difficult to say how much of his verse was composed in India. We can speak with certainty of only one *ghazal* which has a Hindī half-line. On the other hand, it is certain that in his autobiography the sections dealing with India were written there.

A number of poets, including some from Herat, accompanied or followed Bābur to India. They must have written some Turkish verse. Their work has, however, not been preserved. The only other remarkable poet who wrote in Turkish as well as in Persian was Humāyūn's general and minister, Bayrām Khān.[128] The quality of his verse is inferior to that of

Bābur. Humāyūn himself wrote verses in Persian, but it appears from the evidence of the Turkish admiral, Sidī ʿAlī Reis, that the literary taste of his court was bilingual, and that Turkish poetry was appreciated with as much receptivity as the Persian.[129] But the decisive victory of Persian over Turkish took place during the reign of Humāyūn for two main reasons: firstly, the influx of Persian poets into India, which became a steady stream under Akbar and Jahāngīr, and secondly, the withering away of Turkish genius among the Mughal nobility of Turkish stock, while in Central Asia under the Uzbeks the well-springs of the Turkish genius dried up.

Turkish continued to be learnt by some rulers and by members of the Mughal ruling family. Jahāngīr mentions his own proficiency in it; but he chose to write his autobiography, even though in the tradition of Bābur, in Persian.[130] Turkish remained a part of the princely curriculum of the Mughals, at least until the end of the eighteenth century, and a Mughal princeling, Ẓahīr-ad-dīn Aẓfarī, shows, in his memoirs, to have studied it.[131] ʿAbd-al-Jalīl Bilgrāmī (d. 1700), a theologian and poet, was also a scholar of Turkish.[132]

Even before the Mughals, Turkish, of an undetermined Eastern variety, had reached as far as the Deccan and the Bahmanid Mujāhid Shāh (1375–68) is credited with having been able to speak it.

EIGHT

LITERATURE IN URDU AND THE REGIONAL LANGUAGES

1. Urdu[1]

Muslims in India evolved, within the subcontinent, a literary – principally urban – language of their own, Urdu. The name 'Urdu', which was crystallized in the eighteenth century, is derived from the old Turkish 'Ordu',[2] either directly from Chaghatāy Turkish or through its Mongol derivative 'Orda', and is cognate with the modern English 'horde'. Its first literary use occurred in Persian in al-Juwaynī, who was presumably using Mongol sources.[3] It was first used in India by Khiḍr Khān towards the close of the fourteenth, and the beginning of the sixteenth century, under the Tīmūrid influence, but the word was used for the army and not for a language.[4] It was used in the same sense under the Mughals, and it is possible that the indigenous language, which had various names in medieval India, came to be called 'Urdu-yi muʿallā', or the language of the exalted camp, in the reign of either Shāh Jahān or Awrangzīb in the second half of the seventeenth century.

In medieval India pre-Urdu, or various dialects of early Urdu, was called 'Hindī' or 'Hindawī' and was confused with regular medieval Hindī dialects. In these dialects: Rājasthānī, Braj Bhāshā, Maythilī, Awadhī and Haryānī, literature was composed – a fraction of it by Muslims – which does not stand in an ancestral relationship to modern Urdu. Rather, these medieval, north-Indian dialects have a unity of content and a literary continuity with modern literary Hindī, which developed as a twin of Urdu in the eighteenth century.

Amīr Khusraw called pre-Urdu 'Hindawī' or 'Hindī'; Abū-l-Faḍl called it 'Dihlawī'; in the Deccan it was known as 'Dakanī' or 'Dakhanī, or 'Hindī'; in Gujarat it was known as 'Hindī', or 'Gujarī' or 'Gujarātī', and must not be confused with the Gujarātī language, which was evolving independently about the same time. As late as the early nineteenth century, poetry written in Urdu was described as *rīkhta* (literally 'spilled'), which was also an Indo-Persian musical mode.[5]

Urdu most probably originated in the Ghaznavid Punjab. With exaggerated exactitude T. Grahame Bailey's notice of its birth runs thus: 'Urdu was born in 1027; its birthplace was Lahore, its parent Old Punjabi: Old Khari was its step-parent; it had no direct relationship with Braj. The name Urdu first appears 750 years later.'[6] Actually Bailey has crudely tried to sum up the elaborate thesis of Maḥmūd Shērānī, now generally accepted,[7] that in the eleventh century, after the consolidation of the Ghaznavid rule in the Punjab, the Muslim ruling class and the soldiers came in contact with Hindu populations and used their language, Eastern Punjābī, for intercourse with them. In so doing they changed the character of the language they borrowed, impregnating it with a high percentage of Persian vocabulary. When the Ghūrids conquered Delhi, where the Muslim Sultanate was established, this mixed language was imported by the Muslim elements from the Punjab to Delhi. Among the Muslim immigrants to Delhi those from the Punjab formed the largest percentage. Contact between Delhi and the Punjab remained intimate because of the Mongol pressure and the consequent constant garrisoning of the frontier outposts. This language was conveyed to the Deccan by the armies of 'Alā'-ad-dīn Khaljī and, later, during Muḥammad ibn-Tughluq's temporary transfer of the capital to Dawlatabad, where a large number of Indian Muslims settled down. In the Deccan this pre-Urdu developed into one of the first Urdu literary dialects.[8]

There is striking linguistic evidence supporting the thesis of the East Punjābī origin of Urdu. The two languages have common verbal suffixes, gender-formation and identical vowel-endings in nouns and adjectives. They resemble one another in their conjugation of verbs. Differences between Urdu and Punjābī belong to a later stage of development in both languages.[9]

While, as we shall see, the first literary development of Urdu took place in the Deccan and Gujarat, there is documented evidence to suggest that pre-Urdu – and later a refined dialect of Urdu – was spoken by the Muslims of Northern India, developing with elegance from the fourteenth to the eighteenth century, when it burst forth suddenly into literary expression. Ibn-Baṭṭūṭa, who visited India in the early fourteenth century, used a large number of words of Indian origin. Some pre-Urdu nouns found their way into Bābur's *Tuzuk* and he composed at least one verse, half of which is in Turkish and the other half in pre-Urdu.[10]

Theories that Sindhī or Haryānī were the origins of Urdu have also been advanced, but they are far-fetched. It is, however, certain that during the sixteenth century north Indian spoken-Urdu came under the influence of the Hindī dialect, Braj Bhāshā, at Agra, which was the imperial capital, from the reign of Sikandar Lōdī to that of Jahāngīr. Contact with Braj was specially significant under Akbar, and lexicographically Braj usage had an authoritative prestige until the eighteenth century.[11]

The other stream of Urdu developed in the Deccan. Linguistic evidence shows that the early Muslim colonists of the Deccan, who wrote in 'Dakanī', were either from the Punjab or from the areas where Haryānī or similar dialects were spoken[12]; though it has also been suggested that not one single dialect, but several closely related dialects found their way to the Deccan, and a standard literary pattern did not emerge at Golconda and Bijapur until the sixteenth century.[13] Linguistic evidence, however, underlines the resemblances between East Punjābī and the standard Dakanī Urdu. Both have several common grammatical forms and share considerable common vocabulary, some of which has not been inherited by modern Urdu.[14] It is more likely that Dakanī Urdu developed dialectal features locally, and was influenced by the Hindu population of the Deccan and its languages, Telugu, Marathi and Kanarese. The Dakanī Urdu dialects merged into a single literary language in the sixteenth century.

Dakanī Urdu developed in isolation from the more refined, but unwritten, Urdu spoken in northern India. This northern stream was the first to be called Urdu, in the late seventeenth century, about the time when it came in direct intimate contact with Dakanī, after the completion of the Mughal conquests in the Deccan under Awrangzīb.[15] The intellectual élite of Golconda and Bijapur migrated to Awrangabad, the secondary capital of Awrangzīb, during the second half of his reign. Awrangabad thus became the meeting-place, and the habitat, for the merger of north Indian and Dakanī Urdu, towards the close of the seventeenth century.

The first literary use of Urdu in north, as well as south and west, India was made by the Ṣūfī shaykhs.[16] Two factors in the life of the *khānqāhs* brought the Ṣūfīs closer to Indian vernaculars. One of these was their closeness to the masses, both converted Muslims and un-converted or semi-converted Hindus – among whom they carried out their missionary work – who could only understand the vernaculars; and the other factor was their inclination towards music, including Indian music composed in Hindī dialects, as an aid to spiritual ecstasy. Hagiographies have recorded a number of pre-Urdu phrases, coloured with dialectal features, and attribute them to shaykhs, like Farīd-ad-dīn Ganj-i Shakar, as early as the thirteenth century.[17] Similar phrases, with other dialectal features, have been attributed, in other parts of India, to Shaykh Ḥamīd-ad-dīn Nāgorī, Makhdūm-i Jahāniyān, and Sayyid Muḥammad, the Mahdī of Jawnpur; these date from the fourteenth to the sixteenth century.[18]

Others wrote *dohrās*, verses composed to music and sung in 'Hindi' dialects. Some of these may be spurious, like those attributed to Abū-ʿAlī Qalandar; others, especially those composed in Gujarat by mystics like Bahā'-ad-dīn Bājan (d. 1388) can be safely regarded as authentic. In the next stage, which began in the fourteenth century, some Ṣūfī shaykhs progressed from the occasional dicta or verse in early Urdu to a more sustained literary form in verse as well as in prose. Sayyid Muḥammad al-Ḥusaynī 'Gisūdarāz' wrote *Miʿrāj al-ʿāshiqīn* (1421), which is generally regarded as the first prose work in Urdu. In Gujarat, Shams-al-ʿUshshāq Mirānjī (d. 1496) with his *Khūb tarang* established Urdu, coloured with Gujarat dialectal features, as a recognized medium for Ṣūfī narrative verse. Another early mystic poet of Gujarat was Burhān-ad-dīn Jānam. Urdu was also used by the ulema, at an early date, for theological writing. Shaykh ʿAyn-ad-dīn Ganj-al-ʿilm (1307–1392) wrote three treatises on religious ritual in early Dakanī.[19]

It was in the Deccan that Urdu had its first literary efflorescence in the courts of Golconda and Bijapur, which rose as successor states to the Bahmanid sultanate early in the sixteenth century.[20] It is a curiosity of literary history that, in its original home in northern India, Urdu remained from the sixteenth to the eighteenth century, a mere spoken language, while in the Deccan it produced a rich and vigorous literature. The influence of Persian, though active in the Deccan was not as masterfully ascendant as in north India. In the Deccan the Muslim sense of identity chose Urdu rather than Persian, or any of the Hindu local languages, for self-expression, though the language continued to be influenced by, and to borrow from the vocabulary of both.

At Golconda one of the rulers, Sultan Muḥammad Qulī Quṭb Shāh (1580–1611), was himself a poet of unique genius. Artistic to the core, he founded the city of Bhagnagar, later known as Hyderabad – as a gesture to his love for a Hindu courtesan Bhāgmatī – and introduced into it a new variety of architecture. He had a musical ear and was sensitive to the rhythm and beauty of Telugu, the Dravidian language spoken by Hindus in his kingdom, and from this he borrowed an extensive vocabulary for his Urdu verse. Sensitive to the beauty of Indian women, to the fragrance of Indian flowers, and to the colour and pageantry of Indian life, he is one of the two Urdu poets (the other being the northerner Naẓīr Akbarābādī in the eighteenth century) who assimilated Indian life and background into their verse, which is generally rejected, under Persian and extra-Indian influence, in Urdu poetry. His *Kulliyyāt*, one of the earliest collections of verse in Urdu, consists of lyrical *ghazals* which have a musical lilt, narrative poems on Indian themes, and martyrological poems. Other poets at the court of Golconda include Ibn-Nishāṭī, author of a *mathnawī Phūlban* adopted from a Persian original and obliquely linked to the cycle of Alexander romances; the more eminent Ghawwāṣī (c. 1625), who rendered into Urdu, *Sayf-al-mulk wa Badī'-al-jamāl*, a romance adopted from the *Arabian Nights*, and *Ṭuṭī Nāma*, an Indian cycle of tales based on Nakhshabī's earlier Persian rendering.

The first remarkable work in Urdu prose, *Sabras*, was written at the court of Golconda by Mullā Wajhī (*c.* 1630). It is a courtly allegory of love, the quest of the Princess Huṣn (Beauty) by Prince Dil (Heart) with all the conventions of the poetry of love personified as characters. This first narrative romance is based on the Persian original *Dastūr al-ʿushshāq*,[21] by Muḥammad Yaḥyā Sībak Fattāḥī Nīshāpūrī, which has unexplained affinities in theme and narrative with the Western cycle of the *Roman de la Rose*.[22]

In the court of Bijapur one of the first great poets of Dakanī, Nuṣratī (*c.* 1665), wrote his famous epic, *ʿAlī Nāma*, celebrating the victories of his patron, ʿAlī ʿĀdil Shāh II, and also a number of love romances, the most famous of which is *Gulshan-i ʿishq*, a story with an indigenous theme. Nuṣratī has a powerful and eloquent narrative style and an amazing command over the nascent language. Other poets at the court of Bijapur include Hāshimī, who wrote a narrative poem on the familiar theme of the love of Zuleika for Joseph; and Dawlat, who is the author of a verse romance derived from a Persian original, *Bahrām wa Gul Bānū*.

With the Mughal conquest of Golconda and Bijapur, these capitals yielded their precedence to Awrangabad, which became in the last decades of the seventeenth, and early decades of the eighteenth century the principal centre of Urdu poetry. Here, Walī (1668–1744), the father of modern Urdu poetry, introduced the diction and style of the Deccan, but after his two visits to Delhi, in 1700 and 1722, he adopted the language of the north, the *Urdū-yi muʿallā*, and became a link between the old Dakanī and the new, rising, northern school of Urdu poetry, based at Delhi. Apart from the unique historical role he played, he is a consummate artist in verse and a master of the *ghazal* style, which was soon imitated by the poets of Delhi. On the advice of his preceptor in mysticism, and disciple in versification, Saʿd-Allāh Gulshan, Walī turned for inspiration to the vast range of Persian poetry, and brought the Urdu *ghazal* close to the Persian, borrowing most of its conventions, and establishing a tradition, which was to last until 1857. Till this date Dakanī poetry was original, and uninhibited in its borrowings of theme and vocabulary from indigenous cultures and languages. With Walī begins the alienation from Indian themes and, to some extent, from the vocabulary of South Indian languages, though the lyricism of the Hindi diction of love is still fully exploited. With Walī, Urdu poetry turned to the Mughal culture at a time when decadence had set in, and in this process it gained in charm and elegance, but lost in vitality and dynamism, which had been the characteristics of earlier Dakanī literature. Another poet writing at Awrangabad about the same time, Sirāj, also reflects, like Walī, two styles, an earlier Dakanī and a later northern. He shares most of the characteristics and qualities of Walī at a lower level of inspiration and artistry.

In Delhi in the early eighteenth century, Urdu verse, or *rīkhta*, as it was then called, was taken up by a number of poets who were born in the cities near by, and most of whom held military offices as *manṣabdārs*. Most eminent of these pioneers of the Delhi school was Sirāj-ad-dīn 'Alī Khān Ārzū (1689–1756), who also wrote in Persian, and was a lexicographer of repute. He transferred some elements of the traditions of Persian *Sabk-i Hindī*, as represented by Bīdil, into Urdu. His influence on the younger generation of poets was profound. Lesser luminaries among these very early Urdu poets included Najm-ad-dīn Shāh Mubārak 'Abrū', a journeyman in verse; Shāh Ḥātim (1699–1791), whose poetic output covered a wide range, including polished as well as vulgar or satiric verse; 'Abd-al-Ḥayy Tābān, a gifted poet who died young, and Sharaf-ad-dīn Maḍmūn (d. 1754) and Muḥammad Shākir Nājī, whose verse is hardly distinguishable by any individual characteristics from their contemporaries. The Naqshbandī Ṣūfī, Maẓ'har Jān-i Jānan, wrote Urdu verse impregnated with the sublimity of mystical ethics, and some of his writing, expressed in straightforward diction, has a compelling emotional and spiritual appeal.

The next generation of Delhi poets includes some of the greatest names in Urdu literature. Khwāja Mīr Dard (1720–1784), a Naqshbandī Ṣūfī like Maẓ'har, carried his tradition of mystical verse to greater maturity in style and appeal. His diction is simple, almost colloquial, and he employs it with lyrical fervour. In Urdu verse, Dard has not been superseded in mystical expression.

The antithesis to Dard was his famous contemporary Mirzā Rafī' Sawdā (1713–81), a mundane poet, and the most powerful satirist Urdu has ever produced. Sawdā's *ghazal* suffers from artifice, and occasionally sounds prosaic; but in satire and the topical poem he has no equal. His language and imagery is chiselled out to suit his satiric objective. His satire on men is cruel and merciless. But it is in the satire on his times, reflecting the decline of Mughal culture and the decay of Muslim society, that one finds a documentation of profound historical significance, accomplished in inimitable expression and imagery.

The political chaos through which Delhi passed during these years, and the resultant economic collapse, affected the mind and genius of Mīr Taqī Mīr (1733–1810), the most moving composer of *ghazals* in Urdu. Mīr's profoundly sensitive nature subjectively absorbed, and expressed in plaintive tones, the shocks of an age of economic and cultural insecurity, which led in turn to emotional pessimism. This pessimism, translated into the passion of love, inspired Mīr's genius and his mastery of the lyrical style. His emotionalism is self-sufficient; it can rise to sublime heights; it can crystallize anguish into experience and experience into expression; it can capture depths of suffering in direct statement with or without the aid of imagery. In addition to the *ghazals*, Mīr's sensitive genius found expression in *mathnawīs* of rare charm, and in other direct descriptive 'complaints'. His autobiography, *Dhikr-i Mīr*, written in Persian, is helpful in any study of his psychology and the environment he lived in. He compiled one of the first biographical dictionaries of Urdu poets, *Nukāt ash-shuʿarā'*, also written in Persian, which apart from its documentary value reflects the norms of Mīr's standard of critical judgement.

Another *tadhkira* of Urdu poets was compiled by his contemporary, Mīr Ḥasan (d. 1786), who was a poet of a different order; though he experimented in many varieties of verse, he is best known for his narrative *mathnawī Saḥr al-bayān*, a fairy-tale of love. This, incidentally, records valuable details of contemporary social life with descriptions of women's dress, marriage ceremonies and other customs. The style is flowing and torrential and many of its verses have become proverbs.

Both Sawdā and Mīr migrated from insecure, chaotic Delhi to the stability of Lucknow where the Nawwāb-wazīrs held promise of patronage. Two other poets originally from Delhi, Inshā'-Allāh Khān (d. 1817) and Ghulām Hamdānī Muṣ'ḥafī (1750–1824), laid in Lucknow the foundations of what later became the Lucknow school of poetry.[23] Of these Muṣ'ḥafī, in the dignity of his style, and in his thematic emphasis on other-worldly ethics, remained close to the school of Delhi. His expression is direct and polished and at its best is capable of an emotional tranquillity which balances his sensitiveness. A very different style of verse was that of Inshā'-Allāh, which is fluent and spontaneous but whose content is forced and artificial. Inshā'-Allāh is a master of virtuosity, of exuberance and extravagance. With him the style of Lucknow comes into its own, close as it is to the decadent life of luxury of the court and élite, effeminate in its courtship of women of pleasure, witty, unserious and preoccupied with colloquialism and the *bon mot.* This style reached its peak in the verse of Shaykh Qalandar Bakhsh Jur'at (d. 1810), a blind poet who mastered the art of colloquial pun or *ḍil' jugat*, as it is known, in the language of classical Urdu literary criticism. Jur'at's verse is fluent, almost conversational, yet vulgar, and occasionally obscene. Inshā'-Allāh and his friend, Sa'ādat Yār Khān Rangīn, invented a new type of verse, *rīkhtī*, written in the colloquial language of women, which in a segregated society was different from that of men. *Rīkhtī* was written as a *jeu d'esprit*, the language it imitates being that of the courtesans rather than of refined ladies; occasionally it lapses into obscenity. A later poet of Lucknow who specialized exclusively in *rīkhtī* is Jān Ṣāḥib, whose work, though much admired by his contemporaries, and though a store-house of feminine vocabulary and linguistic expression, suffers from artificiality and lacks the frivolous spontaneity of the earlier *rīkhtī* of Inshā'-Allāh and Rangīn. Inshā'-Allāh is also the author of a lively treatise in Persian, *Daryā-i laṭāfat*, on Urdu (and Persian) grammar and prosody, one of the first works of its kind in the subcontinent. Mus'ḥafī compiled, in Persian, several biographical dictionaries (*tadhkiras*) of Urdu poets. These studies of poetry show that the age seems to have taken poetry seriously, though the general trend of it in Lucknow was gay, even frivolous.

Poetry came closer to social life with the advent of the *mushā'ira* or poetic assembly. The *mushā'ira* was held at the house of a poet or a nobleman, who played the host; poets and their admirers sat in a circle on the floor reclining against large sausage-shaped cushions; either the host or an eminent poet presided over the assembly; a wax candle passed on from poet to poet, who recited his verse to acclamation – or occasionally a caustic remark – from the members of the audience. Younger or inferior poets recited first, the masters recited later; and the greater the master, the later he would expect his turn. The origins of the *mushā'ira* are obscure. Probably it grew out of the recital of *qaṣīdas*, at the Delhi court, in the early eighteenth century. Later in that century, as already mentioned, *mushā'iras* were held at the house of Dard. In Lucknow these poetic assemblies became very lively; and sometimes led to bitter feuds between rival masters like Inshā'-Allāh and Muṣ'ḥafī and their disciples.

In the next generation of poets of the school of Lucknow, the two principal rivals were Imām Bakhsh Nāsikh (d. 1848) and Khwaja Ḥaydar 'Alī Ātish (d. 1846). Nāsikh, an athlete of singular habits, was a purist in language. More than any other single individual he was responsible for the rejection in Urdu of archaisms and of several expressions of indigenous or Hindī origin, and for bringing the Urdu *ghazal* closer to the classical style of the Persian. At its best Nāsikh's verse has a certain eloquent loftiness, at its worst it is a mere exercise in expression. His rival, Ātish, though less polished in style, shows real flashes of genius. The *ghazal* of Ātish is forceful, vehement, novel and at times intensely lyrical. His inspiration in his best verse is genuine, and has influenced generations of widely-ranging poets.

In its last phase the school of Lucknow came close to the court of Oudh. Its last ruler, Wājid 'Alī Shāh (reigned 1847–1856), was himself a poet of some merit, though his theme is decadent and his style rather stale. Under his patronage, verse drama was written, which is close to opera and differs from it mainly in its literary quality. The most remarkable work in this genre was Amānat's *Indar Sabhā*, which in a way was the swan-song of the dying, licentious culture of Lucknow. Amānat also wrote a long elegy of love, or *wāsūkht*, in similar sentiment and style.

In the last phase, a reaction to the decadent poetic tradition of Lucknow developed in the martyrological epic, the *marthiya*, which, in Urdu, had its beginning in the Deccan. Its rise in Lucknow is an independent growth, brought to considerable polish by the late eighteenth-century poets Ḍamīr and Khalīq. The *marthiya* is a Shīʿī poem mourning the massacre at Kerbela, by the army of the Umayyad, Yazīd ibn-Muʿāwiya, of Ḥusayn ibn-ʿAlī and his seventy companions.

The development of the *marthiya* shows another aspect of the culture of the Shīʿī élite of Lucknow: intensely religious, safeguarding middle-class ethical values and possessing a world-view with a much wider horizon than the one revealed in the traditional sensuous verse of Lucknow. Yet the *marthiya* was conditioned by the social life of Oudh. Its characters, especially women, are more like the inhabitants of Lucknow in their feeling, sorrow and mourning than Arabs of the seventh century.

The *marthiya* rose to great heights in the voluminous and inspired work of Mīr Bābur ʿAlī Anīs (1802–74), a poet of rare genius. His range of vocabulary is the most extensive in Urdu. He introduced a novel treatment of descriptive themes like the dawn in the desert, the swiftness of the horse, the sharpness of the sword, the pangs of hunger and thirst, the pathos of suffering, and the epic grandeur of a hero resisting with his back to the wall and fighting against overwhelming odds. With Anīs and his contemporary, Mirzā Salāmat ʿAlī Dabīr (1803–1875), an epic tradition was established in Urdu poetry, filled with the grandeur of heroic verse and the depths of intense, passionate tragedy. It has been rightly pointed out that the revolution which transformed Urdu poetry, after the Mutiny of 1857, was, in fact, heralded by the impact of the *marthiya*,[24] for this contributed several elements to the new poetry, which were later developed under Western influence. Among these was a sensitiveness to the beauties and severities of nature, the identification of poetic emotionalism with religion and a break away from the shackles of the *ghazal* to a freer form of versification.

A poet who contributed a great deal in theme and diction to the formation of the new poetry in the nineteenth century belongs neither to the Delhi nor the Lucknow school; he forms a category by himself. He was Walī Muḥammad Nadhīr Akbarābādī (d. 1830). He began his life as a profligate and ended up as a syncretistic Ṣūfī. In both these stages, sacred and profane, he remained very close to the soil. He wrote in the demotic, occasionally vulgar language of the people, used, indiscriminately, dialectal features of the Hindī of Agra and of various ethnic groups of north India, and in this process pulled Urdu in a direction contrary to that of Persianized purists like Nāsikh, thereby enriching it and preparing it to cope with the familiar aspects of nature and of the collective life of the people. Much of the vocabulary he used found its way later into Urdu; but some of it was so colloquially rustic or local and dialectal that it did not gain currency. For his subject-matter he chose the interests, occupations, joys and sorrows of the people. He wrote about the bear led by a mendicant street performer, about birds in flight and in love, about fairs, about Hindu, Sikh and Muslim festivals, with a liberal eclecticism unfamiliar in Urdu poetry; about the situation, conditions and frailty of man, and about the mortality of all humanity typified by the *banjāra* of the tribe of rustic travelling salesmen, who goes unaccompanied on his last profitless journey on the way of all flesh. No other Urdu poet, before or since, has been capable of such closeness in sentiment and expression to the masses of Indian people, Muslim as well as those belonging to other persuasions. He was also capable of the traditional style in his *ghaẓals*; but it is on his demotic poems that his fame principally rests.

Comparative peace, though not prosperity, came to Delhi in 1765. In that year the powerless Mughal emperor Shāh ʿĀlam II assigned the *dīwānī* (revenue collection) of the north-eastern provinces of India to the British East India Company. In fact he became a pensioner and a protégé of the Company; and at last under British protection Delhi became safe from the depredations of the Marāṭhas, the Jāts and Rohillas. Gradually the Delhi school of poetry rehabilitated itself in this new-found security. Shāh ʿĀlam II was himself a poet of indifferent merit. There were a number of minor poets writing in Delhi, most prominent among whom, in the early decades of the nineteenth century, was Shāh Naṣīr (d. 1840), who chose for himself long and difficult rhymes as an intellectual exercise. But the school of Delhi reached its zenith in the second quarter of the nineteenth century with a galaxy of poets including Mu'min, Dhawq, Ẓafar and Ghālib.

Mu'min Khān Mu'min (1800–51) wrote with consummate charm the lyrical *ghaẓal* of heterosexual love. He was also a

9. *Mausoleum of Iletmish*, 1235

devout Sunnī and an admirer of the movement of *jihād* led by Sayyid Aḥmad Barēlwī. His poetry of love, as of faith, has a unique polish and a refined dignity. Shaykh Muḥammad Ibrāhim Dhawq (1789–1854), attached to the court of the powerless Mughal emperor at the Red Fort in Delhi, was a consummate artist in *qaṣīda* (panegyric); he used diction and rhyme-schemes of pomp and magnificence, which suffer from overtones of artifice. His distinguished disciple was Bahādur Shāh Ẓafar (reigned 1837–58; d. 1862), the last Mughal emperor, who wrote voluminous *dīwāns* of *ghazals* and could occasionally rise to heights of inspiration. Most moving of Ẓafar's verse is that written after his dethronement and exile in Burma between 1858 and 1862 when he mourned plaintively his own tragic lot and that of the Muslim élite of Delhi and their culture.

Mirzā Asad-Allāh Khān Ghālib (1796–1869) is generally regarded as the greatest of Urdu poets.[25] In his Persian verse he had inherited the style of Bīdil, which he transplanted into Urdu. His Urdu verse has a richness and intellectuality, a calibre of wit and image, rarely met with elsewhere. He uses the traditional material of poetry but transforms it either by novel experience or by exceptional imagery. His powerful intellect renders his expression challengingly difficult, at times; at other times he could compose in a simple, but quite inimitable style which has come to be known as 'impossibly easy' (*sahl-i mumtanaʿ*). His analysis of the nuances of emotions is achieved by an intense intellectualization of the process of analytical technique. Despite all the difficulty of expression and imagery, his verse has a direct and irresistible appeal and much of it has already become proverbial. His greatness bridges the gulf between medievalism and modernity in Urdu poetry. By carrying the older tradition to the point of inimitable subtlety of perfection he brings it to a consummation and an end; and with his inventive skill he paves the way for the future frontiers of the intellectual and lyrical *ghazal*.

No doubt a traditional stream of the Urdu *ghazal* survived him into the next generation, represented by Amīr Aḥmad, known as Amīr Mīnā'ī (1828–1900) and Nawwāb Mirzā Khān Dāgh Dihlawī (1831–1905), roughly disciples of the classical styles of Lucknow and Delhi respectively; but they are both

10. *Mughal carpet, 17th century*

concerned primarily with the refinement of language and with the beaten tracks of profane love. The mainstream of the Urdu *ghazal*, from Ḥālī in the nineteenth century to Fayḍ in the twentieth, was inspired by Ghālib, though he was not very well imitated.

The Mutiny of 1857–8 is the dividing-line between medieval and modern norms of life as well as of literature in Islamic India. With the failure of the Mutiny and the consequent consolidation of British rule, the Muslim élite faced squarely the problem of modernization. In poetry this meant the acceptance not only of a great many critical criteria of Western origin, as outlined by Ḥālī in the famous *Muqaddima* to his *Dīwān*,[26] but also a recognition of the Indian social and political milieu and an assessment of the situation of the Muslims in India. The way to new approaches was no doubt prepared by early pioneers like Naẓīr Akbarābādī, and by Ghālib's novel handling of the medium of the *ghazal*; but the immediate and principal influences were two. One of these was the direct, though rather superficial and limited contact which early post-Mutiny poets like Muḥammad Ḥusayn Āzād and Alṭāf Ḥusayn Ḥālī had with British officers of the Education Department. The other was the forceful, motivating inspiration of the religious, political and educational movement of Sayyid Aḥmad Khān.

The new poetry continued to some extent to use the *ghazal*, but changed its theme from stale, conventionalized love to ethics and general observation of life. In this transformation it turned to some of the classical Persian poetry, especially Saʿdī, for inspiration; and it is not surprising that Ḥālī, who is the chief representative of the new *ghazal*, is also the author of an intelligent study of Saʿdī. But the main stream of Urdu poetry chose for its expression the freer poem, or *nazm*, which had greater continuity of style and was not fettered like the *ghazal* with an inhibiting rhyme-scheme and an atomistic structure.

Alṭāf Ḥusayn Ḥālī (1837–1914)[27] was a leading supporter of Sayyid Aḥmad Khān, as well as a spiritual and intellectual disciple of Ghālib. His dynamic but simple genius forms a link between Ghālib and Iqbāl, giving to Urdu a unique position among modern Islamic languages with a succession of three great poets in three succeeding generations from the nineteenth to the twentieth century. Ḥālī's most outstanding work is his *Musaddas-i madd-u jazr-i Islām*, a poem on the decline of Islam in general in modern times, and in India in particular, written under the direct inspiration of Sayyid Aḥmad Khān. Much of the remaining poetry of Ḥālī, like that of his contemporary Muḥammad Ḥusayn Āzād, tackles modern themes, but is insipid where it lacks the influence or inspiration of Sayyid Aḥmad Khān's movement. Āzād's verse is more artificial and occasionally a little ornate, like his prose. Among the younger contemporaries of these two early Urdu poets were two talented Hindu poets, Durgā Sahāy Sarūr (1873–1910) and Chakbast, whose verse is mellow with Hindu devotional elements and a more Indianized imagery.

Sayyid Akbar Ḥusayn, known as Akbar Allāhābādī (1846–1921), is, next to Sawdā, the most prominent satirist in Urdu. In political and social satire his work is unique. Fiercely anti-Western, antipathetic to all modernization, he had an inspired, though piecemeal, style and an unrivalled mastery of rhyme. In his anti-modernism he constitutes something of an antithesis to Sayyid Aḥmad Khān and his Aligarh Movement. Akbar was also capable of writing non-satirical, serious verse of considerable dignity.

Muḥammad Iqbāl (1875–1938), whom we have already considered as a modernist religious thinker and as a distinguished poet of Persian, is by far the most eminent Urdu poet of the twentieth century.[28] Though his more intellectually sustained work was composed in Persian, the same elements – his philosophy of the human self and its relation to society, his defence of freedom for all humanity, especially men of the Muslim east, his preoccupation with the values of movement, power and evolution, his devotional aspiration to love divine rooted firmly in phenomenological monism, his forcefulness of expression, and the dynamism of his personality – are atomistically interspersed in his Urdu verse which ranges over four decades.

The first collection of Iqbāl's Urdu verse, *Bāng-i Darā*, is divided into three parts. The first of these includes poems for children, poems on Indian regional patriotism, which are still dear to Hindus and to nationalist Indian Muslims, and poems on vaguely philosophical themes. The second part, consisting of poems, written in Europe between 1905 and 1908, which are either lyrical or Islamic, mark the transition from Indian nationalism to pan-Islamism. The third phase of his Urdu verse from 1908 to 1924 established him as perhaps the greatest poet in the entire Muslim world of the theme and drama of Islam in modern times; this is seen at its best in his Complaint to God (*Shikwa*) with its Answer (*Jawāb-i Shikwa*), in a poem marking the advent of Islamic socialism, the *Khiḍr-i rāh*, and in a powerfully sustained narrative lyric, *Shamʿ-u shāʿir*. After a decade of intense poetic activity in Persian, Iqbāl turned again to Urdu during the last years of his life. His *Bāl-i Jibrīl* (1935) contains some of his greatest work, and includes among a collection of *ghazals*, general and topical, philosophical and political, a poem called the *Masjid-i Qurṭuba* (Mosque of Cordova), which is perhaps the finest in the Urdu language. The next collection of Urdu poems, *Zarb-i Kalīm* (1936), is more directly political and polemical in its treatment of the West's imperialist impact on the world of Islam. His last collection, *Armaghān-i Ḥijāz*, published posthumously in 1938, includes his Persian as well as his Urdu verse.

With Iqbāl, Urdu poetry was thoroughly revolutionized. The poem established itself as the dominant form. Western literary influences were accepted. Poetry became dynamic and revolutionary in the social verse of Josh Malīḥābādī or the Marxist verse of Fayḍ Aḥmad Fayḍ,[29] who was awarded a Lenin Prize. The *ghazal* was also influenced by Iqbāl and became more intellectualized than the otherwise traditional verse of his contemporaries: the lyricist Ḥasrat Mohānī, the mystic Aṣghar Gondawī, the pessimist Fānī Bādā'ūnī, and the devotional and overflowingly lyrical poet Jigar Murādābādī.

It is difficult to perceive any continuity between the older prose of the Deccan and the prose written later in the eighteenth century in northern India. One of the earliest specimens of this later category was a martyrological work, *Dih majlis*, written by Faḍlī, in 1732, in a very highly ornate style with artificially balanced and rhymed sentence structure. The same style is even more conventionalized in the *Naw ṭarz-i muraṣṣaʿ* of ʿAṭā' Khān Taḥsīn written in 1798.

This conventional prose style burdened with euphemisms, lacking clarity in meaning, and difficult to employ in ordinary usage, was not found useful by the officers of the British East India Company, who were interested, at the beginning of the nineteenth century, in the development of a simple, straightforward vernacular prose which could replace Persian at the lower levels of administration. The British efforts towards the evolution of a pragmatic Urdu style were concentrated at the Fort William College at Calcutta under the able direction of John Gilchrist (1759–1841). Himself the author of several works on Urdu philology and lexicography, he developed the policy of employing *munshīs*, who were instructed to write Urdu narrative in a plain, almost conversational style. The most eminent of these was Mīr Amman Dihlawī whose *Bāgh-u bahār*, composed in 1801, is the first classic of modern Urdu prose. Several other Urdu works were compiled at Fort William College by Shīr ʻAlī Afsūs (1735–1809), Bahādur ʻAlī Ḥusaynī and Ḥaydar Bakhsh Ḥaydarī (d. 1833). The last is the author of, among numerous other works, *Ṭoṭā kahānī*, which is based on the cycle of tales familiarized in Persian and Dakanī Urdu by Nakhshabī and Ghawwāṣī respectively. Kāẓim ʻAlī Jawān translated the Qur'ān into Urdu, although earlier Urdu versions of the Qur'ān had been prepared in the eighteenth century by Shāh Walī-Allāh's sons, Rafīʻ-ad-dīn and ʻAbd-al-Qādir. In his *Madhhab-i ʻishq* Nihāl Chand gave a rendering of the story of Bakāwalī, which is the mystic quest of a woman who is symbolized by a flower. Other *munshīs* of Fort William College were Mirzā Luṭf ʻAlī Wilā, who translated several works from Persian, and Lallū Lāl Jī, who wrote in Urdu, but occupies a unique position as the inventor of modern Hindi by writing Urdu in the Devanāgarī script with a Sanskritized vocabulary.

Beyond the sphere of the direct influence of Fort William College, the need for a simpler and more practical style in Urdu was also felt in Delhi, and this is reflected in Ghālib's Urdu letters, which have a charming, conversational style, and in Sayyid Aḥmad Khān's first major work, *Athār as-ṣanādīd*, on the archaeology of Delhi, published before the Mutiny. The swan song of the older, conventionalized, artificial style is Rajab ʻAlī Bēg Sarūr's *Fasāna-i ʻajā'ib*, written in 1824 but which, nevertheless, could not escape certain modern features.

Sayyid Aḥmad Khān's movement of reform thoroughly

revolutionized Urdu prose. Urdu suddenly found itself preoccupied, and capable of dealing successfully, with a very extensive range of religious, polemical, controversial, historical, social and personal writing. The chief architect of the new prose was Sayyid Aḥmad Khān himself. His journal, *Tahdhīb al-akhlāq*, set a standard which elevated Urdu to a rank equal to the three other older Islamic languages, Arabic, Persian and Turkish. In his *Tafsīr* of the Qur'ān and other exegetical works, including the *Tabyīn al-Kalām*, a unique commentary on the Bible, his Urdu is capable of dealing with the minutiae and nuances of very controversial or polemical subject-matter. His *Lectures* substituted fluency and appeal for the older rhetoric. His influence inspired a number of his associates, who developed individual styles of their own. Muḥsin-al-Mulk and Chiragh ʿAlī wrote on religious and juristic themes. ʿImād-al-Mulk Bilgrāmī and his brother Sayyid ʿAlī Bilgrāmī had simple and chaste narrative styles.

Sayyid Aḥmad Khān's most distinguished literary associates were the historians Shiblī Nuʿmānī (1857–1914) and Zakā-Allāh (1832–1910), the novelist Nadhīr Aḥmad (1831–1912), and the poet Ḥālī, who was also a critic and biographer of distinction.

Shiblī Nuʿmānī[30] was one of the ulema but held enlightened and, to a moderate degree, Westernized views. At Aligarh he taught Arabic in the early years of his career, and there he came in contact with T. W. (later Sir Thomas) Arnold. Soon he turned to the history of Islam and wrote studies of the life and work of ʿUmar I, al-Ma'mūn, Abū-Ḥanīfa, al-Ghazālī and Jalāl-ad-dīn Rūmī. His most ambitious biographical work was *Sīrat an-Nabī*, a life of the Prophet in several volumes, which was completed after his death by his disciple, and successor, Sulaymān Nadwī. Shiblī was especially interested in Medieval Muslim scholasticism and wrote two books on *kalām*. In literary criticism his monumental work is *Shiʿr al-ʿAjam*, a history of Persian poetry in five volumes, which has a unique position in *tadhkira* literature and was among the sources of E. G. Browne's *Literary History of Persia*. Shiblī's *Mawāzina-i Anīs wa-Dabīr* is one of the first works of applied literary criticism in Urdu.

Zakā-Allāh was much more Westernized as a historian; but

though he has a fluent historical style, most of his voluminous material is merely an Urdu rendering of English sources dealing with the history of the British rule in India. Urdu historiography in the hands of Shiblī and Zakā-Allāh and their successors remained far inferior to the Indo-Persian chronicles. It was only partly influenced by Western methodology while losing its classical tradition.

Ḥālī carried something of his poetic genius into his prose style which, in his essays often has a delicate cadence and, in his monumental biographies of Sayyid Aḥmad Khān and Ghālib, is capable of expanding into vivid narrative or analytical criticism and valuable documentation. The biographies written by Ḥālī and Shiblī follow the Victorian model, the first part dealing with the life and the second with the work of the person in question. Modern Urdu literary criticism can be said to have begun with Ḥālī's *Muqaddima*, which deals with the theory of poetry in general and its application to Urdu in particular.

Nadhīr Aḥmad was only obliquely connected with Sayyid Aḥmad Khān's movement. His theological views, as reflected in his *al-Ḥuqūq wa-l-farā'iḍ*, were much more conservative. On the other hand, his translation of the Qur'ān is colloquial to the point of being unfaithful to the original. One of his novels, *Ibn-al-Waqt*, is regarded generally as a satire on Sayyid Aḥmad Khān's Western style of living. Nadhīr Aḥmad had originally turned to domestic fiction under the patronage of British officials of the Education Department. His first two novels, *Mir'at al-ʿarūs* and *Bināt an-naʿsh*, are narratives prescribing private-style education and a refined upbringing for young ladies of the lower middle class. *Tawbat an-Nuṣūḥ*, which followed them, made a more powerful impact, being the story of a worldly man and his family shaken into a life of reform, which meant a religious, God-fearing life. Closest to the modern novel is his *Fasāna-i Mubtila*, the story of a rake who is plagued by his own bigamy. The novels of Nadhīr Aḥmad suffer from an excess of didacticism not merely in the plot, but through lengthy sermonizing which is directly religious or ethical. But it was to him that the Urdu novel owed its beginning.

Earlier in the nineteenth century, a type of intricate story of romance, magic and trickery written in an ornate, balanced, artificial and rhymed style was very popular. It was known as the *dāstān*, and its material was a labyrinthine extension of the Amīr Ḥamza cycle, which was popular all over the Muslim world from Turkey to Indonesia. With the beginnings of the novel the literary *dāstān* came to an end; though the oral *dāstān* continued well into the twentieth century.

Muḥammad Ḥusayn Āzād (d. 1910) was a prose-stylist of unique charm, totally unconnected with Sayyid Aḥmad Khān's Movement. His style has a musical clarity, an instinct for life-like description and for picturesqueness in detail. He has a remarkable command over the natural and artificial resources of the language. His *Āb-i Ḥayāt*, the first chronological history of Urdu poetry, brings to life the successive generations of Urdu poets, and though its accuracy has come to be doubted by modern research it is still unsurpassed in its panorama of the infinite variety of the life of Urdu poets and their productions. His *Sukhandān-i Fars* is very inferior to Shiblī's *Shi'r al-'Ajam* as a history of Persian poetry. His *Darbār-i Akbarī* mixes fact with fiction in describing Akbar's court on the basis of the accounts of 'Allāmī and Badā'ūnī. *Nayrang-i khayāl* consists of ornate allegories.

Lucknow made its debut in Urdu prose with a humorous periodical, *Awadh Panch*, that was first published in 1877 and included political and social satire as well as the serialized novel of caricature, a genre in which its editor Sajjād Ḥusayn (d. 1915) excelled.

Pandit Ratan Nāth Sarshār (d. 1902) serialized his novels in another periodical published in Lucknow, the *Awadh Akhbār*. His *Fasāna-i Azād*, which is the story of a vagrant hero, in the tradition of the English novel of the eighteenth century, is remarkable for its portrayal of the cross-currents of the life of all sections of people in Lucknow and its environs, and for the chastity and beauty of its language, descriptive as well as conversational. This voluminous work can perhaps be regarded as the best work of fiction written in Urdu. Sarshār's other novels are picaresque, in the Western style, and his *Khudā'ī Fawjdār* is based on Cervantes' *Don Quixote*.

'Abd-al-Ḥalīm Sharar is the principal historical novelist in Urdu. He was familiar with the Arabic sources of Islamic history, and had an eye for the scandalous and the polemical. His treatment of Islamic history, ranging from Spain to India, is over-sentimental, romanticized, dramatized to the point of infidelity to his sources, but absorbing and vivid.

Another type of novel which found vogue in India for several generations was the one dealing with courtesans. It began with *Nishtar*, written originally in Persian, but known only through its Urdu translation. Mirzā Muḥammad Hādī Ruswā's *Umrāo Jān Adā*,[31] the life story of a courtesan of some education and taste is the best known novel of this genre. The most recent specimen of this type of fiction is Qāḍī ʿAbd-al-Ghaffār's *Laylā kē khūṭūṭ*.

An outstanding figure among Urdu novelists is Munshī Dhanpat Ray, who wrote, under the name of Prēm Chand, in both Urdu and Hindī. He is the novelist of the middle classes whose social and economic problems he analyses with consummate skill. The vast canvas of his works reflects the political ferment in India, when the movements for national liberation had a direct impact on the psychology of Indians of all classes. There is a certain classical purity, an economy of expression, and a direct forcefulness in his style.

About the middle of the twentieth century the Urdu novel, with the works of Krishna Chandra, ʿIṣmat Chaghtā'ī, ʿAzīz Aḥmad and Qur'āt-al-ʿAyn Ḥaydar, came to reflect various degrees of Westernization. The short story flourished more than the novel and is represented by a large number of 'progressive' or semi-Marxist writers, most prominent among whom are Krishna Chandra and Saʿādat Ḥasan Manto.

A great deal of theological literature has been published in Urdu since the middle of the nineteenth century. After the creation of the State of Pakistan this trend has increased. In recent years a large number of religious classics including almost the entire corpus of classical *ḥadīth* have been translated into Urdu.

The future of Urdu literature as of the language is now almost entirely linked up with West Pakistan because of the adverse developments in the northern states of India and in East Pakistan. In West Pakistan the Urdu language and its literary style are bound to be influenced by the regional languages and their literatures.

2. Regional Literatures[32]

In addition to Urdu, Islamic culture found expression in a number of languages written and spoken in the predominantly Muslim areas of the subcontinent.

Of these, Bengali has a special position. It is regional in the sense that it is confined to a particular region, i.e. Bengal; but it is also, along with Urdu, one of the two national languages of Pakistan. This position is made more piquant by the fact that it has a richer and greater non-Muslim literature, and this has influenced, and continues to influence, the Muslim writing in Bengali. This explains the intellectual pull of Calcutta felt in East Pakistan.

We are concerned here only with the Muslim element of Bengali literature.[33] The principal feature of this element is its use of Arabic and Persian loan-words, which originated with the advent of Ṣūfīs like Jalāl-ad-dīn Tabrīzī (*c.* 1303). This Islamized vocabulary continued to be used by the Bengali Muslim poets until the eighteenth century, when the British imposed the Permanent Settlement in Bengal, in 1793, which led to the advancement of the Hindu middle classes and Hindu élite at the expense of the Muslims, and to the Sanskritization of the Bengali language. The Muslim reaction to this trend became manifest with the annulment of the partition of Bengal in 1911, for this partition had been favourable to the Muslims, and its annulment came as a political shock which was also an intellectual challenge. It led to the foundation of Bangla Muslim Sāhitya Samītī, which aimed once again at bringing Bengali closer to Arabic, Persian and Urdu. Poets like Kayqubād and Nadhr-al-Islām worked to the same end.[34]

Early trends in Bengali were eclectic and the line between the Hindu and Muslim elements of its literature was blurred. After the Muslim conquest the Pathān kings of Bengal encouraged local literature, and under their patronage Hindu classical epics, *Rāmāyana* and *Mahābhārata*, were translated into Bengali. Among these early patrons of Bengali literary enterprise were Shams-ad-dīn Yūsuf Shāh (1474–81) and Nuṣrat Shāh (1518–33), as well as Paragal Khān, an *amīr* of the court of Ḥusayn Shāh (1493–1518). In the reign of Ghiyāth ad-dīn Aʿẓam Shāh (1393–1410), Shāh Muḥammad Saghīr, the earliest Muslim to compose in Bengali, wrote his epic of love, *Yūsuf Zulaykhā*, presumably modelled on Firdawsī's *mathnawī* on the same theme.[35] Zayn-ad-dīn, the author of *Rasūl Vijay* (Victory of the Prophet), was the court poet of Yūsuf Shāh. The work is probably the translation of a Persian original.[36] Among early Bengali poets is Shaykh Fayḍ-Allāh, author of *Ghazī Vijay*, a hagiographical poem, written in praise of a Muslim missionary Ismāʿīl Ghāzī (*c.* 1460), and *Rāg Nāma*, a versified treatise on music.

Ḥusayn Shāh had Hindu scriptures and other Hindu classics translated into Bengali. A narrative poem, *Vidyā Sundar*, was composed during his reign by Kākā, a Brahmin converted to Islam. Also during his reign a Muslim poet, Yasorāj Khān, composed his *Krishna Mangla*, a narrative poem on a Hindu devotional theme.[37] The literature of pre-Mughal Muslim Bengal during the fifteenth and sixteenth century consists of narrative poems on Muslim or Hindu themes, religious poems and poems with an eclectic content. There are also poems dealing with arts and sciences like music and astronomy. Much of the Bengali poetry written by Muslim poets in the Pathān and Mughal periods is syncretistic, synthesizing Hindu and Muslim devotional elements. To the syncretistic genre belong two forms of mystical lyrics, the Hinduized *bol*, and its Muslim counterpart, the *maʿrifatī*.

Punthī, or popular hagiographical narrative, survived during several centuries and shows a certain amount of Shīʿī martyrological proclivity. It is represented by such works as Badīʿ-ad-dīn's *Ṣūrat-nāma-i Fāṭima* or Ḥayāt Muḥammad's *Muḥarram Parva*. Muḥammad ibn-al-Ḥanafiyya (one of ʿAlī's sons) often figures as the hero of a *punthī* poem, and also as the central character of several other Bengali religious poems. *Punthī* poems have a considerable percentage of Arabic and Persian loan-words.

Medieval popular Bengali literature is rich in folk-romances and old wives' tales, some of which like *Madhūmālā* are of Hindu origin, others like *Dīwānī Madīna* are partly Islamized, and yet others, like *Āʾīna Bībī*, have a purely Islamic strain. The folk-poetry of rural Bengal is intensely realistic, reflects a sensitive observation of life and landscape and breathes a note of moral purity.

Bengali prose originated in the pre-Mughal era, towards the close of the sixteenth century, curiously enough with Portuguese missionary works.

During the Mughal period Persian became, in Bengal, as elsewhere, the exclusive language of administration at all significant levels, and also of higher culture, with the result that the works of poets like the Muslim, ʿAlāʾul (1607–80),[38] and the Hindu, Bhārat Chandra (1712–60), even though they were not directly connected with Mughal Bengal, are imbued with Persian influences.

Bengali literature of the Mughal period included popular poems explaining points of religious ritual, stories relating to the lives of the Prophet and various saints, martyrological epics, Ṣūfistic verses, love *mathnawīs* based on Persian models, historical or pseudo-historical narratives and allegories. A remarkable genre was the *padāwalī*, a syncretized mystical poem. Among the early poets of Mughal Bengal was Sayyid Sulṭān (*c.* 1576), author of a number of hagiographical poems relating to the life of the Prophet. He was also a historian and a writer of songs. Ṣūfistic trends were represented by his contemporary Ḥājī Muḥammad, and it is interesting to note that early in the seventeenth century he adhered to the doctrine of phenomenological monism (*waḥdat ash-shuhūd*) which was being propagated about the same time by Shaykh Aḥmad Sirhindī in the Punjab.[39]

The predominance of Persian, however, inhibited the flowering of Bengali genius in Mughal Bengal. It was in the autonomous states of the eastern marches, where culture was eclectically a synthesis of Hindu and Muslim elements, that the greatest Muslim, Bengali poets flourished and wrote under the direct or oblique patronage of Hindu rājas. One of these states was Rozanga, which covers approximately the same area as modern western Arakan. Hindu rājas here added Muslim titles to their names and recruited Muslims among their officials.

One of the illustrious poets of this court was Dawlat Qāḍī (1600–38). His famous narrative poem, *Satī Moina*, has a Hindu theme, and has a narrative pattern falling into three stages, union, separation and re-union. He is the author of another poem, *Lore-Chandrānī*. He mingled Bengali with the Hindu devotional language Brajabolī.[40] His scholarship in

Arabic, Persian and also Sanskrit raised Bengali in his hands to a high literary standard. He was also a fine lyric poet and is the author of an exquisite calendar-poem, the *Bāra Mashya*.

The most distinguished poet of the court of Rozanga was ʿAlā'ul (1607–80), remarkable for his imagery, narrative skill and style. He translated Malik Muḥammad Jā'isī's historical allegory *Padmāwat* from Hindī into Bengali and completed Dawlat Qāḍī's *Satī Moina*. Among his poems, his *Sayf-al-mulk wa Badīʿ-al-jamāl* is more Islamic in theme, a story of Arabian Nights origin, which, as we have seen, had also inspired the Dakanī Urdu poet, Ghawwāṣī. Two other narrative poems of ʿAlā'ul, *Haft Paykar* and *Sikandar Nāma* are modelled on the *mathnāwīs* of Niẓāmī.

Another regional court where Bengali poetry flourished was that of Tripura where a Muslim poet, Shaykh Chānd (d. 1625), wrote his religious poem *Qiyāmat Nāma*.

In the early seventeenth century a literary genre of the Bengali dialect, Brajabolī, was the lyrical *pad*, which had for its theme the Hindu lore of the loves of Rādhā and Krishna, but which was written by both Hindus and Muslims.

As we have seen, the Bengali language, and therefore Bengali literature, underwent a change during the British period following the Permanent Settlement of 1793 when the old eclectic tradition which was a meeting-ground of Hindu and Muslim elements was lost in the Sanskritization of the language and Hinduization of the literature. Especially in the later nineteenth and early twentieth century the purely Hindu stream of Bengali literature was revolutionized by two generations of great reformers and writers: Ram Mohan Roy, the founder of the modernist Brahmā Samāj sect; the anti-Muslim novelist Bankim Chandra Chatterjī; the mystic Viveknanda; and finally the eminent lyrical poet Rabindra Nāth Tagore. For several generations Muslims remained entrenched in a conservative religious heritage and were unresponsive to the new movement's creative activity.

Mīr Musharraf Ḥusayn (1848–1911), a novelist, playwright, essayist and poet was the first modern Muslim writer of Bengal to accept Western influences. Another pioneer of modern ideas was the poet Kayqubād (1852–1951), who enjoyed a long, productive life. The thematic emphasis in his historical epic about Aḥmad Shāh Abdālī, the *Mahā shamshān kāviya*, was distinctly pro-Muslim and anti-Hindu. This poem, written in 1904, is one of the early literary landmarks of Muslim nationalism in the subcontinent. Kayqubād was also the author of several other epics and narratives and his verse has a musical quality.

One of the most distinguished poets of modern Muslim Bengal is Nadhr-al-Islām (b. 1899), a fiery genius of remarkable vitality and dynamism. In content his verse covers a wide range, protesting against social injustices and inequalities, generating a revolutionary impulse, struggling against conservative conformities, and glorifying historical and contemporary Islam. He introduced the *ghazal* into Bengali, and enriched the language with an extensive range of Urdu loan-words and poetical epithets.

Another stream of Muslim reaction to the Hindu, modernist-revivalist domination of Bengali literature was more conservative. Some Muslim writers, like Ismā'īl Ḥusayn Shīrāzī, chose to emphasize the glorification of Islam. This tradition was continued in the twentieth century by some writers who were also political leaders, like Akram Khān. In the later nineteenth century some Muslim Bengali writers used Arabic script, whereas the language is generally written exclusively in Devanagari. Among modern Bengali poets, Ghulām Muṣṭafā (b. 1895) shows a concentrated Islamic bias. He has translated Ḥālī's *Musaddas* into Bengali. He has also experimented in Bengali with Arabic metres to which they are alien.

Jasīm-ad-dīn (b. 1902) is the poet of rural life, whose poetry is based on the folk-songs he has so studiously collected. One of his collections has been rendered into English under the title *The Field of Embroidered Quilt*. The Muslim Sāhitya Samāj of Dacca, founded in the 1930s by 'Abd-al-Ḥusayn and 'Abd-al-Wadūd, has introduced progressive and modernist elements into Muslim Bengali literature.

There is a group of young writers, poets and novelists in East Pakistan, who are proud of their heritage, show Western influence to a marked degree, and are building up the new traditions of an East Pakistani, Bengali literature.

In comparison, the regional literatures of West Pakistan have a much stronger Islamic strain, and in some languages they show or retain hardly any Hindu elements. Even where these elements have been retained, as in the case of Sindhi, they are no longer syncretistic or eclectic, but thoroughly absorbed into local Islamic culture and into Ṣūfism.

The oldest of the regional languages of West Pakistan is Pashto,[41] which is close to Pahlavi. With Abū-Muḥammad Hāshim al-Bastī, Arabic vocabulary found its way into Pashto in the ninth century. In the succeeding centuries Persian literary genres, like the *qaṣīda* (panegyric) and *marthiya* (martyrological epic), were introduced into it.

The first period of Pashto poetry extends from the tenth to the sixteenth century; the second, from the sixteenth to the nineteenth, and the third, or modern phase begins with the British occupation of the region in 1840 and continues to the present day.

The earliest Pashto poetry is traced traditionally, though it is difficult to say to what extent apocryphally, to the work of Amīr Karor of Ghūr, a thousand years ago. On this claim the Pathans, the people of the north-west of West Pakistan and of Eastern Afghanistan, base the argument of the antiquity not only of their language, but also of their literature and culture.

Early Pashto poets whose work is individualized are Shaykh Raḍī and Bayt Bābā (twelfth century); Shaykh Tīmūr (thirteenth century); Akbar Zamīndārawī (fourteenth century); Shaykh Ṣāliḥ, Zarghūn Khān and the poetess Bībī Rabī'a (fifteenth century). Through these four centuries their work shows certain common characteristics. It is Islamic in content, and epic in theme and treatment. It deals with the exploits of heroes or consists of love poetry, simple in statement and imagery. In the fifteenth century mystical elements begin to be telescoped with the themes of love.

Pashto literature was created by and for a war-like people, and is rich in epic ballads. These ballads date as far back as the last decade of the twelfth century; one of the earliest was by Malik Yār Gharshīn, who accompanied Muḥammad ibn-Sām Ghūrī on one of his expeditions into India. Romances in Pashto are based on folk-tales, but seldom reach the level of artistic achievement one comes across in Punjabi or Sindhi. In Pashto lyrical poetry, represented by 'Abd-al-Ḥamīd 'Alī Khān and 'Abd-al-Qādir Khān, there is an earthiness and a masculine tenderness. Earthly love often crosses the frontier into the mystical.

Whereas pantheistic Ṣūfism is reflected in the literature of the Rawshaniyya movement, the orthodox variety is more usual and is represented in the work of Mirzā Khān Anṣārī, Dawlat Labānī and others. Controversy between the Rawshaniyya and its opponents, led by Akhūnd Darwīza, contributed to the growth of tractarian literature in both camps. These tracts covered a wide range of ethical and religious subjects.

Khushḥal Khān Khattak (1613–89) remains the most eminent of Pashto poets. He rebelled against Awrangzīb, was imprisoned, and on his release continued the conflict in the Pathān uprising against Mughal rule. He was a prolific writer and is the author of a voluminous *dīwān* of verses.[42] His love poetry is gallant and vivacious; but most remarkable is his self-dramatization in the situation of war, extolling the ideals of manliness and chivalry.

Raḥmān Bābā (sixteenth century) is closer than Khattak to the inner experience of Islamic spirituality. The theme of his work is religious and pietistic, and to some extent mystical. His style is generally lyrical. Another lyrical poet of the sixteenth century, ʿAbd-al-Ḥamīd, has a rare sense of beauty, showing the marked influence of the Persian heritage.

Pashto is rich in folk-songs, which are divided into several varieties: the oldest, *tappa*, which corresponds to the *doha* in Sindhi; the *chārbayta*, or quatrain, which is used also in epic ballads; the *nīmka'ī* and *bagtā'ī* which are forms of folk-song sung by women. Folk-songs are sung by the Pathāns to the accompaniment of a tambourine or a pitcher.

With the British occupation of trans-Indus regions, in 1840, the Pathāns came in touch with Western literature; then followed a period of translations from Urdu and Persian. Rasūl Riḍā and Samandar Khān are the two most representative poets of the first half of the twentieth century. There is also a young group of Westernized writers, some of whom are bilingual, using both Urdu and Pashto; others only the latter. In Afghanistan there is considerable emphasis on the preservation of the Pashto literary heritage and on its advancement. The same movement is flourishing also in Pakistan and is symbolized by

11. *The Tāj Maḥall, Agra*, c. 1635

12. *Detail from one of the alcoves of the Tāj Maḥall*

the Pashto Academy which receives active aid and support from the government of Pakistan.

Ethnically very close to the Pathāns of the north-west are the Balochis inhabiting Baluchistan or eastern Makran, which is a part of West Pakistan. But the literature produced in Balochi is much more modest.[43] The landscape of the Balochi poetry is the rugged, inhospitable countryside, enlivened by flashes of beauty with the seasonal changes. It is not urban and reflects very little of town life. Balochi literature is rich in its descriptions of mountain scenery, of the nomadic life of the Baloch people, their migrations, their internecine feuds and their feeling for their clans.

There are two dialects of Balochi. Sulaymānī is spoken in the north and the north-east, while Makrānī is spoken in the west and south-west. Makrānī is very close to modern Persian with which it shares as much as half its vocabulary.[44]

Balochi poetry in both dialects is wholly oral, handed down from generation to generation by professional minstrels, or *doms*, who sing it at gatherings of clans. Some Balochi verse is amatory, some religious and didactic; often a religious or mystical under-current runs through the love poems. 'Balochi poetry is simple and direct in expression and excels in pictures of life and country which it brings before us without any conscious description on the part of the singer. As might be expected in a parched up land where water is scarce and rain seldom falls, the poet delights in describing the vivid thunderstorms which occasionally visit the mountains, and the sudden transformation of the countryside which follows a fall of rain.'[45] This closeness to nature explains to some extent the underlying mystical strain.

The epic poetry of the Balochis consists of heroic ballads of traditional tribal migrations to the north. Some ballads describe the warfare between Rind and Lashārī tribes during the fifteenth and sixteenth centuries. Others celebrate the feud between the Rind and the Dodai tribes in the sixteen-twenties, while yet others treat of the exploits of the Baloch expedition, under Shāhzād, to help Humāyūn to regain his kingdom in Delhi. There are other ballads of tribal feuds dating as recently as the eighteenth and nineteenth century; some of these are spirited and fiery, others are mere lists of names of warriors. Makrānī poetry reflects the tribal rivalries of the two warring tribes, the Rind and the Kalmatī.

The principal lyric poet writing in Balochi in the eighteenth century was Jām Durrāk, court poet of Nāṣir Khān of Kalat. A particular type of love-song is *dastanāgh* sung to the accompaniment of a *narī* or Balochi pipe. Some of the *dastanāghs* are love poems of great tenderness, others are witty or comic.

Balochi prose literature is underdeveloped. Its subject-matter is either religious, dealing with the lives of the Prophet and the saints, or it consists of love romances. Some of these are of common Islamic heritage, such as the story of Layla and Qays, while others by Murīd Ḥānī and Muḥabbat Khān Samri contain indigenous folk-material.

The élite of the Punjab have been using Urdu – and before that Persian – as the language for cultural expression, but, like the common people of the area, they speak Punjabi, which has a forceful popular literature.[46]

In antiquity, some Punjabi verses are attributed, possibly apocryphally, to the Chishtī mystic Farīd-ad-dīn Ganj-i Shakar. But probably the language goes back to a period even earlier than the thirteenth century, possibly to the period of the Ghaznavid occupation of the Punjab in the eleventh century.

Literary Punjabi begins with the founder of Sikhism, Gurū Nānak (1469–1538). The literature produced by the Sikhs was of a syncretistic nature at the outset, but later it developed an anti-Muslim bias. Sikh literature was written in the indigenous Devanāgarī script known as Gūrmakhī whereas the Muslims wrote Punjabi in Arabic script.

Much of the earlier Punjabi literature written by Muslims seems to have been lost. A number of religious tracts written in the seventeenth century, inspired probably by the Sikh challenge, still survive. Outstanding in this group is the work of Aḥdī (*c.* 1640). His contemporary Pīlū was among the first to give the tragic folk-romance of *Mirzā Ṣāḥibān* a literary form.

This romance and *Ṣassī Pannū*, a tale of Sindhi origin, together with the most popular Punjabi folk-romance *Hīr Rānjhā*, were versified by the poets of the time of Awrangzīb. The early versions of *Hīr Rānjhā* used the genre known as *sī ḥarfī*, consisting of thirty stanzas, each beginning with one of the thirty letters of the Punjabi alphabet.

Popular Ṣūfism,[47] usually pantheistic in expression, is represented in the Mughal period by the 'second' Farīd (d. 1554); a syncretistic mystic Mādhō Lāl Ḥusayn (1539–99), who wrote *kāfis* (short lyrical poems meant to be sung) of divine love in a devout and musical style; and Sulṭān Bā-hū (d. 1691), who is reputed to have written in Arabic and Persian in addition to Punjabi, but whose fame rests on his Punjabi *sī ḥarfī*, in which every line ends with the mystic cry *hū*. Sulṭān Bā-hū belonged to the Qādirī order, but was given to the excesses of the qalandars.

During the period of political and economic chaos that followed the collapse of the Mughal empire and was marked in the Punjab by the invasions of Nādir Shāh and Aḥmad Shāh Abdālī and the rise and tyrannical rule of the Sikhs, insecurity did not inhibit the popular genius. To this period belong the two most outstanding Muslim Punjabi poets, Bul'hē Shāh and Wārith Shāh.

Bul'hē Shāh (d. *c.* 1758), a Ṣūfī poet of eminence, used a simple, popular rural idiom to relate profound mystical experience, which, in that age of mutual religious strife, preached a doctrine of humanistic, almost syncretistic love. He shows an unmistakable similarity to the Hindu Bhaktī poets of earlier centuries, in ranking the inner religious experience higher than religious ritual; and like them he makes fun of the externalist religious leaders.[48]

Wārith Shāh, the greatest of Punjabi poets, is known for his version of *Hīr Rānjhā*, a powerfully moving story of fatal love. He had, himself, undergone a harrowing experience of unrequited love, and pours out his soul into his version of the famous folk-romance. It is written in colloquial speech, is steeped in the life and milieu of rural Punjab, has an amazing linguistic range and weaves popular idioms with naturalness.

Contemporaries of Bul'hē Shāh and Wārith Shāh include two martyrological poets Muqbil Shāh and Ḥāmid Shāh ʿAbbās, who wrote *jang-nāmas* or narrative epic elegies on Ḥusayn ibn-ʿAlī, and ʿAlī's other son Muḥammad ibn-al-Ḥanafiyya respectively. They also wrote narrative poems on familiar folk-romance material.

ʿAlī Ḥaydar (d. 1785) wrote musical verses in the Multani dialect. Hāshim (d. 1823), though the court-poet of the Sikh ruler Ranjīt Singh, composed romances on Muslim themes. Under the Sikhs, Punjabi began to accept influences from literary Urdu and underwent a change. This Urdu influence increased under the British in the nineteenth century. The *ghazal* was borrowed into Punjabi from Urdu.

Among the eminent poets of the nineteenth century was Faḍl Shāh (d. 1890) whose rendering of the rural romance *Sohinī Mahinwāl* is famous. It is the story of a village maiden's love for a young man and how, in order to keep tryst with him, she crossed the river every night floating on a baked-clay jar. Her sister-in-law, guessing her secret, substituted one night a jar of unbaked clay, and the maiden Sohinī, who could not swim well, was drowned. Her lover also flung himself in the water to die with her. Faḍl Shāh is a master of diction, and fully exploits the use of a word in all its nuances.

Hidāyat-Allāh (d. 1920) is known for his *Bārān māh*, a poem which recites the pangs of separation from the loved one through each of the twelve months of the year. Punjabi, like most other regional languages of the subcontinent, has also a rich collection of folk-songs.

Ṣūfistic poetry had a temporary revival in the moving pantheistic poems of Ghulām Farīd (d. 1900), who wrote in the Multani dialect. His verses are impregnated with pantheistic, ontological monism.

During recent years there has been some revival of Punjabi among the élite. Ṣūfī Ghulām Muṣṭafā Tabassum writes in Punjabi and also in Persian and Urdu. Another promising Punjabi poet is the communist Aḥmad Rāhī.

South of the Punjab in the valley of the Indus Sindhi is spoken and written as a popular language.[49] 'The Sindhi language' remarks Sorley 'is a beautiful instrument of precision admirably adapted to the civilization for which it was intended – a peace-loving, agricultural and pastoral culture elaborated by an industrious and non-martial people.'[50]

Sind had been closely allied to Persia in various stages of its history and accepted considerable Persian linguistic influence. Sindhi epic verses, meant to be sung by professional musicians (*bhāts*), were modelled on Persian epic poetry. The most eminent poet of Sind, Shāh 'Abd-al-Laṭīf, shows considerable influence of Jalāl-ad-dīn Rūmī's *Mathnawī*. In the early nineteenth century, under the Tālpūrs, Sind recognized the suzerainty of the Qāchārs and imitated Persia's patterns of culture and literature. Most of the Sindhi poets were bilingual, writing in Sindhi as well as Persian. Colloquial Sindhi vocabulary incorporates today twenty-five per cent Persian loan-words.[51]

Arab geographers of the tenth century inform us that Arabic and Sindhi were both spoken in the region of Sind in the tenth century. By the fifteenth century, if not earlier, Sindhi came to be written in Arabic script, into which useful diacritical modifications were introduced by the British linguists in the nineteenth century.

The beginnings of Sindhi verse have been traced by some historians, presumably apocryphally, to the times of the ʿAbbāsid minister Faḍl ibn-Yaḥyā al-Barmakī (d. 808).[52] Under the Sumrā dynasty (1051–1351), which was of indigenous origin, Sindhi literature certainly showed its first signs of development through folk-songs, oral epics, and romances of tribal rivalry, including the semi-historical tale of *Dūdē Chanēsar* composed in rhymed couplets (*dohā*).

Under the Summas, who succeeded the Sumrās, Sindhi poetry emerged particularized in the hands of individual poets like Qāḍī Qāḍan, whose diction has a fascinating lilt. In this period riddles were composed and some religious verse was written. Under the Arghūns, the Tarkhāns and the Mughals, from 1520 to 1719, there flourished the remarkable mystical poets Rājū Darwīsh (d. 1569), ʿAbd-al-Karīm Bulrī (d. 1622), who used linguistically interesting archaisms, and ʿUthmān Iḥsānī (*c.* 1640), whose *Waṭan Nāma* deals with the mystical themes of annihilation (*fanā*) and survival (*baqā*) in divine love. Technically the *dohā*, which used to be a rhymed couplet, became an independent genre in this period, comprising sometimes as many as six or seven verses.

Under the Kalhōras (1719–83) Sind became independent of the Mughal rule. This is the golden age of Sindhi literature. Poetry flourished both at the cultivated and the unlettered levels. *Dohās* were attuned to music; the narrative poem was used to revive the old folk-romances of Sind; and popular vocabulary found its way into poetry. In mystical verse Vedantic elements were fused with Ṣūfistic. The *kāfī* or *wā'ī*, a short mystical or devotional poem, meant to be sung, was developed, and some theological verse was composed. A well-known poet of the age, Shāh ʿInāyat (d. 1747), composed narratives of old love-stories of Sind and employed nineteen musical modes in his verse.

The most eminent figure in that age, as indeed in the whole corpus of Sindhi poetry, is that of Shāh ʿAbd-al-Laṭīf (1689–1752) of Bhit. His mysticism, steeped in the Islamic tradition, and slightly tinged with Shīʿism, is eclectic to the extent that the poetic content and the environment through which it operates has certain Hindu elements. Some of the folk-tales which are the vehicle of his mystical expression are of pre-Islamic Hindu origin. It is a mysticism based on, and expressed in, terms of human love. Love between the sexes sublimates itself into religious significance without any doctrinaire philosophical presumptions. 'The commonest image . . . is the struggle of the "path" or the "way" to the Beloved, the dangers of the journey and the affliction of pursuit.'[53] This is reinforced by the symbolism of the sand on the road, the dust on the way and the ruggedness of the mountains in the path of the lover. The poems have a dual artistic aim, literary as well as musical.

Literature of the age of Tālpūrs (1783–1843) saw the development of Sindhi poetry in the direction of the narrative of love and the martyrological epic. In this period Sindhi prose begins with Akhund ʿAzīz-Allāh (d. 1824). The *ghazal* was introduced into Sindhi by such poets as the famous pantheistic mystic Sachal Sarmast (d. 1826). Thābit ʿAlī Shāh (d. 1810) wrote martyrological poems under the patronage of Shīʿī Tālpūrs, and also developed the art of satire. Nabī Bakhsh Laghārī (*c.* 1834) composed a much-admired romance of love on the populer tale of *Sasuī Punhūn*.

Sindhi literature received a new lease of life under British rule. Sindhi replaced Persian as the language of subordinate offices. But strangely enough, perhaps due to the influence of Urdu, Sindhi poetry lost much of its indigenous character in theme and image, and remodelled itself on the classical conventions and the stock-in-trade imagery common to Persian and Urdu. The idiom became urbanized, and the best of the new poetry lost contact with the mass of the people. Aristocrats like Ḥusayn ʿAlī Khān (d. 1909) and Mīr ʿAbd-al-Ḥusayn Sāngī

(d. 1924) emerged as outstanding literary figures, composers of dynastic epic and elaborate *ghazal*. Rhymed and highly conventionalized prose was also developed on the model of classical Persian.

Sindhi drew closer to Urdu with the birth of Pakistan in 1947, as a large number of middle-class immigrants settled into the heartland of Sind at Karachi and Hyderabad. But there is an officially-encouraged movement for the preservation of Sindhi literature, its chief instrument being the Sind Adabī Board, which is working under the direction of Ḥusām-ad-dīn Rāshidī.

Kashmiri, the language of the people of Kashmir, has a literature of its own, influenced by Persian and later by Urdu. Kashmiri narrative verse is modelled on the Persian *mathnawī*, from which it has borrowed its subject-matter in such works as *Yūsuf Zulaykha* and *Layla Majnūn*. A remarkable work in Kashmiri narrative verse is the more indigenous *Hīmal*, written by Walī-Allāh Mattū interspersed with lyrics composed by Ẓarīf.

Kashmir was particularly susceptible to the mystic strain in Persian poetry. With Ṣūfistic subject-matter Kashmiri verse adopted much Persian imagery and poetic expression. Lāl Dēd (Lallā the poetess), writing in the fourteenth century, marks a fusion of Ṣūfism with Hindu mysticism in her exquisite lyrical verse. Shaykh Nūr-ad-dīn, a younger contemporary of Lāl Dēd, maintains a balance between the spiritual and the material in his mystical poetry.

A sixteenth-century poetess Ḥabba Khātūn, the rustic consort of Yūsuf Shāh Chak revived the lyrical tradition initiated by Lāl Dēd. She writes in the simple and spontaneous but genuinely poetic language of the people, and reflects the joys and sorrows of rustic life.

In the fifteenth century, under Sulṭān Zayn-al-ʿĀbidīn, *razmiyya* or epic narrative was developed in imitation of the Persian. Firdawsī's *Shāh Nāma* was rendered into Kashmiri verse, and an epic, *Banasura-vadha*, was composed. A narrative poem extolling the reign and achievements of Zayn-al-ʿĀbidīn *Zaynacarita* was also written. Much of the literature of this age however, has been lost.

There was a revival of Kashmiri poetry in the nineteenth

century in the work of Maḥmūd Gāmī, author of narrative poems and mystical romances, and Wahhāb Pārē, well known for his command of the historical narrative. His contemporary, Maqbūl Kralawarī, wrote realistic satires on contemporary life and manners. The nineteenth century was an age of extension and experiment in Kashmiri verse. An interesting genre in poetry was *roh*, a song to be accompanied by folk music. Rasūl Mīr developed the Kashmiri *ghazal*, which is sensuous in content and lyrical in cadence. In the *ghazal* the tradition of Rasūl Mīr was continued by Mahjūr (1885–1952).

Gujarati has some Islamic – especially Bohra – literature; but its literary personality is not Islamic. Marathi has borrowed a large number of Persian loan-words but it was not used for writing by Muslims. With the policy of the discouragement of Urdu in some states of the Republic of India it is possible that the Muslim diaspora in India may use regional languages for self-expression and an Islamic stream may develop in them.

NINE

FINE ARTS

1. Architecture

The opulent Hindu architecture of India bears the stamp of the forest, of luxuriant vegetation, thick with the imagery of multiplying processes and the mechanism of nature. It is so covered with decoration 'that its only purpose appears to be to set off the exuberant form in which life manifests itself',[1] it is a 'twofold symbol of mystery and splendour of the deity'.[2] On the other hand Islamic architecture before its arrival in India had adapted itself to the conditions of the desert, to an austerity and strength which Muslim monotheism encouraged. The contrast of the spiritual content of the two forms of architecture can best be studied in the construction of the Hindu temple and the Muslim mosque. 'Compared with the clarity of the mosque,' observes Percy Brown, 'the temple is an abode of mystery; the courts of the former are open to light and air, with many doorways inviting publicity, the latter encloses "a phantasma of massive darkness", having sombre passages leading to dim cells, jealously guarded and remote.'[3] The Muslim approach to architecture is formal, the Hindu rhythmical; Hindu architecture developed out of a code of hieratic and conventional rules and the Muslim out of an academic tradition.[4] In the matter of architectural construction the basic Hindu principle was trabeate, the basic Muslim principle arcuate.

When the Muslims brought their architectural concepts to India in the tenth and twelfth centuries, various styles of Muslim architecture had already fully developed elsewhere in the world of Islam, and the great mosques of Cairo, Baghdad, Cordova and Damascus had been built long before. The general principles of these Islamic schools were no doubt brought to India, though the construction itself, in the new environment and climate, adapted itself to indigenous technical processes. The Quwwat al-Islām mosque, for instance, is in the Arab tradition and reminiscent of the mosque architecture at Samarra, Cairo and Raqqa.

Indian building material and the skill of Indian masons in working stones, as well as the requirements of the sub-tropical climate modified to a considerable extent the architectural concepts imported from Dār al-Islām. The nature of Muslim architecture, especially its decorative element, was essentially industrial; this made the employment of the Hindu mercenary mason or architect easy. His labour and technique could be bought and adapted to the ideas of the Turco-Afghan architectural planners as far as possible. On the other hand, the nature of Hindu architecture, as of Hindu art in general, was essentially religious, and this made Muslim participation difficult.[5]

Some features of Persian architecture, for instance the glazed tile, could not stand the rigours of India's torrid monsoon zones. This, and other architectural refinements in vogue in Persia had to some extent to be discarded by the Indian masons, who regarded architecture as essentially a 'heavy industry' of quarrying and working stones.[6] But the Persian use of the vault and the dome was accepted and reproduced by Indian techniques from the very beginning of Muslim architecture in India. The dome became its distinctive feature in the Indian skyline. In ancient India because of temple architecture the skyline had been pyramidal, but after the Muslim conquest it became ovoid.[7]

It is difficult to concede the theory that the 'bulbous' dome was borrowed by Islamic Persia from the Buddhist stupa-dome.[8] The Buddhists, though they employed circular roofs and built topes with domical forms externally, did not attempt internal domes, at least in stone, though this was a technique not unknown to Hindu and Jain architecture within the subcontinent. Since the domical structure was the principal feature of Muslim architecture before its arrival in India it seized upon the skill of Hindus and Jains who could be employed to build it, and thus there came into existence a domical style, characteristic of the Muslim architecture in India, with the ever-recurring problem of a unity of composition which could strike a balance between the façade and the dome.[9]

The arch, copied from post-Roman examples by the Seljūqs,[10] borrowed the arch-niche probably from Buddhist models[11] and became a practical proposition in the Muslim architecture of India by the indigenous use of mortar as a cementing agent.[12] It was, however, a foreign construction, and the Indian mason who was used to trabeate processes applied in the beginning an indigenous method of reinforcing it with supporting beams.

With the advent of the Muslims, the topography of at least the Muslim quarters of the cities they occupied also changed. Hitherto the distinctive features of a Hindu city were the choice of its site and two wide streets running through the city at right angles. While preserving the broad features of Hindu town-planning the Muslims added to it spacious mosques, gateways, fountains in open spaces, domes, arches and town-walls.[13] In most cities Muslims and Hindus lived in separate localities of a town, a feature which has persisted to some extent up to modern times.

The Arab tradition of making the mosque a central focal area in a camp city was preserved in the architectural design for the mosque, introduced into the Indian plains by Quṭb-ad-dīn Aybak.[14] Rectangular panels in the spandrel of archways in this architecture, are a survival of the method of lighting which prevailed in the Arabian mosques.[15] The symbolic importance of the mosque can be felt by the name *Quwwat al-Islām* (the might of Islam) given to one of his mosques by Aybak. The architectural material for these early Muslim monuments of the twelfth and early thirteenth centuries were the carved stones of demolished temples, put together in a patchwork by Indian masons according to the direction of Muslim 'clerks of works'. From this ready-made 'raw material' not only were the images of Hindu mythology effaced, but Hindu floral decorations were replaced by Qur'ānic inscriptions or stylized 'arabesque' patterns.[16] The Quṭb Minār near Delhi and La Giralda in Seville were built about the same time, and in architectural spirit these two towers at the opposite ends of the Dār al-Islām in the twelfth century have more in common than Quṭb Minār and the earlier Indian obelisks or towers. On the other hand Hindu elements like fluted pillars with brackets,[17] used in such structures as the mausoleum built by Iletmish for his son, show that the pillage of 'raw material' in the hands of Hindu masons lent itself easily to the transfusion of some Indian features into the Muslim style of architecture.

Towards the end of the thirteenth and the beginning of the fourteenth century, during the influx of craftsmen fleeing from Mongol persecution, more features of extra-Indian styles of Muslim architecture were introduced into India. Thus, the Khaljī technique of laying stone masonry in two different courses was derived from the Seljūq treatment of the ancient Parthian – and Syrian – practice.[18] The Seljūq technique, visible to some extent in the 'Alā'ī Darwāza near Delhi, combined the Islamic decorative treatment with the post-Roman solid walling, pointed arches and vaulting. The severe simplicity of the Tughluq architecture was an expression of Muslim puritanism against the borrowings from exuberant Hindu architecture, and by 1321 when Ghiyāth-ad-dīn Tughluq founded Tughluqabad 'the Muslims worked themselves entirely free from Hindu influence'[19]; the 'true' arch found as early as 1287 in Balban's tomb had by now fully asserted itself as the key-note of Tughluq architectural strength,[20] along with enormously thick walls sloping inwards, and austere exterior decoration with bands and borders of white or occasionally black marble against large surfaces of sandstone. The austerity of this architecture was not derived from Persia, but the suggestion that it was of Meccan origin[21] is not improbable in view of Muḥammad ibn-Tughluq's relations with the Arab world and his hospitality towards foreigners from all Muslim lands. The octagonal tomb of Khān-i Jahān – Fīrūz Tughluq's famous chief minister – which replaced the former square style set a vogue that lasted for two centuries, and was probably copied from the Dome of the Rock at Jerusalem.[22]

Other Islamic, and specifically Persian, elements borrowed by Muslim architecture in India were glazed tile-work, brick and woodwork in the towns of Sind and southern Punjab where the semi-desert conditions and proximity to Persia encouraged their introduction at Multan, Uch and Tatta. The twelfth-century tomb of Shāh Yūsuf Gardīzī relies for its effect, like Persian monuments, on the brilliant colour scheme of encaustic tiles and on geometrical patterns. Glazed tile industry still flourishes in Multan. Wooden doors with projecting bosses and ornamental niches were in the tradition of the Muslim architecture of Western Asia.[23] Of Central Asian origin was the *rawḍa* or the walled garden with the architectural monument set in the middle of it, as well as the terraced garden, which was later developed in exquisite beauty by the Mughals. Pendentives in the 'Pathān' mosque-architecture of the early fifteenth century, filled with a number of small imitation arches, bracketing out one after the other, remind one of the honeycomb or stalactite vault of the Moorish architecture of Spain, even though the process of construction is different.[24]

Among the indigenous elements absorbed by the Muslim architecture of the Delhi Sultanate, in its various phases, was the Jain arrangement of pillars. The colonnaded courts of Jain temples, offered material for a ready-made mosque; in the process of construction, iconoclastically, the temple was removed from the centre of the building and a new wall added to the west, in the direction of the Kaʿba, adorned with *miḥrābs* (niches). The Muslim super-structure soon came to dominate the Hindu element architecturally: 'there is a largeness and a grandeur about the plain, simple outline of the Muhammedan arches which quite overshadows the smaller parts of the Hindu panes....'[25] Pierced stone screens or lattices were also borrowed from the Hindu tradition by Muslim architects who, unlike their Hindu predecessors, avoided the chiselled animal figure because of its iconic suggestiveness and concentrated on geometrical and stylized art-forms, and 'developed the art of designing and executing stone lattices to a degree of perfection unknown to other schools'.[26] In this process of transformation original Indian decorative motifs came to be synthesized with West Asian geometrical patterns, scroll-work and Byzantine acanthus. The most beautiful of the borrowings of Hindu origin were the lotus and the vase symbols, though it is debatable whether the 'lotus dome' in India was of Hindu origin, based on the pattern of the lotus dome at Ajanta.[27] As a decorative design the Indian lotus was used in the tomb of Iletmish and in Muslim edifices of some of the regional styles, such as the Golden Mosque at Gawr constructed about 1500. *Amrak* or *amalaka* or the ribbed front is a Hindu element, and so is possibly the metal pinnacle on the top of a dome, borrowed from the Hindu *kalasa*. In outline the Hindu elements influenced the essentially ovoid trends of Muslim architecture in the direction of the angular, the rectangular and the pyramidal to some extent. They also broke the austere monotony of vast surfaces by encouraging the filling up of the walls.

Mughal architecture, essentially Central Asian, seems to have made its first impact on India during the invasion of Tīmūr, who was creating a new and composite architectural style in Samarqand. The vogue for the bulbous dome and the glazed colour tile is probably due to Tīmūrid influence.[28] But the architecture of the 'Sayyids' and the Lodis was not Tīmūrid enough to satisfy Bābur, who complains of its 'Indian-ness'.[29] About the palace architecture of Gwalior his comment was that though singularly beautiful it gave the impression of patchwork and had no regular plan.[30] Culturally the most Turkish of all Muslim rulers of India, Bābur sought architectural inspiration from the Ottoman style, and sent for Yūsuf, a disciple of the celebrated Sinān.[31] In this way the Mughal architecture of India was able to form its first contours, though hardly any specimens of it have survived.

Persian architectural influences were brought back by Humāyūn, and they can be seen at their best in his tomb, built by a Persian architect Mīrak Ghiyāth. In this, one of the most 'Persian' of the Mughal edifices, the *kāshī*-work and the complex of arched alcoves and rooms, the arrangement of the four-corner cupolas, the narrow-necked dome, and the plan of the *rawḍa* are Persian and Central Asian importations, while the fanciful kiosks and the stone and marble tracery are Indian contributions, though familiar in Indian Islamic architecture since the time of Fīrūz Shāh Tughluq.[32] Humāyūn's tomb, built in the style of Shah Jahān, was the chief 'classical' inspiration for the breakaway from Akbar's architectural eclecticism, and served as a model for the tomb of 'Abd-ar-Raḥīm Khān-i Khānān and the Tāj Maḥall. With the style which Humāyūn's tomb established in India, the old conception of solidity and mass changes to lightness; symmetry is re-emphasized, the arched alcove reminds one of Moorish architecture in Spain, and a new tomb-construction is introduced.

Akbar's architectural eclecticism was in line with the stamp of Imperial heresy which left its mark on every field of creative activity in his reign. Like the Pharaoh Ikhnaton, whom he resembled in several ways, he strove to create a new style of architecture, but unlike the architecture at Tal al-Amarna this tended to be syncretistic rather than egocentric. It was essentially experimental, an attempt to form an imperial style which was to be the museum of all provincial styles. Actually this trend had its beginning before Akbar in some of the edifices of Shīr Shāh Sūrī. 'It all began in great sobriety and elegance and ended in something nearly approaching to wildness and exuberance of decoration, but still very beautiful.'[33] It consciously set itself to mix the two styles, the Hindu and the Muslim, the trabeate and the arcuate 'in almost equal proportions'.[34] The vast army of architects which was employed in Fat'ḥpur Sikri to create an extensive architectural image of Akbar's mind, was recruited from all over the Mughal empire, including Gujarat where a fused Hindu-Muslim architecture had already evolved.[35] Akbar's eclectic architecture used red sand-stone as its common material with insertions of white marble for emphasis. In principle the construction was trabeate and the arcading was generally decorative. It showed influences of the wooden architecture of the Punjab and Kashmir; its domes were hollow, never double; its pillar-shafts were multisided with capitals in the form of bracket-supports; its decoration was of carved and inlaid patterns using Indian motifs; and it used decorative painted design for its interior.[36] Akbar's palace-architecture, exemplified by the Jahāngīrī Maḥall in the Agra fort, combined features of both Muslim and Rājpūt palaces. The Red Palace at Agra fort, especially its court, is of purely Hindu style and 'would hardly be out of place at Chitore or Gwalior'.[37] The Panch Maḥall at Sikri and Akbar's tomb at Sikandra, the latter presumably planned by Akbar though completed by his son Jahāngīr, borrowed the structural design of the Buddhist *vihāra*[38]: the circumambulation path round the stupa. This style of tomb-planning was preserved in the tombs of Jahāngīr and Nūr Jahān at Lahore. On the other hand, purely Persian elements[39] also survived in isolation in Akbar's architecture, for instance, in the form of the magnificent gateway, Buland Darwāza, at Fat'ḥpur Sikri. Akbar's forts at Agra and Attock were also planned externally in the traditional Mughal style without much experiment or Hindu influence.

In architecture as in other fields of administrative, diplomatic and cultural activities, the reign of Shāh Jahān was the antithesis of that of his grandfather Akbar. The change was sudden, almost complete and unparalleled in the history of architecture.[40] Goetz dates the crystallization of Indian Mughal civilization at about 1623–7: 'It is based on the triad of white, red and green, with delicate touches of blue and gold: palaces, mosques and tombs of white marble on red sandstone substructures in green gardens.... But the white prevailed and endowed everything with that unreal, dreamy atmosphere, enhanced by the delicate incrustations of the buildings with costly stones....'[41]

The tomb of Iʿtimād-ad-dawla at Agra marks the sudden transition from the synthetic style of Akbar to the re-Persianized style of Shāh Jahān with its delicate use of marble garnished with gold and precious stones. The style which Shāh Jahān developed and encouraged was essentially Persian. Marble replaced sandstone, and with this change the Mughal architecture entered the era of its greatest glory. Because of the sensitiveness of Jodhpur marble the architectural tone was softened, delicacy and lightness were aimed at instead of massive outlines; decoration ceased to be plastic, and was obtained by means of inlaid patterns in coloured stones. This also implied changes in the architectural elements of the style; the glazed brick double domes and recessed arcades of the Persian style were adopted, though coloured tile was sparingly used. Pillars with tapering shaft-bracket capitals and foliated bases were also introduced. This style expressed itself in such masterpieces as the audience halls and palaces in Agra, Delhi and Lahore forts, in the Pearl Mosque at Agra and in the Tāj Maḥall. Though of Persian derivation it was distinct from the contemporary Ṣafavid style, because of its reluctance to use coloured tile (except in such conscious Persian imitations as Wazīr Khān's Mosque at Lahore) and because of its adoption and complete acclimatization of the Italian technique of *pietra dura* as the chief decorative process.[42] It developed open-work tracery to great perfection using purely Islamic motifs, such as geometrical patterns, floral designs and calligraphy, as well as the Persian cypress and the wine-jar. In its own right it became one of the richest architectural styles of the world, in which 'spacious grandeur of design is combined with feminine elegance'.[43] Much of this inlay-work, technically Western but artistically and thematically Islamic, was done in the case of the Tāj Maḥall by Hindu

13. *The Shālīmār garden, Lahore, built by the Emperor Shāh Jahān in 1647*

craftsmen from Qannuj, but most of the architects employed in designing and building this exquisite 'dream in marble', perhaps the most beautiful edifice ever built by man, were Muslim foreigners like 'Īsā Effendī and Ismā'īl Khān Rūmī who were Turkish, while the calligraphists who did the scroll-work came from Shiraz, Baghdad and Syria.[44]

While Shāh Jahān was building in marble, the western province of the Punjab was re-importing the Persian style of brick-masonry and mural decoration in such buildings as Chawburjī and Wazīr Khān's mosque. The Central Asian garden architecture had already reached its zenith in the Shālīmār Gardens at Delhi and Lahore and in the Shālīmār and Nishāt gardens near Srinagar.

The various provincial or regional styles developed by the Muslim successor-states to the Delhi Sultanate show acceptance or rejection of Hindu influences in varying degrees. Regional Muslim styles sometimes developed further the mutations of earlier regional Hindu schools of architecture[45] and sometimes adhered to the Islamic principles of construction imported from abroad.

In the early Muslim settlements of Bengal Muslim architecture had its beginning in the improvised re-assembling of the pieces of demolished Hindu temples; Hindu elements like short, thick pillars were incorporated, while the Bengali *miḥrāb* seems to have grown out of the canopied niche of the Buddhist stupa.[46] The style of Gawr developed locally, built on Hindu ruins, and had a massiveness not found in the Muslim architecture of India elsewhere.[47] Of distinctly Hindu origin are the chain and bell motifs and local tree patterns. Conversely the trabeate style was not suited to Bengal because of the dearth of stones with which to chisel pillars or beams. Relying on brick, the Bengalis developed a pointed arcuate style and invented a curvilinear form of roof in imitation of the thatched bamboo roof.[48]

Throughout, the architecture of Jawnpur shows an admixture of Hindu and Muslim styles; Hindu and Jain pillars were rearranged in Muslim styles; the pillared arrangement of the Atala Mosque, completed in 1408, follows the pattern of a Hindu temple, and its cells – though copied from Buddhist monasteries – open outwards, while its gateway is 'purely

14. *MS painting from the* Akbar Nāma, c. 1600. *Designed by Miskin and painted by Paras*

saracenic'.[49] Some other features of the Jawnpur style have Central Asian similarities, such as the use of fine geometrical patterns, and especially the prominence given to *maqṣūrā* (façade) vis-à-vis the dome.

Of all the regional Muslim styles the one nearest to the Hindu was that of Gujarat,[50] a strange fact in view of the zeal with which the convert-rulers administered their kingdom, its active trade and diplomatic relations with the Ṣafavids and the Ottomans, and the hospitality and chances of employment it offered to the stream of Muslim settlers from abroad. But its mosque architecture, follows the design of Hindu or Jain temples; the lower parts of the minarets of the mosque at Ahmadabad are of Hindu construction though slightly elongated; niches of Hindu temples seem to have been denuded of their images and filled with 'saracenic' tracery.[51] During the reign of Sultan Maḥmūd Begra (1459–1511) some of the Hindu features came to be replaced by those of the metropolitan Muslim architecture of Delhi, in such monuments as the tomb of Mubārak Sayyid at Mahmudabad; while the tomb and mosque of Sardār Khān, built under the Mughals in 1680, are distinctly Persian in style.[52]

The architecture of the Central Indian Muslim kingdom of Malwa, at its first capital Dhar, began, as in Gujarat, on the ruins of Hindu temples, using their material, decoration and pillared arrangements[53]; but unlike Gujarat, there began in Malwa a distinct and deliberate rejection of the Hindu tradition[54] in favour of the Muslim metropolitan style of the Tughluqs from which several features were borrowed, such as the bastion of the pointed arch with spearhead 'fringe' and the arch-lintel-bracket combination, while the 'boat-keel' dome and the pyramidal roof were taken over from the Lōdī style.[55] As the capital of Malwa shifted from Dhar to Mandu, Muslim elements of architecture became even more dominant; the Jāmiʿ Masjid at Mandu, unlike the one at Dhar, is in pure arcuate style 'without admixture of the trabeate structural methods followed by the native Hindus'.[56] The architecture of Malwa was adapted to the local background and landscape, but this did not inhibit the increasing trend to use colour-work in the Persian tradition, introduced presumably by artists from Multan.[57]

The types of Muslim architecture evolved in the Deccan

were a fusion of the styles of the Delhi Sultanate and influences freshly imported from Persia and probably Turkey, though more and more Hindu elements came to be absorbed in later stages. The massive Dravidian scheme and detail were however rejected throughout. In Bahmanid times the Persian style occasionally blended with the Indian Islamic as in the Jāmiʿ Masjid at Gulbarga, while it often managed to preserve its separate design and construction. The 'bulbous' or Tīmūrid dome became the vogue in Golconda; the fortress architecture of the Muslim Deccan has features akin to Syrian fortresses during the Crusades; the later Bahmanid palace-architecture at Bidar became a kind of 'provincialized' Persian, relying for its effect entirely on mural painting and coloured tile.[58] Maḥmūd Gāwān's school, constructed at Bidar in 1472, has all the particulars of north Persian or Transoxianan architecture, 'in short it might have been moved bodily from the Rijistan at Samarkand'.[59] The Barīd architecture (1487–1619) at Bidar reveals Turkish elements, and makes a return to the structural formation which provides scope for an imposing scheme of coloured tile-work.[60] To the Turco-Persian elements one may trace the 'largeness and grandeur' of the architecture of Bijapur, in which Turkish influences are clearly discernible.[61] Hindu elements seeped into the architecture of Bijapur with the passage of time, as in the elegantly ornamented gateway of Mihtarī Maḥall.[62]

In Sind and in the Punjab Muslim architecture borrowed more freely and retained with less inhibition outstanding Persian features like wood and brick work and the coloured tile. Some of the edifices at Multan, Uch and Tatta have more in common with the architectural glories of Tabriz and Isfahan than with Agra or Delhi or even Lahore.

2. Painting

In the fourteenth century, under the Tīmūrids, a revolution in painting took place in Central Asia; Chinese influences became interfused with Persian, and the art of painting reached the peak of perfection in the work of Bihzād at the court of Sulṭān Ḥusayn Bayqara at Herat. The Mughals came to India deeply steeped in this artistic tradition.[63] Humāyūn on his return from Persia brought with him Persian artists like Sayyid ʿAlī Tabrīzī and ʿAbd-aṣ-Ṣamad Shīrāzī, close followers of Bihzād.[64] The former had worked under Ṭahmāsp and had contributed to the formation of the Ṣafavid style of painting. With this background and these traditions these artists laid in India the foundations of Mughal painting.

Thus Mughal painting in India was a continuation and a transplantation of the integrated traditions of the Tīmūrid and the early Ṣafavid schools; it had no links with the past nor with the already lost Indian tradition of mural painting exemplified by Ajanta. Its palette was Persian. The colours it used were imported from Persia. Its landscape was purely Persian. The manuscripts chosen for illustration were Islamic romances like the *Khamsa* of Niẓāmī or the *dāstān* of Amīr Ḥamza. It developed the Tīmūrid technique of portraiture,[65] which exploited opportunities of colour harmonies and intricate combinations of lines.[66] Unlike the static human figure in medieval Indian art, the human form in Tīmūrid-Persian heritage was, within its limits, active.[67] The human image in Mughal, as in Persian, painting is round with a three-quarter profile; the same technique is used for drawing the contours of limbs and the eyes.[68] In manuscripts like *Bābur Nāma* every detail of Persian design, colouring and general treatment is preserved.[69] Chinese influences, which came through the Tīmūrid school, also survived in Mughal painting, and are sometimes clearly discernible.[70]

The early style of Akbar's court-painters, seen in works like the later paintings of *Amīr Ḥamza*, represents a 'patchwork' of contemporary calligraphic art; the predominant tendency was still to concentrate on the pattern.[71] The partial Indianization of Mughal painting which followed during his reign was due partly to his cultural eclecticism, partly to the representational necessity of reproducing the glory of his court in pictorial art as realistically as the framework of Persian style would permit, and partly to the employment of Hindu artists, whose iconographical talents could easily adapt themselves to a foreign technique of painting under the guidance and supervision of Persian masters. Hindu court-painters like Daswant received their training under ʿAbd-aṣ-Ṣamad and other Persians. Of the painters of Akbar's court mentioned by Abū-l-Faḍl, thirteen were Hindus and only four Muslims; and to Hindu painters Abū-l-Faḍl pays the compliment that 'their pictures surpass our conception of things. Few, indeed, in the whole world are found equal to them.'[72]

In the visual subject of the painting of Akbar's reign Indian man and Indian fauna and flora took their place with the human, animal and nature elements of Persian convention. The Indianization of human contours is especially noticeable in miniatures illustrating Hindu works like *Raẓm Nāma* (*Mahābhārata*).[73] Indian animals appeared along with the familiar animals of Persian painting, and the treatment of some animals, like horses, was naturalized.[74] The treatment of the horizon remained Persian. Persian flowers came to be partly Indianized, partly replaced by Indian flowers; the treatment of the leaves of a tree developed in a direction divergent from the Persian school. The architectural landscape remained largely Persian with its tents and tapestries, but became partly realistic.[75] It has been suggested that the later *Amīr Ḥamẓa* paintings show some influence of Indian murals[76]; conversely the wall-paintings of Akbar's palaces at Fat'ḥpur Sikri are enlarged versions of the Mughal miniature and not descendants of the Indian fresco or tempera such as at Ajanta or Bagh. With its Indianization, especially in the hands of Hindu artists, the Mughal school lost some of its original sensuous beauty in line and colour and its exquisite feeling for texture, but gained in intensity. The development of linear perspective ceased and the human character became the painter's focal point.[77] On the other hand the Persian technique survived in its purity in the works of Persian artists of the Mughal court like Farrukh Beg.[78]

One of the most extraordinary things in the history of art that happened about this time was the emergence of Rājpūt painting, its divergence from the Mughal school, and its rejection of the secular thematic basis of Mughal painting in favour of a revival of Hindu religious content and image. What the cultural eclecticism of Akbar led to, was not the merging and fusing of the Indian and Tīmūrid-Persian pictorial traditions, but their ultimate thematic separation despite their close technical proximity, and despite the unique fact that the very same Hindu artists could paint with equal perfection in both styles, Mughal and Rājpūt. 'Curiously enough,' remarks Goetz, 'it was not under Akbar that the Indian tradition became victorious. It penetrated in innumerable details, but the spirit of

Akbar's age, full of vitality and joy of life, loved the representation of battles, sieges, sports, hunts, all subjects needing a complicated composition which Persian painting, but not early Rājpūt, could provide.'[79]

The miniatures of *Razm Nāma* (*Mahābhārata*) can be regarded, though situated well within the Mughal school, as the milestone for the parting of the way by Rājpūt painting. Its Hindu artists, like Kānha, Jaswant and Tārā, seem to be steeped in an artistic consciousness which is essentially Hindu.[80] The soul of Hindu art, lost for centuries, suddenly seems to find itself on the threshold of a renaissance though in a technically foreign medium. As if by a semi-conscious cultural impulsion, its technique branched off from that of the Mughal school, and lent itself to a reconstruction of Hindu artistic imagination in order to serve, from its iconographic depths, the requirements of Hindu religious and mythographic subject-matter in the work it was illustrating. It is in this work that the essential characteristics of Hindu painting reasserted themselves in the drawing of animals and plants and in the use of indigo-blue as the colour of the skin of Hindu gods.

The split personality of the Hindu artist who was equally at home in the Mughal and Rājpūt styles is not as enigmatic or contradictory as it appears at first sight. The Persian tradition, transplanted into India by the Mughal school, had no individual style. The artist was in his technical essentials a craftsman, a decorator. Works of Mughal painters, though signed, are difficult to distinguish one from the other on the basis of individuality of style.[81] The greatness of the artist lay not in his individuality but in his perfection in a given technique. If the painter's approach were subjective he could, perhaps, have brought about a unity or fusion of Hindu and Muslim elements. Since it was objective and detached, the only unity he could give to both the schools in which he painted was one of certain technical forms. Because of the objectivity of his approach to his art, he was equally at home in two different styles, according to the needs, and the nature, of the commission assigned by his patron.

Yet in the case of the Hindu artist of the Mughal period who painted in both styles, there lay below the surface of technical objectivity an inner layer of deep religious feeling which sharply distinguished him from the Muslim artist for whom painting had no religious, in fact a barely tolerated anti-religious, significance. Whereas the Muslim artist was wholly concerned with transferring into the given scope of the art of painting the pageantry and history of the court, the Hindu artist could establish in his art the identity of his religion. Rājpūt painting is essentially a rejection by the Hindu artistic and religious mind of the Persian-based Mughal miniature-theme, while it harnesses the Mughal miniature technique for Hindu religious subject-matter. Akbar's mission of cultural eclecticism through art was thus subverted by inner religio-cultural tensions.

Rājpūt painting brought to pictorial art some of the characteristics of its own bardic and folk literature. As Binyon has observed, the Rājpūt painters 'seek to express the emotions of a race through line and colour in the same way that ballad-writers express them through rhythmical words, with the same reliance on traditional forms, the same love of cherished legends, and the same sort of limitations. It is an art that never becomes very complex, and always retains a strong affinity with dance and song.'[82] In its linear system of surface organization Rājpūt painting seems to go beyond the Mughal school, back to the compartmental sectioning of the Gujarati miniature, and a hypothesis has recently been advanced that its origins could be indigenous, going back through murals in Rājpūt palaces to a possible school of painting developed in Vijayanagar, from where its style might have travelled via Bijapur to Rajputana.[83] Its chief vehicle of expression is line, 'the *music* of the drawing'[84] symptomatic of the association of the arts of painting and music, both intimately connected with religious ritual in the Hindu mind.[85] This explains the growth and popularity of the *Rāgamālā* genre of Rājpūt painting, in which musical modes are externalized and symbolized in pictorial art. The treatment of the human form or the human group in Rājpūt painting is not the crystallization of an accident of appearance, but is much more self-conscious, concrete, rounded; at times it is as hieratic as the mural figure in ancient Egyptian art, set against a background of glowing colours.[86]

Because of the close association of the Rājpūt chiefs with the Mughal court, the Rājpūt style developed first in the seventeenth century in the courts of Jaipur, Jodhpur and Bikaner, and later in the eighteenth century in the Rājpūt marches of Kangra, Jammu and elsewhere.

In the court of Jahāngīr the Indian element inherited from Akbar was strong and was encouraged to develop in the Mughal painting, where it is visible in the emphasis on the profile, in the treatment of landscape like a theatre-stage; but its naturalism, its subdued colour-scheme and its rich but delicate decoration were 'the very opposite of the Rājpūt ideals'.[87] Because of Jahāngīr's realistic interest in nature, the conventional make-believe Persian landscape yielded to a naturalism[88] which was Indian in situation, but neither oriented towards, nor influenced by, the rising Rājpūt painting; it was in fact a naturalist re-composition of the earlier Mughal style, and in its representation of mountain landscape it retained the Persian semicircular design and even passed it on to the Rājpūt school.[89]

During the reigns of Jahāngīr and Shāh Jahān the subject-matter and technique of Mughal painting changed from manuscript illustration to court painting with the emperor as the main figure. Portraiture achieved perfection under Shāh Jahān. In portrait painting the main difference between the Mughal and the Rājpūt schools is that in the former faces are individualized; in the latter, under the influence of Hindu iconography, faces are not differentiated. The Mughal portrait also developed a unique technique of rich margin decoration.

The influx of Tīmūrid-Persian tradition continued under Jahāngīr, especially during the years of his close friendly relations with the Ṣafavid 'Abbās I. His envoy to Persia, Khān-i 'Ālam, brought back an album of the paintings of Khalīl Mirzā Shāhrukhī, reputed to be the teacher of Bihzād.[90] The Tīmūrid influence was reinforced by such artists as Āqā Riḍā of Herat whom Jahāngīr had employed while still a prince, and whose son Abū-l-Ḥasan remained his favourite court painter. The *siyāhī qalam* (portrait with black contour) was developed in Jahāngīr's court by the Central Asian painters Muḥammad Nādir Samarqandī and Muḥammad Murād.[91] Jahāngīr's love of animal life led Ustādh Manṣūr to specialize in animal painting, an art in which the Hindu painters of the court, like Govardhan and Manohar, also excelled. Another Hindu painter Bishandās, who was sent by Jahāngīr to paint the portrait of 'Abbās I,[92] must certainly have absorbed certain features of the contemporary Ṣafavid style. The purity of Persian tradition, combined with Jahāngīr's love of the painted figure of the animal can be seen in such manuscripts of his reign as the *Dīwān-i Ḥāfiẓ*.[93] On the whole, the Mughal palette under Jahāngīr and Shāh Jahān remained Persian and aimed at luminous colours, juxtaposition of vivacious tonalities and frequent use of gold.

In the reign of Awrangzīb the original Mughal tradition was discouraged, and it declined. Rājpūt elements crept into Mughal painting in the eighteenth century. Even in its decadent phase the Mughal school retained some of its former elements like composition, decoration and colour scheme, but lost its depth and space and its heroic vitality.[94] This process of decay is visible in the illustrated manuscript of Ghanīmat Kunjāhī's *Nayrang-i 'Ishq*.[95]

In the Mughal 'times of troubles' Hindu as well as Muslim artists sought patronage at the courts of petty regional rulers; this patronage was granted in the eighteenth century chiefly at the Rājpūt courts of Kangra, Jammu and other northern hill territories. Here and elsewhere from the ruins of Mughal painting was fed the renaissance of the Rājpūt. From these ruins there also rose Sikh painting in a different and not very elegant style. In the more Westernized cities like Calcutta whatever was left of the Mughal tradition sank into 'bazaar painting'.

In the twentieth century, under the inspiration of modern Western movements, Hindu and Muslim painting re-emerged; but while modern Hindu painting adapted Hindu iconography to modernist tendencies, the essentially Islamic style of Chaghtāi re-introduced the linear, decorative and spiritual heritage of Mughal and Ṣafavid painting in a soft, subdued slightly anaemic, but highly individualistic, revivalism.

3. Music

Music is perhaps the only art in which something like a synthesis between the Muslim and Hindu artistic traditions was achieved, though not without a series of tensions.

The Muslim orthodox attitude to music was the chief arena of conflict between the ulema and the Ṣūfīs under Iletmish and Ghiyāth-ad-dīn Tughluq. The Ṣūfī attitude was cautious in the beginning, but within limits it encouraged the Indian Muslim spiritual proclivity to music. Hujwīrī regarded listening to music permissible for mystics, but under very rigid conditions; it was not to be listened to without a deep spiritual urge, only after long intervals, and only in the presence of one's spiritual preceptor. Of the four Ṣūfī orders popular in India, the Chishtīs alone sought ecstatic inspiration in music. The Suhrawardīs were generally indifferent to it, and recommended instead the recitation of the Qur'ān; the Qādirīs were opposed to music generally, and to music with instruments (*samā' bi-l-mazāmīr*) in particular. The Naqshbandī attitude to music was even more hostile.

Khwāja Mu'īn-ad-dīn Chishtī, the founder of the Chishtī order in India and his successor Bakhtiyār Kākī, both listened to music as a spiritual stimulant.[96] In Delhi this Ṣūfī practice came to be firmly established during the reign of Iletmish, partly because of his devotion to Bakhtiyār Kākī, and partly because of the encouragement of this practice by the *qāḍis* of Delhi, Ḥamīd-ad-dīn Nāgorī, and the historian Minhāj-as-Sirāj Jūzjānī.[97]

In the assemblies of Niẓām-ad-dīn Awliyā *ghazals* of Amīr Khusraw were sung along with other pieces of music, and as some of them were recited again at the court of 'Alā'-ad-dīn Khaljī,[98] music tended to become an oblique cultural link between the Ṣūfī hospice and the court. According to Niẓām-ad-dīn, artistic composition, whether in prose or verse, gives spiritual pleasure, but more so in verse than in prose, and even more so if the verse is sung.[99] Music can be of three kinds; one that makes one laugh, the second that makes one weep, and the third that robs one of one's senses and consciousness.[100] What really counts is the spiritual depth of the Ṣūfī and not the accompaniment or otherwise of musical instruments.[101] Listening to music is permissible only in love of God; and though the verse sung may relate to temporal love, its interpretation and understanding by the Ṣūfī has to be in terms of love divine. The components of a musical assembly are the musicians, the music, the listener and the musical instruments; for music to be permissible the musicians should be adult men and not women or handsome youths, the verses set to music should not be profane or vulgar, the listener's heart should be full of the love of God, and the use of musical instruments should be avoided.

Music, in short, is meritorious if conducive to love of God but sinful if it arouses sensuous passions.[102]

In the wake of other political tensions Ghiyāth-ad-din Tughluq called a congress of 253 ulema to discuss the question of the permissibility of the use of music in terms of religious law. The Ḥanafī ulema Qāḍī Jalāl-ad-dīn and the Shaykh-zāda of Jām opposed music, but Niẓām-ad-dīn Awliyā, who appeared in the Congress as a defendant, based his argument in favour of music on a *ḥadīth*, the authenticity of which was disputed; however the rationalist ʿIlm-ad-dīn Multānī, who had returned from extensive travels in Dār al-Islam, gave evidence to the effect that musical assemblies were a common practice in Ṣūfī hospices all over the world, and Ghiyāth-ad dīn Tughluq decided to make an exception in the case of Ṣūfīs, but prohibited other sects like the *qalandars* or *Ḥaydarīs* from listening to it since in their case a quest for sensuous pleasure was suspected. In his last years Niẓām-ad-dīn himself moved much closer to the orthodox view and is recorded as remarking that whatever is prohibited in *sharʿ* cannot be permissible, but that on the question of music jurists are divided; the Shāfiʿites permit it with instruments but not the Ḥanafites. Therefore, whatever decision a sultan takes at a particular time has to be regarded as legal, though ecstatic dance cannot be allowed.[103]

The Chishtī tradition, however, continued to regard music as an indispensable aid to ecstasy. It relied on Persian verse as the verbal content of musical composition, but in some provinces it soon borrowed or adapted mixed Persian and Hindi wording. Thus, in the fifteenth century one finds Bahā'-ad-dīn Barnāwī composing Persian or hybrid musical tunes like the *khayāl* or *qawl* or the *tarāna* on the one hand, and on the other purely Indian tunes or musical forms like the *jakrī* or the *chutkula*.[104] In these borrowings the purely monistic or ethical tradition of Hindu musical verse was accepted, but Hindu religious and devotional music was exclusively rejected as polytheistic. About this time Gīsūdarāz favoured the composition of Indian melodies inspiring ecstasy 'according to the requirement of the art'[105] and went so far as to justify the ecstatic dance of the Ṣūfīs,[106] which was generally discouraged in Indian Ṣūfism.

The influence of Ibn-al-ʿArabī, which shaped the structural

and intellectual course of Indian Ṣūfism during the fourteenth and fifteenth centuries, was not too favourable to music, possibly because of the Christian ascetic trends which Ibn-al-ʿArabī had assimilated in his outlook. He preferred the recitation of the Qur'ān, and after that of mystical verses, but was opposed to the hearing of sensuous music, to musical instruments, ecstatic dance, applause or artificially inspired ecstasy.[107] In fact, in so far as the Ṣūfī practice of listening to music is concerned, it has been suggested that it was Indian Ṣūfism which accepted it eclectically, and then passed it on to other Muslim lands.[108] The Ṣūfī ecstatic dancing under the influence of music might have been originally a practice of Shamanist origin,[109] but unlike the practice of the Mevleviyya and other orders in Turkey it was generally disapproved of by the Indian Ṣūfīs. The tradition of ecstatic dancing attributed to the Suhrawardite Bahā'-ad-dīn Zakariyyā Multānī,[110] as well as later accounts crediting him with the invention of certain musical modes and tunes like the *multānī*,[111] may be regarded as apocryphal in view of the Suhrawardī discouragement of music.

The attitude of the Naqshbandī order to music, as exemplified by Shaykh Aḥmad Sirhindī, was distrustful. The ecstasy which other orders sought through music, the Naqshbandīs claimed to achieve permanently and personally without any sensuous stimulation. Music they considered to be a means of spiritual inspiration only for those outside their order whose ecstatic experience was unstable.[112]

Convivial parties in the courts of the weaker and more licentious Delhi Sultans were largely an independent growth, and seem to have begun with the patronage of Muʿizz-ad-dīn Kayqubād. The tradition continued in the court of Jalāl-ad-dīn Kahljī where Amīr Khusraw's *ghazals* were sung by beautiful girls like Futūḥa and Nuṣrat Khātūn.[113] Gopāl, a musician of the Deccan was employed in the court of ʿAlā'-ad-dīn Khaljī,[114] where the spiritual side of musical taste was to some extent moulded on the Ṣūfī standards. Amīr Khusraw was the link between the hospice and the court, and his compositions were equally popular in both milieus.

Khusraw had a thorough knowledge of the technicalities of Persian music, and uses musical terms in his works.[115] His knowledge of Indian music is also reflected in his use of its terminology. It is likely that he tried to weld the two musical systems, but in the absence of sufficient reliable evidence it is difficult to determine his exact contribution.[116]

In determining Amīr Khusraw's contribution to the synthesis and development of Indo-Muslim music in India, one has to fall back on much later tradition. He is credited with having invented a number of new melodies such as *muḥayyar*, *ayman*, *'ushshāq*, *muwāfiq*, *zilāf*, *farghāna*, *sarparda*, *firūdast* and *khayal*.[117] It can be safely assumed that at least the musical *ghazal* and the *qawl* (sung in Ṣūfī assemblies) were first introduced by Khusraw.[118] Tradition credits Amīr Khusraw with the invention of the *sitār*, originally a three-stringed instrument, but Waḥīd Mirzā, in his scholarly study of Khusraw, confesses that he was unable to trace any reference to it in his writings, or the writings of his contemporaries and immediate successors,[119] and suggests that the *sitār* may have evolved in Caucasia and not in India; one cannot rule out the possibility that the names of the European musical instruments 'guitar' and 'zither' are cognates of *sitār*. The contemporary musicians mentioned by Khusraw were almost all Muslims, and most of the musical instruments mentioned have Persian names.[120]

The court patronage of music at a refined and cultured level continued under Muḥammad ibn-Tughluq.[121] In the reign of the puritan Fīrūz Tughluq, the patronage of one of his noblemen Ibrāhīm Ḥasan Abūrija inspired, in 1375, *Ghunyat al-munya*, a Persian treatise describing Indian musical instruments, Indian dancing and the code of conduct to be observed in the musical assemblies by the musical profession.[122]

More Central Asian elements such as the *nawbat* were introduced into India during the invasion of Tīmūr.[123] A collection of Indian melodies was compiled during the reign of Sikandar Lōdī and named after him. Participation in the growth of Indo-Muslim music was even more pronounced in the case of regional Muslim rulers during the fifteenth and sixteenth centuries. Sultan Ḥusayn Sharqī of Jawnpur is credited with having invented seventeen Indian *rāgs* (musical tunes) of which twelve were *shyām*, four *todī* and one *asāwari*,[124] genres which are almost purely Indian with very little of the Persian tradition. Another regional Muslim ruler, Muẓaffar II (1511–26) of Gujarat was also a composer of such purely Indian musical varities as *suramba*, *dhyā*, *chhand* and *dohra*.[125] Bakshawa, a musician at the court of Bahadur Shāh of Gujarat (1526–37), is credited with the authorship of a very large number of Indian *dhurpad* melodies.

The Alfī movement in its Mahdawi phase was opposed to music,[126] but it does not seem to have imposed any effective check on Muslim participation in Indian music, and that reached its peak of intensity under the patronage of Akbar. At this stage Indo-Muslim music became syncretistic as well as synthetic. The most renowned musician of Akbar's age, Tān Sen, was a Gaur Brahmin reputedly converted to Islam, and the disciple not only of the eclectic Shaṭṭārī saint Shaykh Muḥammad Ghawth of Gwalior but also of the Hindu poet Harīdās, and a friend of another famous Hindu poet Sūrdās.[127] Subḥān Khān, one of the musicians of Akbar's court is reported to have sung devotional songs (*qawwālīs*) at the tomb of the Prophet in Medina.[128]

In 1666 – commissioned by Rājā Mān Singh – Faqīr-Allāh compiled his famous *Rāg Durpan*, partly a translation from Sanskrit, and one of the most authoritative works on Indian music in Persian. It deals with various Indian melodies –suiting each to the season or the hour of the day or night – and the principles of the composition of tunes. Among his contemporary musicians Faqīr-Allāh mentions fifty, the majority of whom were Muslims,[129] as were the majority of famous musicians attached to the court of Jahāngīr.[130] The patronage of music and dancing continued in the court of Shāh Jahān,[131] and Mirzā Rawshan Ḍamīr translated *Pārijātaka*, a famous Sanskrit work on music into Persian.[132] Though Awrangzīb excluded musicians from his court,[133] scholarly work on music continued during his reign, and a treatise on music *Shams al-aṣwāt* was compiled in 1698.[134]

In the Deccan Ibrāhīm 'Ādil Shāh was a great patron of music as well as a gifted musician and the author of a collection of melodies (*Nawras*),[135] some of which relate to Hindu mythology, others in praise of Gīsūdarāz, and yet others are personal or love-songs. His knowledge of the technicalities of music was not perfect; but his work was translated into Persian by his order. The melodies are Indian, though Persian vocabulary is freely employed in the songs. Ibrāhīm 'Ādil Shāh II is also reported to have founded a special locality, Nawraspur, for the musicians in his capital. In the Deccan the tradition of the patronage of music survived into the age of Tīpū Sulṭān under whom, in 1785, Ḥasan ʿAlī ʿIzzat compiled his *Mufarriḥ al-qulūb*, an interpretative work on music which deals with Indian and Persian musical instruments, and is interspersed with Persian and Urdu (*rīkhta*) verses.[136] Poetry and music were sometimes mixed in the *rīkhta*, which were composed during the eighteenth century especially to be sung.[137] Similarly, Persian verses were set to music along with the Hindi *dohrās*, and sung together. In Bengali a similar process is seen at work in the *Rāga Mālā* which describes various modes of Indian music, mentioning the presiding Hindu deity of each and often illustrating its theme from the poems of the Muslim poet ʿAlā'ul.[138] Similarly the Bengali *Tāla Nama* (1840) contains works of Hindu as well as Muslim composers.

Studying the growth of music, in which the Hindu and Muslim cultures came closer together than in any other art, one is nevertheless faced with the situation in which the Muslim elements are submerged by the Hindu. The process of interfusion of Indian *rāgs* and Persian *maqāmāt*, begun in Khusraw's day, came to be regarded by Wājid ʿAlī Shāh of Oudh, a great connoisseur and patron of music in the mid-nineteenth century, as hybridization.[139] Gradually, however, the classical tradition of Hindu music gained the final ascendancy. It is reflected in *rahas*, a musical novelty invented by Wājid ʿAlī Shāh.

ABBREVIATIONS

Annali = *Annali d'Istituto orientale di Napoli*
ASB = *Asiatic Society of Bengal*
Bibl. Ind. = Bibliotheca Indica
BG = *Bombay Gazetteer*
BSOAS = *Bulletin of the School of Oriental and African Studies*
EI = *Encyclopaedia of Islam*
ERE = *Encyclopaedia of Religion and Ethics*
IC = *Islamic Culture*
ICIE = Aziz Ahmad, *Studies in Islamic Culture in the Indian Environment*
IMIP = Aziz Ahmad, *Islamic Modernism in India and Pakistan*
JAOS = *Journal of the American Oriental Society*
JASB = *Journal and proceedings of the Asiatic Society of Bengal*
JBBRAS = *Journal of the Royal Asiatic Society, Bombay Branch*
JPHS = *Journal of the Pakistan Historical Society*
JRAS = *Journal of the Royal Asiatic Society*
MIQ = *Medieval India Quarterly*
MW = *Muslim World*
REI = *Revue des études islamiques*
RMM = *Revue du monde musulman*
SI = *Studia Islamica*
ZDMG = *Zeitschrift der Deutschen Morgenländischen Gesellschaft*

Short references: Where a single work by one author is cited, the author's name is used as the short reference in the notes. Consult bibliography for details.

NOTES

Chapter One

1. Abū-l-Qāsim Firishta, *Gulshan-i Ibrāhīmī* (Eng. tr. Briggs), i. 113-14.
2. Minhāj-as-Sirāj al-Jūzjānī, *Ṭabaqāt-i Nāṣirī*, Kabul, 1964, i. 461.
3. Amīr Khurd, *Siyar al-awliyā'*, Delhi, 1884, 529-32; 'Abd-al-Ḥayy, *Nuz'hat al-khawāṭir* (Urdu tr.), Lahore, 1965, ii. 167-9.
4. Firishta (Briggs), i. 402.
5. Shihāb-ad-dīn Abū-l-'Abbās Aḥmad, *Masālik al-abṣār*, Eng. tr. in Elliot, iii. 580.
6. *Nuz'hat al-khawāṭir*, ii. 180.
7. 'Abd-al-Bāqī Nihāwandī, *Ma'āthir-i Raḥīmī*, MS in *ASB*, f. 21.
8. Firishta (Briggs), i. 562.
9. 'Abd-al-Ḥaqq Dihlawī, *al-Makātīb wa-r-rasā'il*, Delhi, 1879, 127-8 and *passim*.
10. *Fatāwī-'Ālamgīrī*, Urdu tr. Lucknow 1889, ii. 370-829.
11. See *infra*, pp. 10-11.
12. Aḥmad 'Alī Batālawī, *Nuṣrat al-mujtahidīn*, Lucknow, 1895.
13. Asad-Allāh Tilharī, *Quwwat-i Ḥanafiyya*, Badā'ūn, 1905.
14. For a survey of theological writing written in India see Raḥmān 'Alī, *Tadhkira-i 'ulamā-i Hind*, Lucknow, 1914; M. H. Zubayd Ahmad, *Contribution of India to Arabic Literature*, thesis for the degree of Ph.D. in the University of London; Carl Brockelmann, *Geschichte der arabischen Literatur*, Weimar and Leiden, 1898–1949, ii. 219-22, 415-22, 503-4.
15. Raḥmān 'Alī, 3.
16. Ibid., 23, 179.
17. Baranī, 46.
18. Ibid., 345-6.
19. Muḥammad ibn-Tughluq, Fragment of his memoir in BM Add. MS 25, 785, ff. 316b-317a; Baranī, 464-5; Khwāja Muḥammad al-Ḥusaynī 'Gīsūdarāz', *Jawāmi' al-kalim*, BM Or. 252, ff. 141a-b.

20. ʿAbd-Allāh, *Tarīkh-i Dā'ūdī*, BM Or. 197, ff. 22b-23a; Raḥmān ʿAlī, 101.
21. S. M. Ikram, *Āb-i Kawthar*, Lahore, 1952, 64-5.
22. Zubaid Ahmad, 185.
23. Baranī, 94; Amīr Khusraw, *Maṭlaʿ al-anwār*, Lucknow, 1884, 55-60, 69.
24. Waṣṣāf (Bombay, 1877), 310-11.
25. Ibn Baṭṭūṭa (Cairo, 1870–1), ii. 54.
26. L. Massignon, *Essai sur les Origines du Lexique Technique de la Mystique musulmane*, Paris, 1922, 67.
27. Badā'ūnī, ii. 255; Shaykh Aḥmad Sirhindī, *Maktūbāt*, Lucknow, 1877, i. 47; Akbar's letter to ʿAbd-Allāh Khān Uzbek in Abū-l-Faḍl ʿAllāmī, *Maktūbāt*, Lucknow, 1863, 21.
28. ʿAbd-al-Ḥaqq Dihlawī, *Zād al-Muttaqīn*, BM Or. 217, ff. 10b-41b, 48a-134b.
29. Abū-l-Kalām Āzād, *Tadhkira*, Lahore, n.d. 30-2.
30. Khaliq Ahmad Nizami, *ʿAbd-al-Ḥaqq Muḥaddith Dihlawī*, Delhi, 1953, 242-4, 297-302, 345-77.
31. ʿAbd-al-Ḥaqq Dihlawī, *Ashʿat al-lumʿāt*, Lucknow, n.d.
32. ʿAbd-al-Ḥaqq Dihlawī, *Takmīl al-Imān*, IO Pers. MS 2756, ff. 2a-3b, 9b; *idem*, *Fat'ḥ al-mubīn*, MS (Kalām 76) in Āṣafiyyah Library, Hyderabad, Deccan; *idem*, *Marj al-baḥrayn*, Calcutta, 1831.
33. Hājī Khalīfa, *Kashf aẓ-ẓunūn* (Leipzig), iv. 225, vi. 241, vii. 798, 914.
34. *Nuẓ'hat al-khawāṭir* (Urdu tr.), ii. 140-4.
35. Shāh Wālī-Allāh, *Tuḥfat al-muwwaḥidīn*, Delhi, 1894, 6-29.
36. Wālī-Allāh, *Ḥujjat-Allāh al-bāligha*, Karachi, 1953, i. 4.
37. Ibid., i. 284.
38. Wālī-Allāh, *ʿIqd al-jīd*, Eng. tr. D. Rahbar, *MW*, 155, 347-58.
39. Wālī-Allāh, *Iẓāla al-khafā*, Karachi, n.d. For a general introduction to Walī-Allāh's views see A. Bausani, 'Note su Shah Walīullāh di Delhi' in *Annali*, n.s. x (1961), 99.
40. Abū-l-Ḥasanāt Nadwī, *Hindūstān kī qadīm Islāmī darsgāhen*, Azamgarh, 1936, 97.
41. Shāh ʿAbd-al-ʿAzīz, *Malfūẓāt*, Meerut, n.d., *passim*.
42, Shāh ʿAbd-al-ʿAzīz, *Fatāwā*, Delhi, 1904, 16-17.
43. For Sayyid Aḥmad Barelwī and the movement of his *mujāhidīn* see Ghulām Rasūl Mihr, *Sayyid Aḥmad Shahīd*, Lahore, 1952; *idem*, *Jamāʿat-i Mujāhidīn*, Lahore, 1955, and *Sarguẓasht-i Mujāhidīn*, Lahore, 1956. In English see W. W. Hunter, *The Indian Musalmans*, London, 1871; Aziz Ahmad,

Studies in Islamic Culture in the Indian Environment (*ICIE*), Oxford, 1964, 209-17; I. H. Qureshi, *The Muslim Community of the Indo-Pakistan Sub-Continent*, 's-Gravenhage, 1962, 193-211.

44. M. Nurul Karim, 'Part played by Ḥaji Sharīʿat-Allāh and his son in the socio-political history of East Bengal', *Proceedings of the Pakistan History Conference*, Karachi, 1955, 175-82; Abdul Bari, 'The Farā'iḍī Movement', ibid., 197-208; M. D. Ahmad Khan, *History of the Farā'iḍī Movement in Bengal*, 1818–1906, Karachi, 1965.
45. Fakhr-ad-dīn Aḥmad, *Iẓālat ash-shukūk*, Allahabad, 1880, 66-74.
46. Ibrāhīm Mīr Siyālkotī, *Tārīkh-i Ahl-ḥadīth*, Lahore, 1953; *EI*², i. 256-60; Aziz Ahmad, *Islamic Modernism in India and Pakistan* (*IMIP*), London 1967, 113-22: Raḥmān ʿAlī, 94-5.
47. From Mawdūdī see Aziz Ahmad, *IMIP*, 208-23; some of Mawdūdī's writings are available in English, including his *Towards Understanding Islam*, Lahore, 1960, and *Islamic Law and Constitution*, Lahore, 1960. Outstanding among his voluminous works in Urdu are his Commentary on the Qur'ān; his *Taʿlīmāt*, Lahore, 1955; *Daʿwat-i Islāmī*, Rampūr, 1956; and *Islāmī tahdhīb awr uskē uṣūl-u mubādī*, Lahore, 1960.
48. Mawdūdī, *Towards Understanding Islam*, 3.
49. Ibid., 152-3.
50. Mawdūdī, *Islamic Law and Constitution*, 147-60.
51. Maḥbūb Riḍwī, *Tārīkh-i Deoband*, Deoband, 1952; Ḥusayn Aḥmad Madanī, *Naqsh-i Ḥayāt*, Delhi, 1953. Aziz Ahmad, *IMIP*, 103-13.
52. J. N. Farquhar, *Modern Religious Movements in India*, London, 1924, 350.
53. M. Mujeeb, *The Indian Muslims*, London, 1967, 413-14.
54. Aziz Ahmad, *IMIP*.
55. Sayyid Ahmad Khān, *Tafsīr al-Qur'ān*, Lahore, 1880–95.
56. Sayyid Ahmad Khān, *al-Taḥrīr fī uṣūl at-tafsīr*, 1892, 32-6.
57. Sayyid Ahmad Khān, *Ākhirī Maḍāmīn*, 128-34; *idem*, *Khutbāt-i Aḥmadiyya*, Agra, 1870, 334-5; Chirāgh ʿAlī, *Rasā'il*, Hyderabad, 1918–19, 99.
58. Muḥammad Qāsim Nānotawī in *Taṣfiyyat al-ʿaqā'id*, Delhi, 1901; Ashraf ʿAli Thānawī, *Al-intibāqāt al-mufīda ʿan al-ishtibāhāt al-jadīda*, Lahore, 1952, 33-59, 98-104.
59. Iqbāl, *Reconstruction of Religious Thought in Islam*, Lahore, 1944, 145-6, 164-5.

60. For religious trends in Pakistan see L. Binder, *Religion and Politics in Pakistan*, Berkeley, 1961; Wilfred Cantwell Smith, *Pakistan as an Islamic State*, Lahore, 1951; E. I. J. Rosenthal, *Islam in the Modern National State*, Cambridge, 1965, 125-53, 181-281; Aziz Ahmad, *IMIP*, 237-53.
61. For religious trends in India see Abid Husayn, *Destiny of Indian Muslims*, Bombay, 1965; Aziz Ahmad, *IMIP*, 254-9; Wilfred Cantwell Smith, *Islam in Modern History*, Princeton, 1955.
62. Abid Husayn, 143-4.
63. Ibid., 134.

Chapter Two

1. *Census of India Report*, 1921, i. pt. i. 119; Murray Titus, *Islam in India and Pakistan*, Calcutta, 1959, 238.
2. Fīrūz Tughluq, *Futūḥāt-i Fīrūzshāhī*, Aligarh, 1954, 6-7.
3. G. Yazdānī, 'The Great Mosque of Gulbarga', *IC*, ii (1928), 19; J. N. Hollister, *The Shīʿa of India*, London, 1953, 106-7.
4. Hollister, 109.
5. Ibid., 113-15.
6. Bakhtāwar Khān, *Mir'at al-ʿālam*, BM Add. MS 7657, f. 454b; Mirzā Muḥammad Hadī, *Shahīd-i thālith*, Lucknow, n.d., 15 *et seq.*
7. Nūr-Allāh Shustarī, *Majālis al-mu'minīn*, Tehran, 1852, *passim*.
8. Walī-Allāh, *Izāla al-khafā*, Urdu tr. Karachi, n.d.; ʿAbd-al-ʿAzīz, *Tuḥfa-i Ithnāʿashariyya*, Urdu tr. Karachi, n.d.
9. Hollister, 151.
10. Raḥmān ʿAlī, *Tadhkira-i ʿulamā-i Hind*, 36-7.
11. For a study of the advent of Ismāʿīlīs in India see S. M. Stern, 'Ismāʿīlī propaganda and Fatimid rule in Sind', *IC*, xxiii (1949), 298-307; A. A. A. Fyzee (ed.), *A Shiite Creed*, Bombay, 1942; W. Ivanow, *Guide to Ismaʿili Literature*, London, 1933.
12. Sayyid Sulayman Nadwī, 'Muslim colonies in India', *IC*, i (1927), 221; Hollister, 267, 343; Elliot and Dowson, i. 459, 491; H. F. Hamdani, 'The letters of Mustanṣir billāh', *BSOAS*, vii (1933–5), 308-12; Ivanow, *Brief Survey of the Evolution of Ismāʿīlism*, Bombay, 1952, 20.
13. C. E. Bosworth, 'Ghūrids' in *EI*², ii. 1099-1104.
14. Jūzjānī, i. 461-2; ʿIṣāmī (*Futūḥ as-salāṭīn*, Madras, 1948, 122) erroneously places the rising under Iletmish.

15. D. Menant, 'Les Khodjas de Guzarate', *RMM*, xii (1910), 214-32, 406-24, at p. 224 *et seq.*
16. Amīr Ḥasan Sijzī, *Fawā'id al-fu'ād*, Delhi, 1865, 199.
17. S. T. Lokhandwalla, 'The Bohoras, a Muslim Community of Gujarat', *SI*, iii (1955), 117-35.
18. Ibid.; also Hollister, 246-305.
19. *Bombay Law Reporter*, xxiv (1923), 1070.
20. Lokhandwalla, 127-9.
21. Najm-al-Ghanī Khān, *Madhāhib al-Islām*, Lucknow, 1924, 292.
22. Hollister, 279.
23. Lokhandwalla, 131; Titus, 105.
24. Menant, op. cit. (n. 15); Hollister, 306-412.
25. F. L. Faridi in the *Bombay Gazetteer*, 38; Hollister, 352.
26. Hamid Ali, 'The customary and statutory laws of the Muslims in India', *IC*, ii (1937), 354-69, 444-54, at p. 358; Yusuf Husain, *L'Inde Mystique au Moyen Age*, Paris, 1929, 34.
27. Hollister, 395.
28. Ibid., 353-4.
29. W. Ivanow, 'The Sect of Imām Shāh in Gujarat', *JRAS*, Bombay Branch, xii (1936), 20-45.
30. Najm-al-Ghanī Khān, 333, 350-1.
31. Lokhandwalla, *SI*, iii. 118.
32. H. A. Walter, 'Islam in Kashmir', *MW*, iv (1914), 348; *Cambridge History of India*, iii. 286.
33. H. T. Colebrook, 'On the Origin and Peculiar Tenets of certain Muhammadan sects', *Asiatic Researches*, vii (1801), 339-40.
34. Hollister, 363.

Chapter Three

1. Fīrūz Tughluq, 7.
2. H. Blochmann, Intro. to 'Allāmī, *Ā'īn-i Akbarī*, Calcutta, 1927, i, p. xli.
3. 'Abd-al-Ḥaqq, *Zād al-Muttaqīn*, f. 304; Najm-al-Ghanī Khān, 706.
4. Badā'ūnī, i. 319.
5. S. A. A. Rizvi, 'Mahdawi Movement in India', *MIQ*, 1/i (1950), 14-15.
6. Bandagī Muḥammad 'Abd-ar-Rashīd, *Naqliyyāt*, *passim*; S. A. A. Rizvi, *Muslim Revivalist Movements in Northern India*, Agra, 1965, 100-3.
7. Najm-al-Ghanī Khān, 711-13.

8. Rizvi, op. cit. (n. 6), 101, 106-34.
9. Titus, 113-14.
10. For details see Makhanlal Roychoudhuri, *The Dīn-i Ilāhī*, Calcutta, 1941; Aziz Ahmad, 'Dīn-i Ilāhī' in *EI*², ii. 296-7.
11. For details see M. Shafi, 'Bāyazīd Anṣarī' in *EI*², i. 1121-4; J. Leyden, 'On the Roshenian sect and its Founder Bāyazīd Ansārī', *Asiatic Researches*, xi. 363 *et seq.*
12. Najm-al-Ghanī Khān, 578-80.
13. For the Aḥmadī creed see Mirzā Ghulām Aḥmad, *The Philosophy of the Teachings of Islam*, Rabwah, 1959; Mirzā Bashīr al-din Maḥmūd Aḥmad, *Introduction* to Sher Ali's Eng. tr. of *The Holy Qur'ān*, Rabwah, 1955; *idem*, *Invitation to Aḥmadiyyat*, Rabwah, 1961; *idem*, *Aḥmadiyyat or True Islam*, Washington, 1951. For a general survey of Aḥmadism, Humphrey J. Fisher, *Aḥmadiyyah*, London, 1963, 35-88; Kenneth Cragg, *Counsels in Contemporary Islam*, Edinburgh, 1965, 155-66.
14. J. N. Farquhar, *Modern Religious Movements in India*, London, 1924.
15. Qur'ān 33 : 40.
16. Fisher, 40.
17. Muḥammad Iqbāl, *Islam and Ahmadism*, Lahore, 1936, 18.
18. For the creed of the Lahori Group see Muhammad ʿAlī, *The Aḥmadiyya Doctrines*, Lahore, 1932; *idem*, *The Founder of the Aḥmadiyya Movement*, Lahore, n.d.

Chapter Four

1. Abū-Naṣr as-Sarrāj, *Kitāb al-lumaʿ fī t-taṣawwuf*, ed. R. A. Nicholson, Leiden, 1963, 177, 325, 337; H. Ritter, 'Abū Yazīd al-Bisṭāmī' in *EI*², i. 162; L. Massignon, *Essai sur les origines du lexique technique de la mystique musulmane*, Paris, 1922, 243; A. J. Arberry, *Revelation and Reason in Islam*, London, 1957, 90; R. C. Zaehner, *Hindu and Muslim Mysticism*, London, 1960, 94-5.
2. Tr. into English by R. A. Nicholson, London, 1959.
3. For instance in Ghulām Sarwar, *Khazīnat al-aṣfiya*, Cawnpore, 1902, i. 289.
4. Al-Hujwīrī (Nicholson), 213-14; ʿIṣāmī, *Futūḥ as-salāṭīn*, Madras, 1943, 455-7; Amīr Ḥasan Sijzī, *Fawā'id al-fu'ād*, Delhi, 1865, 133, 137-8.
5. Sarwar, i. 268.
6. Quoted in Amīr Khurd, *Siyar al-awliyā'*, Delhi, 1885, 130-1.
7. Aziz Ahmad, 'The Sufi and the Sultan in Pre-Mughal Muslim India', *Der Isalm*, 38 (1962), 142-53.

8. Sijzī, 40-1; Amīr Khurd, 560-1; K. A. Nizami, *Some Aspects of Religion and Politics in India during the 13th century*, Aligarh, 1961, 257.
9. Sijzī, 205; Amīr Khurd, 363; Ḥamīd Qalandar, *Khayr al-majālis*, ed. K. A. Nizami, Aligarh, 1960, 277.
10. Sarwar, i. 254.
11. Nizami, *Religion and Politics*, 175; *idem*, 'Some aspects of Khanqāh life in Medieval India', *SI*, viii (1957), 51-70.
12. 'Izz-ad-dīn Kāshānī, *Miṣbāḥ al-hidāya*, Lucknow, 1904, 118-21.
13. Ḥamīd Qalandar, 105-6; Nizami, *Religion and Politics*, 212-13.
14. Amīr Khurd, 323; Sijzī, 161.
15. Amīr Khurd, 121-2; Ḥamīd Qalandar, 287.
16. Amīr Khurd, 116-17, 229-31.
17. For details see K. A. Nizami, *Ta'rīkh-i Mashā'ikh-i Chisht*, Delhi, 1953; *idem*, 'Čishtiyya' in *EI*², ii. 50-6.
18. Sarwar, 222.
19. Amīr Khurd, 39-40; K. A. Nizami, 'Čishti' in *EI*², ii. 49-50.
20. Sijzī, 70; cf. Nizami, *Religion and Politics*, 186.
21. For details see K. A. Nizami, *The Life and Times of Shaikh Farid-u'd-din Ganj-i shakar*, Aligarh, 1955.
22. Ḍiyā'-ad-dīn Baranī, *Ta'rīkh-i Fīrūz Shāhī*, Calcutta, 1862, i. 343-4.
23. Sarwar, i. 330.
24. K. A. Nizami, *Salaṭīn-i Dihlī kē madhhabī rujḥānāt*, Delhi, 1966.
25. Sarwar, i. 337.
26. M. Shafi, 'Čiragh-i Dihlī' in *EI*², ii. 47-9.
27. Amīr Khurd, 237; Sarwar, i. 353.
28. Amīr Khurd, 228, 271-2; Sarwar, i. 355, 359-60; Muhammad Habib, 'Shaikh Nasīruddin Maḥmūd Chirāgh-i Dehlī as a great historical personality', *IC*, xx (1946), 129-53.
29. Sijzī, 161; Amīr Khurd, 59, 295.
30. Amīr Khurd, 48, 62-3.
31. For details see K. A. Nizami, *The Suhrawardī Silsilah and its influence on Medieval Indian Politics*, n.d.
32. ʿAbd-al-Ḥaqq Dihlawī, *Akhbār al-akhyār*, Delhi, 1891, 28.
33. Jamālī, *Siyar al-ʿĀrifīn*, Delhi, 1893, 129; *Nuzhat al-khawāṭir*, (Urdu tr.), i. 288-9.
34. Nizami, op. cit. (n. 31), 21-2.
35. Shams Sirāj ʿAfīf, *Ta'rīkh-i Fīrūz Shāhī*, 514; Sarwar, ii. 58.
36. Fuad Köprülü, *Islam Ansiklopedisi*, i. 212; M. Molé 'Les Kubrawiya entre sunnisme et shiisme', *REI*, xxxix (1961), 62.

37. Wā'iẓ al-Kāshifī, *Rashḥāt*, Cawnpore, 1912, 8-9, 18-27.
38. L. Massignon/L. Gardet, 'al-Ḥallādj' in *EI*², iii. 102.
39. 'Alā'-ad-dawla Simnānī, *Chihil Majlis*, BM Or. MSS 9725; Molé, op. cit. (n. 36).
40. Shaykh Aḥmad Sirhindī, *Maktūbāt*, Lucknow, 1877; Aziz Ahmad, *ICIE*, 182-9.
41. Ashraf Jahāngīr Simnānī, *Maktūbāt-i Ashrafī*, BM Or. MSS 267, *passim*.
42. Maẓ'har Jān-i Jānān in *Kalimāt-i ṭayyibāt*, Delhi, 1891, letter 14, 26-7, and *passim*.
43. Yusuf Husain, *Medieval Indian Culture*, London, 1959, 53.
44. M. Mujeeb, *The Indian Muslims*, London, 1967, 298-9.
45. Dārā Shukoh, *Sakīnat al-awliyā'*, Rampur MSS, ff. 139 a-b.
46. Dārā Shukoh, *Safīnat al-awliyā'*, Urdu tr. Karachi, 1961, 102.
47. Hujwīrī (Nicholson), 130, 183-8, 260-6, 416, and *passim*.
48. Abū-l-Faḍl 'Allāmī, *Ā'īn-i Akbarī* (Jarrett), iii. 384-400.
49. Molé, op. cit. (n. 36), 116-17.
50. Ḥamd-Allāh Mustawfī, *Ta'rīkh-i Guzīda*, ed. E. G. Browne, Leiden, 1910, 791; 'Abd-al-Ḥaqq Dihlawī, *Akhbār al-akhyār*, 115.
51. *Nuz'hat al-khawāṭir* (Urdu tr.), ii. 23.
52. Zayn Badr 'Arabī, *Ma'dan al-ma'ānī*, Bodleian Pers. MS 1263, ff. 5b, 31a, and 72a; Aḥmad ibn-Yaḥyā Mānerī, *Maktūbāt*, Cawnpore, 1911; *idem*, *Maktūbāt-i jawābī*, Cawnpore, 1910.
53. Bahā'-ad-dīn Shaṭṭarī, *Risāla-i Shaṭṭāriyya*, IO Pers. MS 2257 (Ethé, 1913) fos. 6b-14b.
54. Sarwar, ii. 306.
55. K. A. Nizami, 'The Shaṭṭarī saints and their attitude towards the state', *MIQ*, i/2 (1950), 57-61.
56. 'Abd-al-Qādir Badā'ūnī, *Muntakhab al-tawārīkh*, Calcutta, 1868–9, iii. 4-5.

Chapter Five

1. Sijzī, 137; Amīr Khurd, 66; Ḥamīd Qalandar, 65-6, 150; J. C. Oman, *The Mystics, Ascetics and Saints of India*, London, 1905; Nizami, *Religion and Politics*, 178-9.
2. Muhṣin Fānī, *Dabistān-i madhāhib* (O'Shea and Troyer), ii. 226-8.
3. Titus, 133.
4. Ibn-Kathīr, *al-Bidāya wa-n-nihāya*, Cairo, 1932–9, xiii. 274, 344; 'Abd-al-Ḥaqq Dihlawī, *Akhbār al-akhyār*, 249-50; H. Laoust, *Les Schismes dans l'Islam*, Paris, 1965, 286; F. Babinger in *EI*¹, iii. 677.

5. Amīr Khurd, 575; Sijzī, 20; Jamālī, 67.
6. ʿAbd-ar-Raḥmān Ḥasanī, *Mirʾat-i Madāriyya*, BM Add. MSS 16,858, ff. 27a, 42 a-b, *passim*; Muḥsin Fānī, ii. 220-6.
7. Mrs Meer Hassan Ali, *Observations on the Mussulmauns of India*, London, 1917, 372.
8. Jaʿfar Sharīf, *Islam in India* (*Qānūn-i Islām*), Eng. tr. G. A. Herklots, Oxford, 1921, 218-82.
9. W. R. Lawrence, *The Valley of Kashmir*, London, 1895, 334.
10. Ḥamīd Qalandar, 46.
11. Sijzī, 178; Ḥamīd Qalandar, 110-17.
12. W. Crooke, *Religion and Folklore of Northern India*, Oxford, 1926, 167.
13. Crooke, 167-8; *Bombay Gazetteer* [*BG*], iv. 281 and *passim*.
14. Crooke, 165.
15. *Nuzʾhat al-khawāṭir*, Urdu tr., i. 180-1.
16. Crooke, 79, 95-8. R. C. Temple, *The Legends of the Punjab*, Bombay, 1884, ii. 104, iii. 301; H. A. Rose, *A Glossary of the Tribes and Castes of the Punjab and North West Frontier Provinces*, Lahore, 1911–19, i. 129, 568; Jaʿfar Sharīf, 143.
17. Crooke, 138-9.
18. Crooke, 198, 422.
19. Ibid., 41.
20. Sijzī, 119, 243.
21. Jaʿfar Sharīf, 35; E. A. Gait, *Census Report: Bengal*, Calcutta, 1902, i. 188; L. S. S. O'Malley, *Census Report: Bengal etc.*, Calcutta, 1913, i. 252.
22. Mrs Meer Hassan Ali, 158; Crooke, 38-9.
23. V. A. Smith, *Akbar, the Great Mughal*, Oxford, 1919, 18.
24. Cf. *Punjab Notes and Queries*, Allahabad, 1883-7, i. 27; Crooke, 143.
25. Shāh Walī-Allāh, *Balāgh al-mubīn*, Lahore, 1890, 33-4.
26. Crooke, 301; *ERE*, x. 93; Jaʿfar Sharīf, 10, 159, 193.
27. *ERE*, 600 *et seq*.
28. Harikishan Kaul in *Census Report: Punjab*, Lahore, 1912, i. 121.
29. *ERE*, vii. 693 *et seq.*; Jaʿfar Sharīf, 38, 67, 135; Titus, 146; Jaʿfar Sharīf, 25 *et seq*.
30. O'Malley, i. 251.
31. *Purnea District Gazetteer* (vol. xxv of *Bengal District Gazetteers*), Calcutta, 1911, 58 *et seq*.
32. *Indore State Gazetteer*, Calcutta, 1908, 59.
33. *Central Provincial Gazetteer*, vol. xiv (*Nīmar*); Allahabad, 1908, 63.

34. Nizami, *Religion and Politics*, 304.
35. Muḥsin Fānī, ii. 234-5; Mrs Meer Hassan Ali, 375 *et seq.*; Ja'far Sharīf, 139; Titus, 147; Nizami, *Religion and Politics*, 304.
36. *BG* ix. pt. i. 365 *et seq.*
37. G. A. Grierson, *Bihar Peasant Life*, Calcutta, 1885, 408; Crooke, 213.
38. Crooke, 170-94.
39. Crooke, 134, 213.
40. Shāh Muh. Ismā'īl, *Tadhkīr al-akhwān*, Lahore, 1947, 25-8, 51-2.
41. *Bulletin of Henry Martyn School*, Aligarh, Oct.-Nov., 1954–5; Titus, 233.

Chapter Six

1. Firishta (Briggs), i. 61, 113-14.
2. Baranī, 341-67; N. N. Law, *Promotion of Learning in India during Muhammadan Rule by Muhammadans*, London, 1916, 36-7.
3. Aḥmad ibn-'Abd-Allāh al-Qalqashandī, *Ṣubḥ al-a'shā'*, Cairo, 1913–20; chapters relating to India tr. into English by O. Spies (*An Arab Account of India in the 14th century*), Stuttgart, 1936, 29.
4. Baranī, 562-66; Firishta (Briggs), i. 464-5; Law, 56.
5. Raḥmān 'Alī, *Tadhkira-i 'ulamā-i Hind*, Lucknow, 1914, 101; Firishta (Briggs), i. 581-9; Law, 74; Yusuf Hussain, *Medieval Indian Culture*, 76-7.
6. Law, 126-7.
7. Abū-l-Ḥasanāt Nadwī, *Hindūstān kī qadīm Islāmī darsgāhen*, Azamgarh, 1936, 22.
8. Law, 160-2.
9. Ghulām 'Alī Āzād Bilgrīmī, *Ma'āthir al-karām*, IO Pers. MS 1320, f. 96a.
10. Khāfī Khān, *Muntakhab al-lubāb*, Calcutta, 1869–1925, i. 249.
11. Nadwī, 26-7.
12. Law, 189.
13. Cf. F. Bernier, *Travels in Mughal India*, Eng. tr., London, 1891, 155-6.
14. Nadwī, 11, 25, 80-1.
15. Ibid., 121.
16. Law, 117.
17. Firishta (Briggs), iv. 236; Law, 200-3.
18. S. M. Ikram, *Rūd-i Kawthar*, Lahore, 1958, 587-8.

19. For the history of Deoband see Maḥbūb Riḍwī, *Ta'rīkh-i Deoband*, 1952; Aziz Ahmad, *IMIP*, 104-9.
20. For its objectives see the Inaugural Address by Shiblī Nuʿmānī in his *Rasā'il*, Delhi, 1898, 91-105.
21. For details see ʿAbd-al-Ḥaqq, 'Marḥūm Dihlī College', *Urdu* 13/50 (1933).
22. Prospectus in ʿAbd-al-Ḥaqq, *Sayyid Aḥmad Khān*, Karachi, 1959.
23. For details, MAO Educational Conference, *Majmūʿa-i resolutionhā-i dihsāla*, 1886–95, Aligarh, 1896.
24. Ministry of Education, Government of Pakistan, *Report of the Commission on National Education*, Karachi, 1959.
25. Ibid., 211-15.
26. Ibid., 215.
27. Abid Husain (ʿĀbid Ḥusayn), *The Destiny of Indian Muslims*, London, 1965, 132.

Chapter Seven

1. For details see Zubayd Ahmad, *Contribution of India to Arabic Literature*, Allahabad, 1946.
2. Ed. U. M. Daudpota, Delhi, 1939.
3. Ibn-Nadīm, *al-Fihrist* (Flügel), 305 and *passim*.
4. Nabi Bakhsh Khan Baloch, 'The Diwan of Abu ʿAṭā of Sind', *IC*, 23 (1949), 136-50; A. Schaade in EI^2, i. 107.
5. Eng. tr. E. Sachau, *Alberuni's India*, London, 1910.
6. Al-ʿUtbī, *At-Tā'rīkh al-Yamīnī*. Cairo, 1869.
7. ʿAbd-al-Ḥalīm Chishtī, 'Ḥasan b. Muḥammad as-Saghānī', *Maʿārif*, Azamgarh, January-September, 1959.
8. Abū-l-Ḥasan ʿAli Nadwī, *Hindustānī Musalmān*, Lucknow, 1961, 41; For a bibliography of Saghānī see C. Brockelmann, *GAL*, i. 613-15; S. i. 443-4.
9. *Nuz'hat a'l-khawāṭir* (Urdu tr.), ii. 58.
10. Zubayd Ahmad (Thesis), 170-1.
11. Ibid., 188.
12. *Nuz'hat*, ii. 87-8.
13. Zubayd Ahmad, op. cit. (n. 1); K. A. Nizami, *Ḥayāt-i Shaykh ʿAbd-al-Ḥaqq Dihlawī*, Delhi, 1953, 171-2.
14. MSS in Āṣafiyya Library, Hyderabad, No. 1320 (Kalām, no. 76).
15. For details see Zubayd Ahmad, op. cit. (n. 1).
16. Shāh Walī-Allāh, *Al-Juz' al-laṭīf*, Delhi, 1897, 27-8.
17. Shah Walī-Allāh, *Ḥujjat Allāh al-bāligha*, Arabic text and Urdu tr., Karachi, 1953.
18. Available in Eng. tr. by Dā'ūd Rahbar, *MW*, xlv (1955), 347-58.

19. S. M. Ikram, *Rūd-i Kawthar*, Karachi, n.d., 413.
20. Abū-l-Ḥasan ʿAlī al-Ḥasanī al-Nadwī, *Mādhā khasira l-ʿālam bi-nḥiṭaṭ al-muslimīn*, Cairo, 1955; also available in Eng. trans. by Muḥammad Āsaf Qidwā'ī, *Islam and the World*, Lahore, 1961.
21. For a survey of Persian literature in the subcontinent see S. M. Ikram, Introduction to *Armaghān-i Pāk*. Karachi, 1953, 13-80; Shibli Nuʿmānī, *Shiʿr al-ʿAjam*, iii, Cawnpore, 1920–3; A. Ghanī, *A History of Persian Language and Literature at the Mughal Court*, Allahabad 1929–30; Aziz Ahmad, *ICIE*, 223-38; A. Bausani, *Storia delle letterature del Pakistan*. Milan, 1958, 45-98.
22. Muhammad ʿAwfī, *Lubāb a -albāb*, ed. Saʿīd Nafīsī, Tehran, 1333 shamsī, 291.
23. Ibid., 419.
24. Masʿūd Saʿd Salmān, *Dīwān*, ed. Rashīd Yāsimī, Tehran, 1318 shamsī.
25. ʿAwfī, 90, 93.
26. Ikram, op. cit. (n. 21), 31-2.
27. ʿAwfī, 557, 764, 169.
28. Ikram, op. cit. (n. 21), 37.
29. A scholarly and comprehensive study of Khusraw is Wahid Mirza, *The Life and Works of Amir Khusrau*, Calcutta, 1935.
30. ʿIṣāmī, *Futūḥ as-salāṭīn*, ed. A. S. Usha, Madras, 1948. See also Aziz Ahmad, 'Epic and Counter-Epic in Medieval India', *JAOS*, 83 (1962), 470-6.
31. Aziz Ahmad, 'Ḥasan Dihlawī' in *EI*², iii. 249; Ḥasan Dihlawī, *Kulliyyāt*, ed. M. A. Maḥwī, Madras, 1933.
32. Badr-i Chāch, *Dīwān*, Lucknow, 1845; *Qaṣā'id*, Cawnpore, 1845.
33. Aziz Ahmad, 'Djamalī' in *EI*², ii. 420-1.
34. The only assessment of Bīdil in a Western language is A. Bausani, 'Note su Mirza Bedil', *Annali*, vi (1957), 163-91.
35. A. Bausani, 'The position of Ğalib (1796–1869) in the history of Urdu and Indo-Persian poetry', *Der Islam*, 24 (1959), 99-127; A. C. S. Gilani, *Ghālib, His Life and Persian Poetry*, Karachi, 1956.
36. Eng. tr. R. A. Nicholson, *Secrets of the Self*, London, 1920.
37. Eng. tr. A. J. Arberry, *Mysteries of Selflessness*, London, 1953.
38. Eng. tr. A. J. Arberry, *Javid-Nama*, London, 1966.
39. French tr. Eva Meyerovitch and M. Achena, *Message de l'Orient*, Paris, 1956.

40. Eng. tr. A. J. Arberry, *The Persian Psalms*, Lahore, 1948.
41. A. Bausani, 'Contributo a una definizione dello "stile indiano" della poesia persiana' in *Annali*, n.s. vii (1958), 167-78; Aziz Ahmad, *ICIE*, 228-31.
42. Ed. Ghani and Fayyaz, Tehran, 1324 shamsī.
43. Ed. Tehran, 1327 shamsī.
44. Ed. published under the misleading title, *Ta'rīkh-i Fakhru'd-dīn Mubārakshāh*, by Sir Denison Ross, London, 1927.
45. P. Hardy, 'Some Studies in pre-Mughal Muslim Historiography', in C. H. Philips (ed.), *Historians of India, Pakistan and Ceylon*, London, 1961, 116.
46. India Office Pers. MSS 647 (Ethé, 2767).
47. BM Add. 1653; for a synopsis of this work see Mujeeb, 179-82.
48. Ed. Bibl. Ind., Calcutta, 1863; ed. A. H. Habibi, Kabul, 1342 shamsī; see also A. S. Bazmee Ansari, 'al-Djūzdjānī', in *EI*², ii. 609.
49. For a notice of this work see von Hammer, *Gemäldesaal der Lebenbeschreibungen grosser Moslemischer Herrscher*, iv. 172-82; also Elliot and Dowson (Allahabad reprint), ii. 204-12.
50. Elliot and Dowson, ii. 206.
51. Pers. text ed. S. M. Haq, Aligarh, 1927; Eng. tr. M. Habib, Madras, 1931.
52. For a study of this period of historiography see P. Hardy, *Historians of Medieval India*, London, 1960.
53. Bibl. Ind., Calcutta, 1862; P. Hardy, 'Baranī' in *EI*², i. 1036-7.
54. P. Hardy 'The oratio recta of Baranī's *Tārīkh-i Fīrūz Shāhī* – fact or fiction;' *BSOAS*, xx (1957), 315-22.
55. India Office Pers. MSS 1149; Eng. tr. in M. Habib and A. V. S. Khan, *The Political Theory of the Delhi Sultanate*, Allahabad, n.d.
56. Bibl. Ind., Calcutta, 1890.
57. Fīrūz Tughluq, *Futūḥāt-i Fīrūz Shāhī*, ed. A. Rashid, Aligarh, 1954; extracts in Eng. trans. in Elliot and Dowson (Allahabad), iii. 374-88.
58. 'Abd-Allāh Waṣṣāf, *Tajziyat al-amṣar wa tajriyat al-athār*, Bombay, 1877, section dealing with the Delhi sultans.
59. Ed. A. S. Usha, Madras, 1948.
60. Calcutta 1931; Eng. tr. Baroda, 1932.
61. BM Or. MSS 137; for an analysis of the work see P. Hardy, 'The Tarikh-i Muhammadi by Muhammad Bihmad Khani' in *Jadunath Sarkar Commemoration Volume*, ii (1958), 181-90.

62. Kamāl-ad-dīn ʿAbd-ar-Razzāq, *Maṭlaʿ as-saʿdayn wa-majmaʿ al-baḥrayn*, BM Or. MSS 1291.
63. Mirza Ḥaydar Dughlat, *Ta'rīkh-i Rashīdī*, Eng. tr. N. Elias and E. Denison Ross, London, 1898.
64. Elliot and Dowson, iv. 288-92.
65. IO Pers. MSS 428.
66. Elliot and Dowson, iv. 213.
67. Khwāndmīr, *Qānūn-i Humāyūnī*, Bibl. Ind., Calcutta, 1940.
68. Bibl. Ind., Calcutta, 1939.
69. BM Or. MSS 1857.
70. BM Or. MSS 197.
71. Ed. S. M. Imamuddīn, Dacca, 1960, 2 vols.
72. BM Or. MSS 1929; BM Add. MSS 11, 633.
73. Bibl. Ind., Calcutta, 1941.
74. Ed. and tr. into Eng. A. Beveridge, London, 1902.
75. Jawhar Āftābchī, *Tadhkirat al-wāqiʿāt*, BM Add. MSS 16, 711; Urdu tr. S. Moinul Haq, Karachi, n.d.
76. Ed. M. Sadiq Ali, Cawnpore-Lucknow, 1881–3; Eng. tr. A. Beveridge, Calcutta, 1948.
77. Eng. tr. i, H. Blochmann, Calcutta, 1927; ii, H. S. Jarrett, Calcutta, 1891; iii, H. S. Jarrett and J. N. Sarkar, Calcutta, 1948.
78. IO Pers. MSS 836 (Ethé 110).
79. Bibl. Ind., Calcutta, 1868–9.
80. Bibl. Ind., Calcutta, 1927–35.
81. King's College, Cambridge, MSS 84.
82. Calcutta, 1924.
83. Eds. Lucknow, 1905; Bombay, 1832; Eng. tr. (Briggs), London, 1829.
84. Ed. Aligarh 1864; Eng. tr. A. Rogers, 1909; for a discussion of the variants, Elliot and Dowson (Allahabad), vi. 251-83.
85. Bibl. Ind., Calcutta, 1865.
86. IO Pers. MSS 1666.
87. IO Pers. MSS 1547.
88. BM Add. MSS 23,513.
89. Bibl. Ind., Calcutta, 1867.
90. Eds. Bibl. Ind., Calcutta, 1923–39; Lahore, 1958–60.
91. For details of and extract from both works, Elliot and Dowson, vii. 73-122, 133.
92. Bibl. Ind., Calcutta, 1868.
93. Eng. tr. J. N. Sarkar, Bibl. Ind., Calcutta, 1947.
94. BM Add. MSS 7567.
95. Storey, I, ii (i), 133.
96. Bibl. Ind., Calcutta, 1869–1925.

97. Elliot and Dowson, vii. 534-64.
98. BM Or. 3288; Rieu, *Supp*. 25.
99. Elliot and Dowson, vii. 569-73.
100. For details see Sayyid Abudllah, *Adabiyyāt-i Farsī men Hinduwon kā ḥiṣṣa*, Delhi, 1942; Aziz Ahmad, *ICIE*, 235-8.
101. BM Add. MSS 16, 863; see also Iqbal Husain, 'Chandra Bhān Brahman', *IC*, xviii (1945), 115.
102. Delhi, 1918.
103. Ed. U. M. Daudpota, Delhi, 1939.
104. Ed. U. M. Daudpota, Bombay, 1938.
105. Ed. S. C. Misra and M. L. Rahman, Baroda, 1961.
106. Eng. tr. M. F. Lokhandwala, Baroda, 1965.
107. Ed. Moinul Haq, Karachi, 1961.
108. Bibl. Ind., Calcutta, 1888–90.
109. Ed. Delhi, 1893.
110. Urdu tr. Agra, 1908.
111. Delhi, 1891.
112. Lucknow, 1872; Urdu tr. Karachi, 1961.
113. *Ma'āthir al-karām*, IO Pers MSS 1320 (Ethé 682); *Sarv-i Āẓād*, IO Pers. MSS 1852 (Ethé 683); *Khiẓāna-i 'āmira*, IO Pers. MSS 2079 (Ethé 685).
114. Abū-l-Faḍl 'Allāmī, *Maktābūt*, Lucknow, 1863.
115. Awrangzīb, *Ruq'āt-i 'Ālamgīrī*, several eds.; Eng. tr. J. H. Bilmoria, Bombay/London, 1908.
116. *Bālmukand Nāma*, ed. S. Abdur Rashid, Aligarh, 1957.
117. *Inshā-i Harkaran*, BM Add. MSS 26, 140.
118. Sharaf-ad-dīn Aḥmad ibn-Yaḥyā Mānerī, *Maktūbāt*, Cawnpore, 1911; *idem*, *Maktūbāt-i Jawābī*, Cawnpore, 1910.
119. Shaykh Aḥmad Sirhindī, *Maktūbāt*, Lucknow, 1877.
120. In *Kalimāt-i ṭayyibāt*, Delhi, 1891; also Maẓ'har Jān-i Jānān, *Khuṭūṭ*, Delhi, 1962.
121. 'Abd-al-Ḥaqq Dihlawī, *al-Makātīb wa-r-rasā'il*, Delhi, 1879; Walī-Allāh, *Siyāsī Maktūbāt*, ed. K. A. Nizami, Aligarh, 1950.
122. M. Habib, 'Chishti mystic records of the Sultanate period', *MIQ*, iii (1950), 1-42.
123. Ed. K. A. Nizami, Aligarh, 1959.
124. Zayn Badr 'Arabī, *Ma'dan al-ma'ānī*, Bihar, 1883.
125. Gīsūdarāz, *Jawāmi' al-kalim*, BM Or. MSS 252.
126. Mirzā Ḥaydar Dughlat, *Ta'rīkh-i Rashīdī*, Eng. tr. E. D. Ross and N. Elias, London, 1898, 173.
127. Fuad Köprülü, 'Babur – Literary Works' in *EI*^{2}, i. 849, which also gives a complete bibliography of Bābur's works.

128. Bayrām Khān, *Persian and Turkī Dīwāns*, ed. E. Denison Ross, Calcutta, 1910.
129. Sidī Alī Reis 'Kātib-i Rūmī', *Mir'at al-mamālik*, ed. Jevdet, Istanbul, 1895, 43-55.
130. Jahāngir, *Tuzuk* (Eng. tr. Rogers), 109-10.
131. Ẓahīr-ad-dīn Aẓfarī, *Wāqi'āt-i Aẓfarī*, Madras, 1957.
132. Raḥmān 'Alī, 108.

Chapter Eight

1. For accounts of Urdu literature in English see R. B. Saksena, *A History of Urdu Literature*, Allahabad, 1940; Muhammad Sadiq, *A History of Urdu Literature*, London, 1964; T. Grahame Bailey, *A History of Urdu Literature*, Calcutta, 1932; Aziz Ahmad, 'Urdu Literature' in S. M. Ikram and Percival Spear, *The Cultural Heritage of Pakistan*, Karachi, 1957, pp. 119-34; *idem*, *ICIE*, 244-62.
2. Maḥmūd al-Kāshgharī, *Dīwān-i Lughāt-i Turk*, Istanbul 1333/1915, i. 112; C. Brockelmann, *Mitteltürkischer Wortschatz nach Maḥmūd la-Kāshgharī: Dīvān Lughāt at-Turk*, Budapest, 1928; Gerhard Doerfer, *Türkische und mongolische Elemente im Neupersischen*, Wiesbaden, 1965, ii. 1932. I am grateful to Dr Turhan Gandjei for drawing my attention to the etymological derivation of 'Urdu'.
3. Al-Juwaynī, *Ta'rīkh-i Jahānkushā*, i. 148, 162.
4. Abū-l-Faḍl, *Ā'īn*, ii. 308.
5. Maḥmūd Shērānī, *Punjab men Urdū*, Lahore, 1928, 14-18.
6. T. Grahame Bailey, *Studies in North Indian Languages*, London, 1938, 1. In 1027 Maḥmūd of Ghazna annexed the Punjab.
7. Shērānī, op. cit. (n. 5); G. A. Grierson, *Linguistic Survey of India*, Calcutta, 1904, ix, pt. i. p. xiii.
8. Shērānī, 21-46.
9. Ibid., 70-86.
10. *Diwān*, ed. A. Samoilovich (*Sobranie stickhotvoroney Imperatura Babura*), Petrograd, 1917; E. Denison Ross (ed.), *Facsimile of Diwan-i Babur Badishah*, Calcutta, 1910, Plate XVII.
11. Cf. Sirāj-ad-dīn 'Alī Khān Ārzū, *Taṣ'ḥīh-i Gharā'ib al-lughāt*, Cawnpore, 1868.
12. Grierson, *Linguistic Survey*, ix, pt. i; S. K. Chatterji, *Indo-Aryan and Hindi*, Ahmadabad, 1942, 184.
13. Chatterji, 185.
14. Shērānī, 87-95.

15. Shams-Allāh Qādirī, *Urdū-yi qadīm*, Lucknow, 1930, 39.
16. For details, ʿAbd-al-Ḥaqq, *Urdū kī nashv-u numā men Ṣūfiyā-i karām kā kām*, Karachi, 1953.
17. Amīr Khurd, 182.
18. ʿAbd-al-Ḥaqq, 13-14, 26-30, 56-78.
19. Qādirī, 40-1.
20. For details, Naṣīr-ad-dīn Hāshimī, *Dakan mēn Urdū*, Hyderabad, 1936.
21. Ed. R. S. Greenshields, Berlin/London, 1926.
22. Aziz Ahmad, 'Sabras kē ma'ākhidh awr mamāthil', *Urdu*, Karachi, 1949.
23. For details Abū-l-Layth Ṣiddīqī, *Lakhna'ū kā dabistān-i shāʿirī*, Lahore, 1955.
24. Saksena, 134.
25. A. Bausani, 'Ghālib' in *EI*², ii. 1000-1; *idem*, 'The position of Ǧalib in the History of Urdu and Indo-Persian poetry', *Der Islam*, xxxiv (1959), 99-127. For an English rendering of some of his Urdu verses, J. L. Kane, *Interpretations of Ghalib*, Delhi, 1957.
26. Alṭaf Ḥusayn Ḥālī, *Muqaddima-i shiʿr wa-shāʿirī*, Lahore, 1953.
27. Aziz Ahmad, 'Ḥālī' in *EI*², iii. 93-4; *idem*, *IMIP*, 97-100, for a synopsis of Ḥālī's *Musaddas*.
28. For translations of selections of his Urdu verse in European languages see *Poems from Iqbāl*, translated by Victor Kiernan, London, 1955; and Iqbāl, *Poesie*, rendered into Italian by Alessandro Bausani, Parma, 1956.
29. Eng. tr., V. G. Kiernan, *Poems by Faiz Ahmad Faiz*, Delhi, 1958.
30. On the methodology of Shiblī's historiography see, Aziz Ahmad, *IMIP*, 77-86.
31. Eng. tr. by Khushwant Singh and M. A. Husaini, Calcutta, 1961.
32. A. Bausani, *Storia delle Letterature del Pakistan*, Milan, 1958; S. M. Ikram and P. Spear, *Cultural Heritage of Pakistan*, Karachi, 1955, pp. 135-66.
33. Inam al-Haqq, *Muslim Bengali Literature*, Karachi, 1957; for a general survey of Bengali literature see D. C. Sen, *History of Bengali Language and Literature*, Calcutta, 1911.
34. Salimullah Fahmi in *Pākistān kī ʿilāqā'ī zabānon par Farsī kā athar*, Karachi, 1953.
35. Inam al-Haqq, 70.
36. Ibid., 75-77.
37. J. C. Ghosh, *Bengali Literature*, London, 1948, 46.

38. Usually transcribed as Alaol. It is difficult to say whether the name is ʿAlā'ul, the first part of a full name, or self-sufficient al-Awwal.
39. Inam al-Haqq, 185.
40. This should not be confused with the Hindi dialect Braj Bhashā spoken and written in the valley of Jumna.
41. J. A. Qidwai, *Pashto Adab*, Karachi, 1951; Ṣādiq-Allāh Rishtin, *Da Pashto da adab ta'rīkh*, Kabul, 1946; J. Darmesteter, *Chants populaires des Afghans*, Paris, 1888; H. G. Raverty, *Selections from the Poetry of the Afghans*, London, 1864; W. Lentz, 'Sammlungen zur afghanischen Literatur – und Zeitgeschichte', *ZDMG* (1937), 711-32; Riḍa Hamdānī, *Adabiyyāt-i Sarḥad*, Peshawar, 1953.
42. English translations of his selected poems: D. N. MacKenzie, *Poems from the Divan of Khushḥal Khan Khattak*, London, 1965; Evelyn Howell and Olaf Caroe, *The Poems of Khushḥal Khan Khattak*, Peshawar, 1963.
43. For details see M. Longworth Dames, *Popular Poetry of the Baloches*, London, 1907.
44. Grierson, *Linguistic Survey*, 1921, x. 327-45; W. Geiger, 'Die Sprache der Belutschen', *Grundriss der Iranischen Philologie*, Strassburg, 1898–1901, i/ii. 231 *et seq.*
45. L. Dames.
46. For details see Muhammad Sarwar, *Panjābī Adab*, Karachi, n.d.; G. A. Grierson, *Linguistic Survey*, Calcutta, 1916, ix. pt. 1.
47. For details see Lajwantī Rām Krishna, *Panjabi Sufi Poets*, Calcutta, 1938.
48. M. Sarwar, 47-54; Ram Krishna, 60-1, 65.
49. For details see Husamuddin Rashidi, *Sindhi Adab*, Karachi, n.d.; U. M. Daudpota, *Sindhi Literature*, Karachi, 1951.
50. H. T. Sorley, *Shah Abdul Latif of Bhit*, London, 1940, 111.
51. Abdul Wahid Sindhi in *Pākistān kī ʿilāqā'ī zabānon par Fārsī kā athar*, 37-44.
52. *Mujmil at-tawārīkh*, Tehran, 343; Rashidi, 16.
53. Sorley, 255.

Chapter Nine

1. Tara Chand, *The Influence of Islam on Hindu Culture*, Allahabad, 1936, 240.
2. Ibid., 235.
3. Percy Brown, *Indian Architecture (Islamic Period)*, Bombay, 1958, 1.

4. Ibid., 2-3.
5. Vincent A. Smith, *History of Fine Art in India and Ceylon*, Oxford, 1911, I, 421.
6. Brown, 8.
7. Ibid., 2.
8. E. B. Havell, *A Handbook of Indian Art*, London, 1920, 108.
9. James Fergusson, *History of Indian and Eastern Architecture*, London, 1910, ii. 56; Brown, 3.
10. Brown, 2, 11.
11. Havell, 107.
12. Brown, 2.
13. K. M. Ashraf, 'Life and Conditions of the People of Hindustan, 1200–1550', *JASB*, 1935, 265-8.
14. Brown, 10.
15. Ibid., 13.
16. Ibid., 10.
17. Brown, 14.
18. Ibid., 6, 7.
19. Fergusson, ii. 215; V. Smith, 398.
20. Fergusson, ii. 227.
21. Smith, 398.
22. Brown, 25.
23. Ibid., 6, 34.
24. Fergusson, ii. 221.
25. Ibid., 197-8, 215.
26. V. Smith, 432.
27. Havell, 145–7; cf. V. Smith, *Akbar the Great Moghul*, London, 1927, 435; K. A. C. Cresswell in the *Indian Antiquary*, July 1915.
28. Fergusson, ii. 286.
29. Bābur, *Tuzuk* (Leyden and Erskine), ii. 533.
30. Ibid., 337.
31. Smith, (n. 5) 406; Brown, 96.
32. *Archaeological Survey of India*, 1902–3, 62; the same, 1903–4, 170; Brown, 92-3, 97-8; Havell, *Handbook*, 133; Havell, *Indian Architecture*, London, 1927, 163.
33. Fergusson, ii. 285.
34. Brown, 99.
35. Ibid., 101-6.
36. Ibid., 99.
37. Fergusson, ii. 293.
38. Ibid., 300.
39. Smith, 410.
40. Fergusson, ii. 307.

41. H. Goetz, *Indian and Persian Miniature Painting*, Amsterdam, 1958, 13.
42. Brown, 8, 109-10; Smith, 412.
43. Ibid.
44. Cf. Havell, *Handbook*, 138-9.
45. Ibid., 118-28.
46. Brown, 37-8.
47. Fergusson, ii. 257.
48. Ibid., 253-4.
49. Ibid., 225-8; Fuehrer, *The Sharqī Architecture of Jaunpur*, Calcutta, 1889.
50. Brown, 48; Fergusson, ii. 229; J. Burgess, *The Muhammedan Architecture in Gujarat*, London, 1896; Burgess, *The Muhammedan Architecture of Ahmedabad*, London, 1900–5; J. Burgess and H. Cousens, *The Architectural Antiquities of Northern Gujarāt*, London, 1903.
51. Brown, 48; Fergusson, ii. 236; Smith, 401.
52. Brown, 57; Smith, 402.
53. Fergusson, ii. 246-50.
54. Ibid., 251, 253.
55. Brown, 62.
56. Fergusson, ii. 251.
57. Brown, 63.
58. Ibid., 71-4; H. Cousens, *Bijāpūr and its Architectural Remains*, Bombay, 1916.
59. Brown, 74.
60. Ibid., 75.
61. Saladin, *Manuel d'Art musulman*, i. 509, 561; Smith, 405; Brown, 78.
62. Fergusson, ii. 279.
63. Bābur (Leyden and Erskine), i. 322.
64. The *Khamsa* of Niẓāmī illustrated by Sayyid ʿAlī Tabrīzī, BM Or. 2265; *Dārāb Nāma*, illustrated by Khwāja ʿAbd-aṣ-Ṣamad, BM Or. 4615; L. Binyon, *The Poems of Niẓāmī*, London, 1928; L. Binyon, J. V. S. Wilkinson and Basil Gray, *Persian Miniature Painting*, London, 1933, 118-20.
65. L. Binyon, *The Court Painters of the Great Moguls*, London 1921, 58.
66. E. B. Havell, *Indian Painting and Sculpture*, London, 1928, 194.
67. Ivan Stchoukine, *La Peinture Indienne*, Paris, 1929, 108.
68. Ibid., 110.
69. *Bābur Nāma*, BM Or. 3714.

70. As in Bhāgvatī's portrait of Humāyūn in BM Add. 18801, and in the miniature 'Princess Humāy and the Polo-players', Binyon, 46, Plate VII.
71. Havell, op. cit. (n. 67), 200.
72. Abū-l-Faḍl 'Allāmī, *Ā'īn-i Akbarī*, i (Blochmann), 114.
73. T. H. Hendley, *The Razm Nāmah Manuscript*, Memorials of the Jeypore Exhibition, iv. 1883; Stchoukine, 110-11.
74. Ibid., 92-3.
75. Ibid., 77-9.
76. E. Wellesz, *Akbar's Religious Thought reflected in Mogul Painting*, London, 1952, 37.
77. Binyon, 45.
78. Farrukh Beg's miniatures in *Akbar Nāma*, Victoria and Albert Museum, London, No. 69.
79. Goetz, 19.
80. Smith, 328.
81. Binyon, 46.
82. Binyon, 38.
83. Wellesz, 36, basing her argument on the internal evidence of *Najm al-'ulūm*, a Bijapur MS dated 1570 in the Chester Beatty Collection.
84. Binyon, 68.
85. Smith, 330.
86. Goetz, 14; Binyon, 68.
87. Goetz, 19.
88. Binyon, 67.
89. Stchoukine, 80, 83, 94.
90. Mu'tamid Khna, *Iqbāl Nāma-i Jahāngīrī*, 132.
91. Stchoukine, 44.
92. Jahāngīr, *Tuzuk*, Aligarh, 1864, 280.
93. BM Or. 7573.
94. Goetz, 20.
95. T. Arnold and J. V. S. Wilkinson, *Library of A. Chester Beatty, Oriental Manuscripts*, London, 1936; Ernest Kühnel, *Moghul-Malerei*, Berlin, 1956, 46-7.
96. Ṣabāh-ad-dīn 'Abd-ar-Raḥmān, *Bazm-i Ṣūfiyya*, 48, 77.
97. Sijzī, 133; 'Iṣāmī, 117-20.
98. Jamālī, *Siyar al-'Ārifīn*, IO Pers. MS 1313, ff. 147 a-b.
99. Sijzī, 38.
100. Ibid., 94.
101. Ibid., 55.
102. Sijzī, 56, 137.
103. Sijzī, 125-6.
104. Shērānī, *Punjāb men Urdū*, Lahore, 1928, 176-8.

105. Muḥammad al-Ḥusaynī Gīsūdarāz, *Jawāmi' al-kalim*, BM Or. 252, ff. 98 a-b.
106. Ibid., ff. 99a.
107. Miguel Asín Palacios, *El Islam Cristianizado*, Madrid, 1931, 187.
108. Ibid., 187-8, 326-32, 389.
109. J. K. Birge, *The Bektashi Order of Dervishes*, London, Hartford, 1937, 213.
110. Sijzī, 77.
111. Faqīr-Allāh, *Rāg Durpan*, IO Pers. MS 1937 (Ethé 2017), f. 12a; Mirzā Muḥammad, *Tuḥfat al-Hind*, BM Add. 16, 868, f. 228b.
112. Shaykh Aḥmad Sirhindī, *Maktūbāt*, i. 235, 367-70.
113. Baranī, 199-200.
114. Mirzā Muḥammad, f. 192a.
115. Amīr Khusraw, *Qirān as-Sa'dayn*, Lucknow, 1885, 163 *et seq.*; Khusraw, *I'jāz-i Khusrawī*, Lucknow, 1876, 180 *et seq.*
116. Wahid Mirza, *The Life and Works of Amīr Khusrau*, Calcutta, 1935, 238.
117. Mirzā Muḥammad, ff. 227a-228a.
118. Wahid Mirza, 239.
119. Ibid., 239-40.
120. S. N. Haidar Razvi, *Music in Muslim India*, *IC*, xv (1941), 331-40.
121. Quatremere, *Notices des Manuscrits*, xii. 185.
122. *Ghunya al-munya*, IO Pers. MS 1863 (Ethé 2008), ff. 46-54a, 54b-86a, 86b-92a.
123. Haidar Razvi, 336.
124. Mirza Muhammad, ff. 228a-b.
125. Sikandar bin Muḥammad 'Manjhū', *Mir'at-i Sikandarī*, Eng. tr. by Farīdī, 130.
126. Haidar Razvi, 336.
127. Mirzā Muḥammad, f. 193a; Abū-l-Faḍl (Blochmann), i. 403, 612.
128. Mirzā Muḥammad, f. 193a.
129. Faqīr-Allāh, ff. 3b-16b, 41b-49b.
130. Mu'tamid Khān, 308.
131. Chandra Bhan Brahmin, *Chahār Chaman*, BM Add. 16, 863, ff. 30a-b.
132. Mirzā Rawshan Ḍamīr, *Pārijātaka*, IO Pers. MS 808 (Ethé 2009).
133. Sāqī Musta'id Khān, *Ma'āthir-i 'Ālamgīrī*, Calcutta, 1947, 52.

134. IO Pers. MS 1746 (Ethé 2022).
135. Ibrāhīm ʿĀdil Shāh II, *Nawras*, ed. Nazir Ahmad, Lucknow, 1955.
136. Hasan ʿAlī ʿIzzat, *Mufarriḥ al-qulūb*, IO Pers. MS 2809 (Ethé 2024).
137. IO Pers. MS 1906 (Ethé 2019); IO Pers. MS 3377 (Ethé 2020).
138. D. C. Sen, *History of Bengali Language and Literature*, 799.
139. Wājid ʿAlī Shāh, *Ṣawt-i Mubārak*, Lucknow, 1853, 42 *et seq.*

GLOSSARY

'ābid, votary.
adhān, call to prayers.
'alam, standard.
Alfī, millennial.
amalaka, *amrak*, ribbed front.
awqāf, pl. of *waqf*, religious endowments.
banjāra, a wandering caste of traders.
bayt al-māl, public treasury.
bazmiyya, courtly *mathnawī*.
berā, fleet.
bī-shar', irreligious.
bhūt, restless soul of a murdered person.
bid'a, innovation, roughly equal to heresy.
Chhattī, celebration on the sixth day of child-birth.
chharī, standard, stick.
chilla, secluded worship.
churēl, ghost of a woman who has died pregnant.
dā'ī, inviter, missionary.
dā'ira, 'circle', camp.
dār al-ḥarb, 'land of war', i.e. countries not under Muslim rule.
dassondh, one-tenth of income payable by the Khojas to the Aghā Khān.
dast-i ghayb, 'hidden hand'.
dāstān, labyrinthine prose romance of heroism, magic and trickery.
dastār-bandān, 'turban-wearers', '*ulamā*'.
da'wa, invitation, claim, mission.
dhikr, liturgical recitation.
dībācha, introduction.
dīwān, collection of *ghazals*.
dohra, Hindi rhymed couplet.

fatwā, juristic ruling.
fiqh, classical Muslim jurisprudence.
futūḥ, unsolicited income received by a Ṣūfī gratuitously.
futuwwa, bountifulness, 'spiritual manliness'.
ghazal, elegy, song of love.
ḥadīth, report of a statement the Prophet is alleged to have made.
iftā', classical legislation.
iḥyā', reviving, cultivation of unproductive land.
ijmā', consensus.
ijtihād, use of individual reasoning.
imām, leader, in Shī'ī doctrine the hereditary head of the community in line of succession from the Prophet through his daughter Fāṭima and his son-in-law 'Alī.
imāmbāṛa, a hall where Shī'ī *ta'ziyas* are kept.
imām ḍāmin, amulet worn on the arm.
inshā', epistle-writing.
ittiḥād, (mystic) union.
jam', conjunction, union.
jamā'a, a (religious) group or party.
jamā'at khāna, Isma'īlī or Ṣūfī hall of worship.
jhāṛ phūnk, 'sweeping and blowing', a magical rite.
kāfī, a short mystical poem composed to music.
kalām, classical Muslim scholastic theology.
kalasa, pinnacle.
kalima, Muslim attestation of faith.
kāshī, architectural decoration originating in Kashan.
khalīfa, successor, vicegerent, caliph.
khānqāh, a Ṣūfī hospice.
khilāfat nāma, certificate of mystic succession.
khirqa, patched cloak.
khuṭba, sermon.
kulāh-i chahār-tarkī, cap of four-fold mystic renunciation.
laylat al-qadr, the night of the 27th Ramaḍān on which the first verse of the Qur'ān was revealed.
mad'ḥ-i ṣaḥāba, Sunnī recitation of the praise of the four orthodox Caliphs.
majdhūb, 'saturated', one attracted by divine grace, and renouncing all worldly concerns.
maktūbāt, letters.

malāmī, blame-worthy.
malfūẓāt, dicta.
manqūlāt, traditional sciences.
maqsūra, enclosure in a mosque; also its façade.
maʿqūlāt, rational sciences.
marthiya, a poem of mourning; especially lamenting the massacre of Ḥusayn ibn. ʿAlī and his companions.
mātam, mourning.
mathnawī, narrative poem composed of distichs corresponding in measure.
miḥrāb, niche.
muftī, a specialist in Muslim law who gives an authoritative opinion.
munshī, composer of epistles.
murāqaba, contemplation, concentrated séance.
mushāʿira, assembly for the recitation of *ghazals*.
mutʿa, temporary marriage.
naẓar, sight, the evil eye.
pad, a musical mode.
panja, a five-pointed symbol.
prēt, departed, wandering evil spirit.
purdah, veiling of women.
qāḍī, the Islamic judge.
qalandar, wandering mendicant; follower of a heterodox Ṣūfī order.
qaṣīda, panegyric in verse.
qiyās, juristic reasoning by analogy.
rawḍa, a building surrounded by a walled garden.
razmiyya, epical *mathnawī*.
rīkhta, Urdu verse.
rīkhtī, Urdu verse in the language of women.
Sabk-i Hindi, Indian school of Persian poetry.
ṣalāt, ritual prayer.
samāʿ, listening to devotional music.
samādhī, Hindu mystic or contemplative séance.
satī, self-immolation of a widow in classical Hinduism.
sharīʿa, the sacred law of Islam.
shirk, polytheistic association.
shughl, employment (in state service).
siflī ʿamal, earthly or vicious magic.

silsila, a Ṣūfī order.
sitār, a stringed musical instrument.
sunna, practices and precepts of the Prophet.
tadhkira, a collection of biographical notices.
tafḍīliyya, doctrine upholding the precedence of the Shīʿī *imāms* over the first three caliphs.
tafsīr, Qur'ānic exegesis.
taqiyya, pious fraud or subterfuge.
taqlīd, traditional conformity.
ṭarīqa, (mystic) path.
taṣawwur-i shaykh, concentration on the image of the preceptor in the Naqshbandī order.
tawakkul, trust in God, resignation.
tawba, repentance.
taʿwīdh, amulet.
ta'wīl, Qu'ānic interpretation.
ta'ziya, a representation of the shrines of Ḥasan and Ḥusayn, sons of ʿAlī.
ʿulamā', pl. of *ʿālim*; men of religious learning.
ʿurs, marriage, hence also the anniversary of a saint's death which is regarded as his union with God.
uṣūl, principles.
vihāra, Buddhist temple.
waḥdat ash-shuhūd, unity of witness, phenomenological monism.
waḥdat al-wujūd, unity of being, ontological monism.
waḥy, divine revelation.
wilāyat, *walāyat*, sainthood, dominion.
walī, saint.
wuḍū', ritual ablution.
yagāna, unique.
zanbīl, a basket of palm leaves, begging bowl.
zāwiya, a small house in which a Ṣūfī lived in retirement.

BIBLIOGRAPHY

1. *Works in Oriental Languages*

ʿAbd-Allāh: *Ta'rīkh-i Dā'ūdī*, BM Or. MS 197.

Abdullah, S.: *Adabiyyāt-i Farsī men Hinduwon kā ḥiṣṣa*, Delhi, 1942.

ʿAbd-al-ʿAzīz, Shāh: *Malfūẓāt*, Meerut, n.d.

—*Fatāwī*, Delhi, 1904.

—*Tuḥfa-i Ithnā ʿashariyya*, Karachi, n.d.

ʿAbd-al-Ḥaqq Dihlawī: *al-Makātib wa'r rasā'il*, Delhi, 1879.

—*Zād al-Muttaqīn*, BM Or. MS 217.

—*Ashʿāt al-lumʿāt*, Lucknow, n.d.

—*Marj al-baḥrayn*, Calcutta, 1831.

—*Takmīl al-īmān*, IO Pers. MS 2756.

—*Akhbār al-akyyār*, Delhi, 1891.

ʿAbd-al-Ḥaqq, Mawlawi: 'Marḥūm Dihlī College', *Urdu* 13/49 (1933), pp. 1-72; 13/50 (1933), 243-85; 13/51 (1933), 461-86; 13/52 (1933), 613-41.

—*Sayyid Ahmad Khān*, Karachi, 1959.

—*Urdū kī nashv-u numā men Ṣufiyā-i karām kā kām*, Karachi, 1953.

ʿAbd-al-Ḥayy: *Nuz'hat al-khawāṭir*, Hyderabad, 1959–62; Urdu tr. Lahore, 1965.

—*ar-Rafʿ wa-t-takmīl fīl-jarḥ wa-t-taʿdīl*, Aleppo, 1964.

—*al-Ajwiba al-fāḍila*, Aleppo, 1964.

Abū-l-Layth Ṣiddīqī: *Lakhna'u kā dabistān-i shāʿirī*, Lahore, 1955.

ʿAfīf, Shams Sirāj: *Ta'rīkh-i Fīrūz Shāhī*, Calcutta, 1890.

Aḥmad ʿAlī Batālawī: *Nuṣrat al-mujtahidīn*, Lucknow, 1895.

Aḥmad Sirhindī, Shaykh: *Mabdaʿ wa maʿād*, Cawnpore, 1891.

—*Radd-i Rawāfiḍ*, Lucknow, n.d.

—*Maktūbāt*, Lucknow, 1877.

Ākhund Darwīza: *Tadhkirat al-abrār wa-l-ashrār*, BM Or. MS 222.

ʿAlī al-Muttaqī: *Kanz al-ʿummāl*, Hyderabad, 1945.

ʿAlī Reis, Sidī: 'Kātib-i Rūmī', *Mir'at al-mamālik*, ed. Jevdet, Istanbul, 1895.

Allāh Diya: *Siyar al-aqṭāb*, Lucknow, 1889.

ʿAllāmī, Abū-l-Faḍl: *ʿĀ'īn-i Akbarī*. Eng. tr. i (H. Blochmann), Calcutta, 1927; ii (H. S. Jarrett), Calcutta, 1891; iii (Jarrett and Sarkar), Calcutta, 1948.
—*Akbar Nāma*, Lucknow, 1881–3.
—*Maktūbāt*, Lucknow, 1863.
Alṭāf ar-Raḥmān: *Aḥwāl-i ʿulamā-i Farangī Maḥall*, Lucknow, n.d.
Amānat Allāh: *Muḥāfiẓ al-īmān min makā'id lā-madhhabān*, Allahabad, 1877.
Amīr Aḥmad: *Sirāt al-Ashraf*, 2 vols, Lucknow, 1949.
Amīr Khurd: *Siyar al-awliyā'*, Delhi, 1302/1885.
Amritsarī, Thanā-Allāh: *Ahl-i ḥadīth kā madhhab*, Amritsar, 1920.
ʿArabi Zayn Badr: *Maʿdan al-maʿānī* (dicta of Sharaf-ad-dīn Yaḥyā Mānērī), Bihar 1301/1883.
Arzū, Sirāj-ad-dīn ʿAlī Khān: *Taṣ'ḥiḥ-i Gharā'ib al-lughāt*, Cawnpore, 1868.
Asad-Allāh Tilharī: *Quwwat-i Ḥanafiyya*, Bada'un, 1905.
Ashraf ʿAlī Thānawī: *al-Intibāhāt al-mufīda ʿan al-ishtibāhāt al-jadīda*, Lahore, 1952.
ʿAwfī, Muḥammad: *Lubāb al-albāb*, ed. Saʿīd Nafīsī, Tehran, 1333 shamsī.
Āzād, Abū-l-Kalām: *Tadhkira*, Lahore, n.d.
Āzād Bilgrāmī, Mīr Ghulām ʿAlī (ed.): *Khizāna-i Āmira*, Cawnpore, 1871.
—*Sarv-i Āzād*, Hyderabad, 1913.
—*Ma'āthir al-karām*, Hyderabad, 1910; 10 Pers. MS 1320.
Āzād, Muḥammad Ḥusayn: *Āb-i Hayāt*, Lahore, n.d.
Aẓfarī, Ẓahīr al-dīn: *Wāqiʿat-i Aẓfarī*, Madras, 1957.
Bābur: *Tuzuk* (ed. N. Ilminski), Kazan, 1856; Eng. tr. A. Beveridge, London, 1931; Eng. tr. Leyden and Erskine, London, 1921.
—*Dīwān* (ed. A. Samoilovich) (*Sobranie stickhotvoroney Imperatura Babura*), Petrograd, 1917; *Facsimile of Dīwān-i Bābur Badishāh*, Calcutta, 1910.
Badā'unī, ʿAbd-al-Qādir: *Muntakhab at-tawārīkh*, Calcutta, 1868–9.
Bahrā'ichī, Naʿīm-Allāh: *Maʿlūmāt-i Maẓhariyya*, Cawnpore, 1858.
Bakhtāwar Khān: *Mir'at al-ʿālam*, BM Add. MS 7657.
Baranī, Ḍiyā'-ad-dīn: *Ta'rīkh-i Fīrūz Shāhī*, Calcutta, 1862.
Bāyazīd Ansārī: *Maqṣūd al-Mu'minīn*, MS Āṣafiyya Library, Hyderabad (cat. I 390/86); Brockelmann, S. II, 991.
—*Ṣirāṭ at-tawḥīd*, Peshawar, 1952.

—*Ḥāl-nāma*, Subḥan-Allāh Oriental Library, Aligarh, no. 920-37.
al-Bīrūnī, Abū-Rayḥān: *Taḥqīq mā li-l-Hind*, Eng. tr. E. Sachau, *Alberuni's India*, London, 1910.
Brahman, Chandra Bhān: *Chahār chaman*, BM Add. MS 16, 863.
Chirāgh ʿAlī: *Rasā'il*, Hyderabad, 1918–19.
Chishtī, ʿAbd-al-Ḥalīm: 'Ḥasan ibn-Muhammad as-Saghānī' in *Maʿārif*, Jan.-Sept. 1959.
Dārā Shukoh: *Safīnat al-awliyā'*, Urdu tr. Karachi, 1961.
Dughlat, Mirzā Ḥaydar: *Tā'rīkh-i Rashīdī*, Eng. tr. E. Denison Ross and N. Elias, London, 1898.
Fakhr-ad-dīn Aḥmad: *Iẓālat ash-shukūk*, Allahabad, 1880.
Fakhr-i Mudabbir: *Ādāb al-ḥarb wa-sh-shujāʿa*, BM Add. MS 1653.
—*Shajra-i ansāb-i Mubārak Shāhī* (*Tārīkh-i Fakhr-ad-dīn Mubārak Shāh*), London, 1927.
Fat'ḥ-ad-dīn: *Shajra-i Naqshbandiyya*, Rawalpindī, 1904.
Faqīr-Allāh: *Rāg Durpan*, IO Pers. MS 1937.
Farīd Bhakkarī: *Dhakhīra al-khawānīn*, Karachi, 1961.
Firishta, Abū-l-Qāsim: *Gulshan-i Ibrāhīmī* (*Ta'rīkh-i Firishta*), Bombay, 1832; Lucknow, 1905; Eng. tr. J. Briggs (*History of the Rise of Muhammedan Power in India*), London, 1829.
Fīrūz Tughluq: *Futūḥāt-i Fīrūz Shāhī*, ed. S. Abdur-Rashid, Aligarh, 1954.
Ghawthī Shattārī: *Gulshan-i Abrār*, As. Soc. of Bengal, MS 259.
—*Gulzār-i Abrār*, Urdu tr. 1908.
Ghulām Aḥmad Khān: *Majmūʿa-i malfūẓāt-i khwājagān-i Chisht*, Delhi, 1906.
Ghulām ʿAlī, Shāh: *Maqāmāt-i Maẓ'harī*, Delhi, 1891.
Ghulām Halīm: *Tuḥfa-i ithnā-ʿashariyya*, Lucknow, 1879.
Ghulām Muḥy-d-dīn: *Siḥr al-Hind*, Delhi, 1876.
Ghulām Sarwar: *Khazīnat al-aṣfiyā'*, Cawnpore, 1902.
'Gīsūdarāz', Khwāja Muḥammad al-Ḥusaynī: *Jawāmiʿ al-kalim*, BM Or. MS 252.
Hādī, Mirzā Muḥammad: *Nūr-Allāh Shūstarī, Shahīd-i Thālith*, Lucknow, 1925.
Ḥājjī Khalīfa: *Kashf aẓ-Ẓunūn*, Leipzig, 1835–52.
Ḥālī, Alṭaf Ḥusayn: *Muqaddima-i shiʿr wa shāʿirī*, Lahore, 1953.
Ḥamīd Qalandar: *Khayr al-majālis* (ed. K. A. Nizami), Aligarh, 1960.
Ḥasan ʿAlī ʿIzzat: *Mufarriḥ al-qulūb*, IO Pers. MS 2809.
Ḥasanī, ʿAbd-al-Ḥayy: *Ath-thaqāfa al-Islāmiyya fī-l-Hind*, Damascus, 1958.
Ḥasanī, ʿAbd-ar-Raḥmān: *Mir'at-i Madāriyya*, BM Add. MS 168.

Hāshimī, Naṣīr-ad-dīn: *Dakan men Urdū*, Hyderabad, 1936.
al-Hujwīrī, ʿAlī ibn-ʿUthmān: *Kashf al-maḥjūb*, ed. Zhukovsky and M. ʿAbbāsī, Tehran, 1957; Eng. tr. R. A. Nicholson, London, 1936.
Iʿjāz Ḥusayn: *Mukhtaṣar ta'rīkh-i adab-i Urdū*, Karachi, 1956.
Ibn-Kathīr: *Al-Bidāya wa-n-nihāya*, Cairo, 1932–9.
Ibn-Nadīm: *Al-Fihrist* (ed. Flügel), Leipzig, 1871–2.
Ibrāhīm ʿĀdil Shāh II: *Nawras* (ed. Nazir Ahmad), Lucknow, 1955.
Ibrāhīm Mīr Siyalkotī: *Ta'rīkh-i ahl-i ḥadīth*, Lahore, 1953.
Ikram, S. M.: *Āb-i Kawthar*, Lahore, 1952.
—*Mawj-i Kawthar*, Lahore, 1950.
—*Rūd-i Kawthar*, Karachi, n.d.
—(ed.): *Armaghān-i Pāk*, Karachi, 1953.
—(ed.): *Darbār-i Millī*, Lahore, 1961.
Imdād-Allāh, Ḥājjī: *Maktūbāt-i Imdādiyya*, ed. Ashraf ʿAlī Thānawi, Lucknow, 1915.
—*Maktūbāt* (ed. Ayyūb Qādirī), Karachi, 1957.
Inʿām al-Ḥaqq: *Muslim Bengalī Adab*, Karachi, 1957.
ʿInāyat-Allāh, Muḥammad: *Tadhkira-i ʿulamā-i Farangī Maḥall*, Lucknow, 1930.
ʿIṣāmī: *Futūḥ as-salāṭīn*, Madras, 1948.
Ismā'īl, Shāh (Shahīd): *Tadhkīr al-akhwān*, Lahore, 1948.
—*Manṣab-i imāmat*, Delhi, n.d.
Jamālī, Ḥāmid ibn-Faḍl-Allāh: *Siyar al-ʿĀrifīn*, Delhi, 1893.
Jahāngīr: *Tuzuk*, Aligarh, 1864; Eng. tr. A. Rogers, London, 1909.
al-Juwaynī, ʿAlā'-ad-dīn: *Ta'rīkh-i Jahānkusha*, Leiden/London, 1912–37; Eng. tr. J. A. Boyle (*The History of the World Conqueror*), Manchester, 1958.
Jūzjānī, Minhāj-as-sirāj: *Tabaqāt-i Nāṣirī*, ed. A. H. Habibi, Kabul, 1964.
Kalīm-Allāh, Shāh: *Kashkūl-i Kalīmī*, Delhi, 1890.
Kāshānī, ʿIzz-ad-dīn: *Miṣbāḥ al-hidāya*, Lucknow, 1904.
al-Kāshgharī, Maḥmūd: *Dīwān-i Lughāt-i Turk*, Istanbul, 1333/1915.
Khāfī Khān: *Muntakhab al-lubāb*, Calcutta, 1869–1925.
Khayr-ad-dīn, M.: *Tadhkirat al-ʿulamā'* (Urdu tr.), Calcutta, 1934.
Khusraw, Amīr: *Maṭlaʿ al-anwār*, Lucknow, 1884.
—*Iʿjāz-i Khusrawī*, Lucknow, 1876.
—*Qirān as-Saʿdayn*, Lucknow, 1885.
Madanī, Ḥusayn Aḥmad: *Naqsh-i ḥayāt*, Delhi, 1953.
Maḥbūb Riḍwī: *Ta'rīkh-i Deoband*, Deoband, 1952.

Mānērī, Sharaf-ad-dīn Aḥmad ibn-Yaḥya: *Maktūbāt*, Lucknow, 1868; Cawnpore, 1911.
—*Maktūbāt-i jawābī*, Cawnpore, 1910.
Maẓhar, Mīrza, Jān-i Jānān: *Kalimāt-i Ṭayyibāt*, Delhi, 1891.
—*Khuṭūṭ* (ed. Khaliq Anjum), Delhi, 1962.
Mawdūdī, Abū-l-Aʿlā': *Taʿlīmāt*, Lahore, 1955.
—*Daʿwat-i Islāmī*, Rampur, 1956.
—*Islamī tahdhīb awr uskē uṣūl-u mubādī*, Lahore, 1960.
Mihr, Ghulām-Rasūl: *Sayyid Aḥmad Shahīd*, Lahore, 1952.
—*Jamāʿat-i Mujāhidīn*, Lahore, 1955.
—*Sarguẕasht-i Mujāhidīn*, Lahore, 1956.
Mustawfī, Ḥamīd-Allāh: *Ta'rīkh-i Guẕīda* (ed. E. G. Browne), Leiden, 1910.
Muḥammad, Mirzā: *Tuḥfat al-Hind*, BM Add. MS 16, 868.
Muḥammad Ḥasan Naqshbandī: *Ḥālāt-i mashā'ikh-i Naqshbandiyya Mujaddidiyya*, Muradabād, 1904.
Muḥsin Fanī (attributed to): *Dabistān-i madhahib*, Eng. tr. D. Shea and A. Troyer, Paris, 1843.
Muḥyi-d-dīn, Shaykh: *al-Balāgh al-mubīn*, Lahore, 1876.
Mushtāqī, Rizq-Allāh: *Wāqiʿāt-i Mushtāqī*, BM Add. 11633.
Muʿtamid Khān: *Iqbāl Nāma-i Jahāngīrī*, Calcutta, 1865.
Nadwī, Abū-l-Ḥasan ʿAlī: *Hindustānī Musalmān*, Lucknow, 1961.
—*Mādhā khasira l-ʿālam bi-nḥiṭaṭ al-Muslimīn?* Cairo, 1955; Eng. tr. *Islam and the World*, Lahore, 1961.
Nadwī, Abū-l-Ḥasanat: *Hindūstān kī qadīm Islāmī darsgāhen*, Aʿzamgarh, 1936.
Najm-al-Ghanī Khān: *Madhāhib-i Islām*, Lucknow, 1924.
Niẓām-ad-dīn Burhānpūrī, etc.: *Fatāwā'i Hindiyya* (*Fatāwā'i ʿĀlamgīriyya*), Urdu tr. by Sayyid Amīr ʿAlī, Lucknow, 1889.
Nizami, K. A.: *ʿAbd-al-Ḥaqq Muḥaddith Dihlawī*, Delhi, 1953.
—*Ta'rīkh-i Mashā'ikh-i Chisht*, Delhi, 1953.
—*Salāṭīn-i Dihlī kē madhhabī rujhānāt*, Delhi, 1966.
Pakistān kī ʿilāqā'ī ẕabānon par farsī kā athar, Karachi, n.d.
Qādirī, Shams-ad-dīn: *Urdū-yi qadīm*, Lucknow, 1930.
al-Qalqashandī: *Ṣubḥ al-aʿshā*, Cairo, 1913–20.
Qāniʿ, ʿAlī Shīr: *Tuḥfat al-karām*, Delhi, 1886.
Qidwā'ī, J. A.: *Pashto Adab*, Karachi, 1951.
Qurayshī, ʿAbd-ar-Razzāq: *Mirẕā Maẕ'har Jān-i Jānān awr unka Urdū kalām*, Bombay, 1961.
Raḥmān ʿAlī: *Tadhkira-i ʿulamā-i Hind*, Lucknow, 1914; Urdu tr. by M. Ayyūb Qādirī, Karachi, 1961.

Rāshidī, Ḥusām-ad-Dīn: *Sindhi Adāb*, Karachi, n.d.
—'Urdū zabān kā aṣlī mawlad: Sind', *Urdu*, 30/2 (April 1951), pp. 9-15.
—'Sind kē Urdū shuʿrā', *Urdū*, 30/4 (October 1951), pp. 5-26.
Ṣabāḥ-ad-dīn ʿAbd-ar-Raḥman: *Bazm-i Ṣūfiyya*, Aʿzamgarh, 1949.
Saghānī, Raḍī-ad-dīn Ḥasan: *Mashāriq al-anwār*, Istanbul, n.d.; Urdu tr. 1894.
Sāqī Mustaʿid Khān: *Ma'āthir-i ʿĀlamgīrī*, Calcutta, 1947.
Sarwar Muḥammad: *Panjābī Adab*, Karachi, n.d.
Sayyid, Aḥmad Khān: *Tafsīr al-Qur'ān*, Lahore, 1880–95.
—*al-Taḥrīr fī uṣūl at-tafsīr*, Agra, 1892.
—*Ākhirī Maḍāmīn*, Lahore, 1898.
—*Khuṭbat-i Aḥmadiyya*, Agra, 1870.
Shaṭṭārī, Bahā'ad-dīn: *Risāla-i Shaṭṭariyya*, 10 Pers. MS 2257.
Shiblī Nuʿmānī: *Rasā'il*, Delhi, 1898.
—*Shiʿr al-ʿAjam*, Cawnpore, 1920–3.
Shēr Khān Lodī: *Mir'at al-khayāl*, Calcutta, 1831.
Shērānī, M.: *Panjāb mēn Urdū*, Lahore, 1928.
Shustarī, Nūr-Allāh: *Majālis al-mu'minīn*, Tehran, 1852.
Sijzī, Amīr Ḥasan: *Fawā'id al-fu'ād*, Delhi, 1865.
Sikander ibn-Muḥammad 'Manjhū': *Mir'at-i Sikandarī*, Baroda, 1961; Eng. tr. Faridi, Dharampur, n.d.
Simnānī, ʿAlā'-ad-dawla: *Chihil Majālis*, BM Or. MS 9725.
Simnānī, Ashraf Jahāngīr: *Laṭā'if-i Ashrafī*, Delhi, 1882.
—*Maktūbāt*, Aligarh, n.d.; BM Or. MS 267.
Suhrawardī, Ḍiyā'-ad-dīn Abū-Najīb ʿAbd-al-Qāhir: *Ādāb al-murīdīn*, Urdu tr. Delhi, 1901.
al-ʿUtbī: *At-Ta'rīkh al-Yamīnī*, Cairo, 1869.
Wāʿiẓ al-Kāshifī: *Rashḥāt*, Cawnpore, 1912.
Wājid ʿAlī Shāh: *Ṣawt-i Mubārak*, Lucknow, 1853.
Wakīl Aḥmad: *Nuṣrat al-mujtahidīn*, Lucknow, 1896.
Walī-Allāh, Shāh: *Ḥusn al-ʿaqīda* (Urdu tr. *Merā ʿaqīda*), in *Ar-Rahīm*, i/x (March 1964), pp. 26-34.
—*Ḥujjat Allāh al-bāligha*, Karachi, 1953.
—*Tuḥfat al-muwaḥḥidīn*, Delhi, 1894.
—*ʿIqd al-jīd*, Eng. tr. Daud Rahbar, *MW*, xlv (1955), 347-58.
—*Al-Balāgh al-mubīn*, Lahore, 1890.
—*Al-Juz' al-laṭīf*, Delhi, 1897.
—*Izālat al-khafā'*, Karachi, n.d.
—*Al-Musawwa min aḥādīth al-Muwaṭṭa*, ed. ʿUbayd-Allāh Sindhī, Hyderabad, Sind, 1963.
Zāhid ʿAlī: *Hamārā Ismāʿīlī madhhab awr uskī ḥaqīqat*, Hyderabad, 1954.

2. *Works in European Languages*

Abdul Bari, M.: 'The Farā'idī Movement', *Proceedings of the Pakistan History Conference* (5th session), Karachi, 1955, pp. 197-208.
Abid Husain: *The Destiny of Indian Muslims*, London, 1965.
Ahmad Khān, M. D.: *History of the Farā'iḍi Movement in Bengal* 1818–1906, Karachi, 1965.
Aïnî, Mehemmed Ali: *Un Grand Saint de l'Islam: Abd al-Kâdir Guilânî*, Paris, 1938.
Anderson, J. N. D.: 'Recent Reforms in the Islamic Law of inheritance', *International and Comparative Law Quarterly*, 14 (1965), 349-65.
Ashraf, K. M.: 'Life and Conditions of the People of Hindustan, 1200–1550', *JASB* (1935), 3rd series.
Aziz Ahmad: *Islamic Culture in the Indian Environment*, Oxford, 1964.
—*Islamic Modernism in India and Pakistan*, 1857–1964, London, 1967.
Bailey, T. Grahame: *A History of Urdu Literature*, Calcutta, 1932.
—*Studies in North Indian Languages*, London, 1938.
Bains, A.: *Ethnography of the Castes and Tribes of India*, Strassburg, 1912.
Baloch, Nabi Bakhsh Khan: 'The Diwan of Abū ʿAṭa of Sind', *IC*, xxiii (1949), 136-50.
Bashīr al-dīn Maḥmūd Aḥmad: *Introduction* to Shīr ʿAlī's Eng. tr. of *The Holy Quran*, Rabwah, 1955.
—*Invitation to Aḥmadiyyat*, Rabwah, 1961.
—*Aḥmadiyyat or the True Islam*, Washington, 1951.
—*The Ahmadiyya Movement*, London, 1924.
Bausani, A.: 'Note su Shah Waliullāh di Dehli', *Annali*, n.s. x (1961).
—*Storia delle letterature del Pakistan*, Milan, 1958.
—'Note su Mirza Bedil', *Annali*, vi (1957), 163-91.
—'The position of Ghalib (1796–1869) in the history of Urdu and Indo-Persian poetry', *Der Islam*, 24 (1959), 99-127.
—'Contributo a una definizione dello "stilo indiano" della poesia persiana', *Annali*, n.s. vii (1958), 167-78.
—'Hali's Ideas on Ghazal', *Charisteria Orientalia* (1956), 38-55.
Bernier, F.: *Travels in Mughal India*, Eng. tr. London, 1891.
Binder, L.: *Religion and Politics in Pakistan*, Berkeley, 1961.
Binyon, L.: *The Court Painters of the Great Moghuls*, London, 1921.

Blumhardt, J. F.: *Catalogue of the Hindustani Manuscripts in the Library of the India Office*, Oxford, 1926.
—*Catalogue of Hindi, Punjabi and Hindustani Manuscripts in the Library of the British Museum*, London, 1899.
Bray, D.: *Census Report: Baluchistan*, Calcutta, 1913.
Brockelmann, C.: *Geschichte der arabischen Literatur*, second edition, two vols., Leiden, 1943, 1949; three supplementary vols., Leiden, 1937–42.
—*Mitteltürkischer Wortschatz nach Maḥmūd al-Kāshgharī: Dīvān Lughat al-Turk*, Budapest, 1928.
Brown, Percy: *Indian Architecture (Islamic Period)*, Bombay, 1958.
Brush, S. A.: 'Ahmadiyyah in Pakistan', *MW*, 45 (1955), 145-71.
Burgess, J.: *The Muhammedan Architecture in Gujarat*, London, 1896.
—*The Muhammedan Architecture of Ahmadabad*, London, 1900–5.
—and H. Cousens: *The Architectural Antiquities of Northern Gujarat*, London, 1903.
Campbell, J. M. *ed.*: *The Bombay Gazetteer*, Bombay, 1874–1904.
Chatterji, S. K.: *Indo-Aryan and Hindi*, Ahmadabad, 1942.
Colebrook, H. T.: 'On the Origin and Peculiar tenets of certain Muhammedan sects', *Asiatic Researches*, vii (1801).
Cousens, H.: *Bijapur and its Architectural Remains*, Bombay, 1916.
Cragg, Kenneth: *Counsels in Contemporary Islam*, Edinburgh, 1965.
Crooke, W.: *Religion and Folklore of Northern India*, London, 1926.
Dames, M. Longworth: *Popular poetry of the Baloches*, London, 1907.
Darmesteter, J.: *Chants populaires des Afghans*, Paris, 1888–90.
Daudpota, U. M.: *Sindhi Literature*, Karachi, 1951.
Dörfer, Gerhard: *Türkische und mongolische Elemente in Neupersischen*, Wiesbaden, 1965.
Dumasia, N. M.: *A Brief History of the Agha Khan*, Bombay, 1903.
Elliot, H. M. and Dowson, J.: *The History of India as told by its own Historians*, Allahabad, 1964.
Encyclopaedia of Islam, 2nd ed. London, Leiden, 1960, continuing.
Encyclopaedia of Religion and Ethics, ed. J. Hastings, Edinburgh, 1908–21.
Ethé, H.: *Catalogue of Persian Manuscripts in the India Office*, Oxford, 1903, 1937.

Faiz, Faiz Ahmad: *Poems*, tr. V. G. Kiernan, Delhi, 1958.
Farquhar, J. N.: *Modern Religious Movements in India*, London, 1924.
Fergusson, James: *History of Indian and Eastern Architecture*, London, 1910.
Fisher, Humphrey J.: *Aḥmadiyyah: A Study in Contemporary Islam on the West African Coast*, London, 1963.
Fyzee, A. A. A. (ed.): *A Shiite Creed*, Bombay, 1942.
—'Materials for an Ismāʿīlī Bibliography', *JBBRAS*, N.S. 11 (1935), 59-65; 16 (1940), 99-101.
Gait, E. A.: *Census Report: Bengal*, Calcutta, 1902.
Geiger, W.: 'Balūcische Texte mit übersetzung', *ZDMG*, 43 (1889), 579-89; 47 (1893), 440-9.
—'Die Sprache der Afghanen', *Grundriss der Iranischen Philologie*, Strassburg 1898–1901, i/ii, 201-30.
Ghani, A.: *A History of Persian Language and Literature in the Mughal Court*, Allahabad, 1929–30.
Ghani, A. R. and Nur Ilahi, K.: *Bibliography of Iqbal*, Lahore, 1955.
Ghosh, J. C.: *Bengali Literature*, London, 1948.
Ghulām Aḥmad, Mirzā, of Qādiyān: *The Philosophy of the Teachings of Islam*, Rabwah, 1959.
—*The Teachings of Islam*, London, 1910.
Ghulam Muhammad: *Festivals and Folklore of Gilgat, Memoirs, Asiatic Society of Bengal*, Calcutta, 1905.
Gilani, A. C. S.: *Ghalib, His Life and Persian Poetry*, Karachi, 1956.
Goetz, H.: *Indian and Persian Miniature Painting*, Amsterdam, 1958.
Grierson, G. A.: *Bihar Peasant Life*, Calcutta, 1885.
—*Linguistic Survey of India*, Calcutta, 1904–21.
Habib, M.: 'Shaikh Naṣīruddīn Maḥmūd Chirāgh-i Delhi as a great historical personality', *IC*, xx (1946), 129-53.
—and A. V. S. Khan, *The Political Theory of the Delhi Sultanate*, Allahabad, n.d.
—'Chishti mystic records of the Sultanate period', *MIQ*, iii (1950), 1-42.
Halim, A.: 'Mystics and mystical movements of the Sayyid-Lodī period', *Journal of the Asiatic Society of Pakistan*, viii/2 (1963), pp. 71-108.
al-Hamdani, Abbās, H.: *The Ismāʿīlī Daʿwa in Northern India*, Cairo, 1956.
Hamdani, H. F.: 'The Letters of Mustanṣir billāh', *BSOAS*, vii (1933–5), 308-12.

Hamid Ali: 'The customary and statutory laws of the Muslims in India', *IC*, ii (1937), 354-69, 444-54.
Hardy, P.: *Historians of Medieval India*, London, 1960.
—'The oratio recta of Barani's *Ta'rīkh-i Fīrūz Shāhī* – fact or fiction;' *BSOAS*, xx (1957), 315-22.
—'The Tarikh-i Muhammadi by Muhammad Bihamdkhani', *Jadunath Sarkar Commemoration volume*, 1958, 181-90.
Harikishan Kaul: *Census Report, Punjab*, Lahore, 1912.
Hassan Ali, Mrs Meer: *Observations on the Mussulmauns of India*, London, 1917.
Havell, E. B.: *A Handbook of Indian Art*, London, 1920.
—*Indian Architecture*, London, 1927.
—*Indian Painting and Sculpture*, London, 1928.
Hollister, J. N.: *The Shī'a of India*, London, 1953.
Hunter, W. W.: *The Indian Musalmans*, London, 1871.
Ikram, S. M. and Spear, P.: *Cultural Heritage of Pakistan*, Karachi, 1955.
The Imperial Gazetteer of India, London, 1907–9.
Iqbal, Muhammad: *Islam and Ahmadism*, Lahore, 1936.
—*The Reconstruction of Religious Thought in Islam*, London, 1934; Lahore, 1944.
—*Poems*, tr. V. G. Kiernan, London, 1955.
—*Poesie*, tr. A. Bausani, Parma, 1956.
Iqbāl Husain: 'Chandra Bhān Brahman', *IC*, xviii (1945).
Ishaq, Muhammad: 'India's Contribution to the study of Hadīth Literature', *Dacca University Bulletin*, xxii (1955).
Ivanow, W.: *Guide to Ismā'īlī Literature*, London, 1933.
—*Brief Survey of the Evolution of Isma'ilism*, Bombay, 1952.
Ja'far Sharīf: *Islam in India or the Qānūn-i Islām*, Eng. tr. G. A. Herklots, 1832; revised by W. Crooke, Oxford, 1921.
Jamil, M. Tahir: *Hali's Poetry*, Bombay, 1938.
Kamāl al-dīn, Khwāja: *The Ideal Prophet*, London, 1925.
—*Islam and Christianity*, London, 1932.
Kaul, J. L.: *Interpretations of Ghalib*, Delhi, 1957.
Khāja Khān: *Studies in Taṣawwuf*, Madras, 1923.
Khan, Mu'in al-din Ahmad: 'Hājī Sharī'at-Allāh, the Founder of the Farā'iḍī movement (AD 1781–1840)', *JPHS*, 11 (1963), 105-26.
—'Muḥsin al-dīn Ahmad *alias* Dudū Miyān (AD 1819–1862)', *JPHS*, 11 (1963), 234-58.
—'Successors of Dudū Miyān', *JPHS*, 11 (1963), 278-89.
—'Ta'aiyyunī Opposition to the Farā'idī Movement', *JPHS*, 12 (1964), 150-64.

Khushḥāl Khān Khattak: *Poems from the Divan*, tr. D. N. Mackenzie, London, 1965.
—*Poems*, tr. into English by Evelyn Howell and Olaf Caroe, Peshawar, 1963.
Kühnel, Ernst: *Moghul-Malerei*, Berlin, 1956.
Laoust, H.: *Les Schismes dans l'Islam*, Paris, 1965.
Law, N. N.: *Promotion of Learning in India during Muhammedan Rule by Muhammedans*, London, 1916.
Lawrence, W. R.: *The Valley of Kashmir*, London, 1895.
Lentz, W.: 'Sammlungen zur afghanischen Literatur – und Zeitgeschichte', *ZDMG* (1937), 711-32.
Leyden, J.: 'On the Roshenian Sect and its Founder Bāyazīd Ansārī', *Asiatic Researches*, xi, 363 ff.
Lokhandwalla, Sh. T.: 'The Bohras, a Muslim community of Gujarat', *SI*, iii (1955), 117-135.
Massignon, L.: *Essai sur les origines du Lexique Technique de la Mystique musulmane*, Paris, 1922.
Mawdudi, A. A.: *Towards understanding Islam*, Lahore, 1960.
—*Islamic Law and Constitution*, Lahore, 1960.
Menant, D.: 'Les Bohras du Guzarate', *RMM*, x (1910), 456-93.
—'Les Khodjas du Guzarate', *RMM*, 12 (1910), 214-32.
Ministry of Education, Government of Pakistan: *Report of the Commission on National Education*, Karachi, 1959.
Misra, S. C.: *Muslim Communities in Gujarat*, Bombay, 1964.
Mohanlāl, Munshi: 'A Brief Account of Masud, known by the name of Shakarganj or Shakarbar', *JASB*, v (1836), 635-8.
Molé, M.: 'Les Kubrawiya entre sunnisme et shiisme aux huitième et nouvième siècles de l'Hégire', *REI*, xxix-xxxi (1961), 16-142.
Muḥammad ʿAli: *English Translation of the Holy Qur'ān with ... Commentary ...*, Lahore, various eds.
—*The Religion of Islam*, Lahore, 1936.
Muḥammad ʿAlī: *The Aḥmadiyya Doctrines*, Lahore, 1932.
—*The Founder of the Aḥmadiyya Movement*, Lahore, n.d.
Muhammad Din, Malik: *Gazetteer of Bhawalpur*, Lahore, 1909.
Muhammedan Anglo-Oriental Educational Conference, *Majmūʿa-i resolutionhā-i dihsāla*, Aligarh, 1896.
Mujeeb, M.: *The Indian Muslims*, London, 1967.
Nadwī, Sulaymān: 'Muslim colonies in India', *IC*, i (1927).
Nizami, K. A.: *The Life and Times of Shaykh Farid-u'd Din Ganj-i Shakar*, Aligarh, 1955.
—*The Suhrawardī Silsilah and its influence on Indian Politics*, n.d.
—'Persian Literature Under Akbar', *MIQ*, iii/1-2 (1957–8), pp. 300-28.

Nizami, K. A.: 'Some Aspects of Khānqāh life in Medieval India', *SI*, viii (1957), 51-70.
—*Some Aspects of Religion and Politics in India during the 13th century*, Aligarh, 1961; referred to as *Religion and Politics*.
—'The Shattari Saints and their attitude towards the State', *MIQ*, 1/2 (1950), 56-70.
Nurul Karim, M.: 'Part played by Haji Shariʿatullah and his son in the socio-political history of East Bengal', *Proceedings of the Pakistan History Conference* (5th session), Karachi, 1955, pp. 175-82.
O'Malley, L. S. S.: *Census Report: Bengal, Bihar, Orissa, Sikkim*, Calcutta, 1913.
Oman, J. C.: *The Mystics, Ascetics and Saints of India*, London, 1905.
Philips, C. H. (ed.): *Historians of India, Pakistan and Ceylon*, London, 1961.
Punjab Notes and Queries, Allahabad, 1883–7.
Qureshi, I. H.: *The Muslim Community of the Indo-Pakistan Sub-Continent*, 'S-Gravenhage, 1962.
Ram Krishna, Lajwanti: *Panjabi Sufi Poets*, Calcutta, 1938.
Raverty, H. G.: *Selections from the poetry of the Afghans*, London, 1864.
Razvi, S. N. Haidar: 'Music in Muslim India', *IC*, xv (1941), 331-40.
Rieu, C.: *Catalogue of the Persian Manuscripts in the British Museum*, London, 1879–95.
Rizvi, S. A. A.: *Muslim Revivalist Movements in Northern India in the Sixteenth and Seventeenth Centuries*, Agra, 1965.
—'Mahdavi Movement in India', *MIQ*, 1 (1950), 10-25.
Rose, H. A.: *A Glossary of Tribes and Castes of the Punjab and North-West Frontier Province*, Lahore, 1911–19.
Rosenthal, E. I. J.: *Islam in the Modern National State*, Cambridge, 1965.
Roychoudhuri, M.: *The Dīn-i Ilāhī*, Calcutta, 1941.
Sabir, M.: 'Cultural and linguistic affinities between Turkey, Iran and Pakistan', in *Papers read at the R.C.D. Seminar on Common Cultural Heritage*, Tehran, 1965, pp. 91-9.
Sadiq, Muhammad: *A History of Urdu Literature*, London, 1964.
Saksena, R. B.: *A History of Urdu Literature*, Allahabad, 1940.
Sell, E.: *The Religious Orders of Islam*, Madras, 1908.
Sen, D. C.: *History of Bengali Language and Literature*, Calcutta, 1911.
Smith, V. A.: *Akbar, the Great Mughal*, Oxford, 1919.
—*History of Fine Art in India and Ceylon*, Oxford, 1911.

Smith, Wilfrid Cantwell: *Pakistan as an Islamic State*, Lahore, 1951.
—*Modern Islam in India*, London, 1946.
—*Islam in Modern History*, Princeton, 1957.
Sorley, H. T.: *Shāh Abdul Latīf of Bhit*, London, 1940.
Stchoukine, Ivan: *La Peinture Indienne*, Paris, 1929.
Storey, C. A.: *Persian Literature, A Bio-Bibliographical Survey*, London, 1927–58.
Tara Chand: *The Influence of Islam on Hindu Culture*, Allahabad, 1936.
de Tassy, Garcin: *Histoire de la Litterature Hindouie et Hindoustanie*, Paris, 1870.
—*La Langue et la Littérature Hindoustanie en* 1870–6, Paris, 1871–7.
Temple, R. C.: *The Legends of the Punjab*, Bombay, 1884.
Titus, Murray T.: *Islam in India and Pakistan*, Calcutta, 1959.
Wahid Mirza: *The Life and Works of Amir Khusrau*, Calcutta, 1935.
Walter, H. A.: *The Ahmadiyya Movement*, Calcutta/London, 1918.
—'Islam in Kashmir', *MW*, iv (1914).
Wellesz, Emmy: *Akbar's Religious Thought reflected in Mughal Painting*, London, 1952.
Wilkinson, J. V. S. and Gray, B.: *Persian Miniature Painting*, London, 1933.
Yusuf Husain: *L'Inde Mystique au Moyen Age*, Paris, 1929.
—*Medieval Indian Culture*, London, 1959.
Zaehner, R. C.: *Hindu and Muslim Mysticism*, London, 1960.
Zubayd Ahmad, M. G.: *The Contribution of India to Arabic Literature*, PH.D. dissertation, University of London.

INDEX

The Arabic article al-, *with its variants* an-, ash-, *etc.*, *is neglected in the alphabetical arrangement.*